S0-AEG-779

THE HOUSE OF EXILE

THE ELDER OF THE HOUSE OF EXILE READS ALOUD

The House of Exile

By
NORA WALN

With Illustrations by
C. LEROY BALDRIDGE

BOSTON
LITTLE, BROWN, AND COMPANY
1933

DS
721
W3

Copyright, 1933,

By Little, Brown, and Company

All rights reserved

Published April, 1933
Reprinted April, 1933 (three times)
Reprinted May, 1933 (three times)
Reprinted June, 1933 (twice)
Reprinted July, 1933
Reprinted September, 1933
Reprinted November, 1933
Reprinted December, 1933

THE ATLANTIC MONTHLY PRESS BOOKS
ARE PUBLISHED BY
LITTLE, BROWN, AND COMPANY
IN ASSOCIATION WITH
THE ATLANTIC MONTHLY COMPANY

PRINTED IN THE UNITED STATES OF AMERICA

For a dear friend
MARGARET HATCH
and a kind stranger
EDWARD WEEKS

As the purpose of this book is merely to tell of everyday life in a Chinese family, I feel that I am justified in withholding actual surnames. These names can have no significance to the Western world. But as my writings have frequently been translated into Chinese periodicals after publication in Europe and America, the clan that I have actually described feel that the use of their name in so intimate a recounting would be an uncomfortable razing of their courtyard walls.

NORA WALN

CONTENTS

ILLUSTRATIONS

THE HOUSE OF EXILE

THE HOUSE OF EXILE
HOPEI PROVINCE, CHINA

LATE in the eighteenth and early in the nineteenth century, Lin Yan-ken selected merchandise for J. S. Waln. Amber, alumroot, beeswax, and cassia lignea. Cinnabar, chinaware, chessmen carved from ivory tusks, and an elbowchair of rosewood. Embroidered fans, grass cloth, ginger in earthen pots. Hemp and indigo. Jute, kaolin, also lily flowers. Musk, nankeens, orpiment, a miniature pagoda of silver, and medicinal rhubarb. Packets of seeds of the melon and of the apricot. Teas, both green and black. Umbrellas, vases, and wall papers with scenes from Chinese life. Writer's ink and xanthein.

These are some of the items neatly entered in a time-yellowed account book, as sent by the Confucian merchant, from Canton in the ancient Empire of China, on sailing ships to the Quaker merchant in Philadelphia, U.S.A.

It is recorded, here at the Ancestral Hall of the Lin homestead, that Lin Yan-ken went to Canton and joined the business of his maternal uncle, Houqua, one of the thirteen men appointed by Ch'ien Lung, then Emperor of China, to trade with foreigners. He arrived on the day following the Festival of the Washing of Flowers, in the Year of the Pig, of the Chihai Cycle. He served there until the Dragon Boat Festival, in the Year of the Horse, of the Jen-wu Cycle. By Western calendar, from May 1779 to June 1822.

Lin Yan-ken returned to his birth-home to enjoy fifteen

years of family life. In this time his descendants, who had numbered but one son of his youth, were increased to the classical family — five sons and two daughters. The last ten years of his life, he was Elder of the House of Exile. Stories from Yan-ken's life and axioms given by him still echo in the homestead, as it is the custom in Chinese courtyards to pass from generation to generation the truths that have been garnered from life by those who have lived.

Lin Wei-sung is now Elder of the House of Exile. It is his habit on summer afternoons to gather us into the cool shade under the interlacing branches of two trees that form a leafy canopy over the library courtyard, and in winter to draw us into the library, where the sun shining through the rice-paper windows lays a warm gold carpet on the floor. The trees that make the courtyard canopy are called "Yan-ken's trees." He planted the one near the east wall on the morning of his departure from home, the one near the west wall forty-three years later on the evening of his return.

At times the Elder reads from the classics. Other days he recounts incidents from his experience. Always he encourages others to contribute what they will. Thus even the littlest child is accustomed to entertain without self-consciousness. Often Fan-lei, wife of the Elder's third son, enthralls us with folklore. Occasionally Keng-lin, an uncle who plays the table lute with charm, joins us, then we chant epic poems, many about Lin heroines and heroes. Once the Elder sent a servant to fetch an ivory box from the green lacquer cabinet. When he had it, he thrust two fingers into the box and withdrew a yellowed envelope. From the envelope he took two sheets of paper. He smoothed them. He handed the three to Ching-mei. He told her to look at them, then to pass them on carefully.

The envelope was marked in English, "Entrusted to the care of Captain Blackinston, Ship *Perseverance*." On one of the sheets the writing was in English. The other was its translation into Chinese. The English page was dated "Philadelphia, Sixth Month 10, 1804," and signed "J. S. Waln." The letter addressed Lin Yan-ken. It expressed satisfaction in the knowledge that any packet with his seal did not need examination to assure the receiver that its contents were of the promised quality. It regretted that conditions of the era did not permit the exchange of other than material goods, and ended with the hope that in later generations, "when suspicion between peoples must certainly disappear," the Lins and the Walns might exchange visits.

We were each permitted to hold the letter a few seconds. Then the Elder put it in the ivory box, locked the box, and had it returned to the green lacquer cabinet. Said he, "We Chinese have a much longer history than any other people in the world. We know our life story for forty-six centuries. We have been a people who keep ourselves to ourselves. Our experience with Westerners has seldom been such as to give us confidence in Western friendship. Too often we trusted and were betrayed.

"Opinion, at the date of the letter I have just shown you, was influenced by previous incidents. Of these I shall tell you three. Should you desire to know more, you can find them in the history portfolios on the west side of this library.

"*Firstly:* In the zenith of the Ming dynasty, a flock of white-sailed ships came up the Canton River. Their commander gave his name as Fernão Peres de Andrade and his birthplace as Portugal. He asked for the privilege of mercantile trade. His manners were charming. The Canton Viceroy was impressed. The Viceroy reported Andrade favorably to the throne.

"Wu Tsung was then Emperor. He used the vermilion pencil to reply, permitting trade and inviting the stranger to Peking. The white-winged ships were filled with our silks, embroideries, porcelain, ivories, teas, and such Chinese things. Andrade dispatched them to Portugal. Then, with royal escort, he journeyed luxuriously to the Court, where he was welcomed and resided as an honored guest.

"The white-winged ships returned with the tidings that the Emperor of Portugal was delighted with the Chinese things. Portugal paid generously for the first shiploads. To facilitate the business, Andrade secured permission for several hundred of his countrymen to dwell along our coast. Most chose to settle in our beautiful southern cities, Ningpo and Foochow.

"Shortly after this, Andrade's brother arrived with an enormous fleet manned by armed men. Our smooth-voiced visitors no longer bothered to be polite. They pirated our warehouses and our temples. One among them insolently slit open the wedding chair of a daughter of the House of Chu at Ningpo with his long sword. To rid ourselves of our guests, we had to rise up and massacre them.

"*Secondly:* Through history we traded amiably with the Filipinos. When Western ships sailed into Manila, the major population was Chinese. The commander of these stranger ships said that his birthplace was called Spain.

"His conduct and the conduct of his companions were gentle on arrival. There was advantageous business for all. But when the Westerners got a foothold, they declared that we Chinese were too numerous. They set upon us, as though we were wild beasts, and slaughtered thousands of us. Our ancestor, Lin Po-chun, was one of the butchered.

"*Thirdly:* Near the end of the Ming dynasty when the decadent Imperial Family were so occupied with base pleasures that the people had to be occupied with civil rebellion, Western ships again sailed up the Canton River. They bombarded our Tiger Forts, landed armed men, and hoisted their flag. Thus they induced China to establish a trading post outside the walls of Canton. They had with them a charter from Charles I of England, dated the year 1635.

"When the Ming dynasty was closed and the Ch'ing dynasty

opened, this trading station was viewed with anxiety. But we had no gunboats with which to drive the bold intruders away. All our precepts were against military power. Then, as now, the soldier was ranked as the lowest creature in society.

"The vermilion pencil was used to protect us. An edict forbidding any man, woman, or child to leave our homeland, under threat of death on return, was posted at each magistrate's office. Runners cried this edict aloud through the provinces three times annually. Thirteen merchants of prudent character were selected and appointed to the Western trade. They and their staffs were the only Chinese permitted to have contact with the intruders.

"There was fortune in the Western trade. Merchants vied with each other for appointment. Each family tried to hold the seal from generation to generation. None other than relatives were taken into the business. The situation was delicate because each merchant had to give the Emperor bond for the Westerners' obedience to regulations. If a Western trader disobeyed an edict, the Chinese merchant bonded for him not only lost his seal of appointment, but he and all his family were ruined — their fortune forfeit to the throne.

"The vermilion pencil forbade Westerners to approach China at any place except Canton, or to anchor there for other than the prompt dispatch of mercantile business. During the reigns of the first three Ch'ing Emperors, regulations restricted the traders to an allotted anchorage and disembarkation unto a quarter-mile square outside the Canton city wall. They were forbidden to ride in river boats, sit in rickshaws or sedan chairs, wander into the country, or attempt to stare in through the city gate.

"But in the reign of the fourth Emperor they were granted the refreshment of a walk. Three of the most powerful merchant sponsors had drawn the Emperor's attention to the fact that in coming to China the traders were confined on their small vessels for four or five months and had a similarly long return journey. So on four days of four moons each year, under the guardianship of their merchant sponsor and in droves of not more than ten, they were permitted an excursion to the Fati flower gardens. On those sixteen days the gardens were closed to Chinese. Our Emperor did not want us near the Westerners, who were judged uncultured savages.

"It was some decades before the Westerners discovered that we had no great military power behind our edicts and that they could wander in where they pleased, to force their religions and their merchandise upon us."

After a long silence, the Elder said, before he dismissed us: "The letter I showed to you is kept and is shown to each generation, not only because of its value as evidence of Yan-ken's integrity, but as proof that all Westerners are not savages. Some can appreciate character even as other men."

2

The life scroll of Lin Pao-lin relates that the Waln letter fired his mind, when he was a very young child, with eagerness to go abroad and discover what the world outside China is like. He was a good student and possessed an unwavering will. So he secured a place in the first group of Chinese scholars permitted by the rulers of China to study in the United States.

He was in America from 1872 to 1881. While there he addressed a letter to the Waln Family, City of Brotherly Love, to find out if they would still like to have one of the Lin Family visit them. His letter was returned to him by the Post Office.

Pao-lin came home to China. He brought with him many dozens of scientific books and much laboratory equipment. With these he fitted up one courtyard of the homestead and taught science to all his boy and girl relatives whom he could interest.

He was killed, in his laboratory, by antiforeign fanatics nicknamed "Boxers," in the summer of 1900.

3

My interest in China began in April 1904. I was then in my ninth year and the guest of my paternal grandparents, Elijah and Ann Waln, on their farm in the Grampian Hills of Pennsylvania. The day was rainy. As I had torn a hole in one of my rubber boots, I had been forbidden to leave the house.

Grandfather was at Philadelphia visiting a vegetarian friend. Grandmother was occupied learning a new tatting pattern from Great-aunt, who had come to keep her company in his absence. I lingered in the doorway, considering a dash down the puddly path to the stable where old William Welty, the hired man, mended harness. Then a finch, dressed in springtime yellow and black, dropped with closed wings to the level of my eyes.

The bird recovered himself with gay flips and whirled upward, breaking into humorous song on the curve of his flight. He mocked me with his freedom. And I was off into the orchard. Vested with authority on the farm, old William Welty still had power to command me when I was nearly nine. He sent me to my Grandmother with soaked black slippers, mud-stained white stockings, and the starch of my grey chambray dress made limp by tall wet grass. Told by Grandmother to go to my room, I went on into the attic. There, in a chest under the eaves, in use to keep the moths from the wedding dress of a slim-waisted Quaker bride, I found copies of the *United States Gazette*.

Later, Grandmother discovered me engrossed with the *Gazettes* and gave them to me. They are on my table before me as I write this prelude to the selections from my Chinese journals which form the body of this book.

Many news items, both domestic and foreign, concerning the world in 1805 now arrest my attention as I turn the pages. But in my childhood, it was only my own name that gleamed from the pages. Each *Gazette* has a column of marine notices announcing vessels "berthed below" (at Philadelphia) with lists of merchandise in them and advertisement to the consignee to take delivery. It was only the goods consigned to Waln that captured my imagination; only the movements of brigs, sloops, schooners, frigates, or ships identified as at some time serving Waln that concerned me.

When I was young, I was never taken to Philadelphia. But one of the *Gazettes* has a page article describing Philadelphia's growth. This article was written by a gentleman who remembered "when there were only three coaches kept by the gentry and at most only two or three ships arrived in a year," but who had "lived to see upwards of three hundred coaches daily display the ease of opulence on the avenues in fair weather and 1,500 sail annually expedited for every quarter of the globe, of which fifteen or twenty double the southern Promontory of Africa and explore the Antipodes for the most costly productions of the east."

Although this description was ninety-nine years old when I found it, I accepted it realistically — just enlarging it with what interesting items my elders mentioned on their returns from Philadelphia. I accepted all cargoes consigned to J. S. Waln as my own. And Canton, in Southern China, immediately became my favorite port of purchase.

My elders used to speak with satisfaction of the quietness in which I sat during the hour of First Day morning silent worship at our Meeting-House; I was troubled by this praise, because I did not always seek the company of God in my quietness, but was sometimes busy planting "lily flowers" or "seeds of the melon and the apricot" that I had received from Canton.

Years passed. I came to possess a row of Chinese histories, and to own Chinese dictionaries. I dipped into the philos-

ophies of Lao-tzu, Mencius, and Mo-ti. I committed to
memory analects from Confucius. I added five volumes of
verse translated from the Chinese to the maps, log books,
and old letters which I collected from relatives. And I
wrote a sad ballad (which was printed in a magazine) about
the little boy Emperor of China, Pu-yi, the last "Son of
Heaven."

Then on a golden autumn morning, when I was an under-
graduate at Swarthmore College, I was called to the telephone.
I took up the receiver. A lady spoke. She explained that
she and her husband, of the Lin Family of China, were on a
tour of the Western world, and, desiring to meet one of the
Waln Family, had looked through the catalogues listing scholars
at the Society of Friends schools, and found my name.

Scarce able to believe that it was not a dream, I arranged to
go to her at Philadelphia by the next train — the 1:23. I
had never seen a Chinese other than those of my mind's
creation. Miss Meeter, professor of Greek and gentle Dean of
Women, happened to cross the station platform, on her way
from the village to the campus, just as I hurried to the station.
She was concerned by my neglect of hat and gloves. But when
I told her what had happened she joined in my pleasure. She
kindly lent me hers — and kissed me before she waved me into
the rear car.

I saw Shun-ko and her husband, Lin Yang-peng, standing
under the clock in Broad Street Station, before I passed through
the exit gate. They were two exquisitely neat slim figures,
with faces of smooth ivory. Both were dressed in high-
collared, heel-length gowns of dark silk, with short sleeveless
jackets of brocade.

Yang-peng wore a round brimless cap with a small red button on his close-cropped head. Shun-ko had no hat. Her
glossy black hair was brushed tidily from a centre parting.
As she turned to look up at the station clock, I saw a tiny flat
bouquet of chrysanthemums in her nape knot. Their de-

tailed perfection of dress and their self-possession, amid the
staring crowd, made me timid.

But when Shun-ko's dark eyes met mine, I was at peace.
From that instant there have been no barriers between us.
Strong, wise, and true, despite our difference in race she took
me into her heart.   She had never had a daughter.   I had lost
my mother four years previously.

We had a week together — seven magic days in which we
found ourselves uncannily akin in seriousness and in humor.
Too soon her husband reminded her that she must travel on,
and an anxious dean reminded me of college routine I had forgotten.   When she was on the train, Shun-ko leaned from her
compartment window and said: "You must come to me."

Through five years I cherished the intent to go.   Shun-ko
and I wrote to each other frequently.   I meant to start soon.
But life was so entrancing.   There are so many things that
capture one's attention.   Time passed, and I did not get off.

Then, in the summer of 1920, when my brothers and sisters
were all still at boarding school and college, we seven decided
to summer where we had not been before.   We took an advertised isolated cottage on a cliff overhanging Lake Erie.   It
was near enough to Cleveland to make a journey there and
back in one day.   I had a desire to see Cleveland.   "I wouldn't
think of it," each of my brothers and sisters replied when I
suggested the trip.

So I went alone.   I lunched at a drug-store counter on
sandwiches and milk, reading the third volume of Mr. Giles's
Chinese Dictionary, which I had taken along for company in
dull intervals.

A lady in brown tapped me on the shoulder.   When I looked
up she smiled and we fell to talking of the readableness of dictionaries.   I found that she also read them.

We spent the remainder of the day looking at Cleveland
together.   I learned that her name was Grace Coppock, and
that she lived in China.   I told her about Shun-ko.   She said,

"You must come to China." I answered that I hoped to go, but that it was an expensive trip and not possible just now.

She studied me for a bit. Then she said: "It must be made possible. China needs girls like you. I am General Secretary of the Y.W.C.A. in China. I invite you to come."

I drew back at this and assured her that I had no mission in life or desire to go anywhere to do people good. She laughed and said no more about it. But when we parted in the late afternoon she said, "Before we mentioned your going out to China with me, you gave an invitation and I accepted it. I am coming to your cottage to spend Wednesday next with you."

She came. We all boated, swam, read aloud, and cooked dinner over our open log fire, as was our custom. We all enjoyed her, and she declared that she enjoyed us. One of my brothers found that she had an interest in the old trading days in China. He asked me to let her look into the chest he had made to hold my collection of eighteenth and early nineteenth century maps, ship logs, newspapers, and so forth. She told my brother that she wanted me to go out to China. He said that would be a splendid winter for me, as I had always wanted to go; but that I should be useless as a missionary, as I should no doubt be converted to something-or-other by the first heathen with whom I had conversation. The others agreed with him.

Miss Coppock came to visit us again. Through the summer and early autumn she wrote to me. Each time she told me that the way was open if I wanted to return with her, and assured me that she would not hamper me in any way. She had read and liked all she had been able to collect of my printed verse and stories. Certainly she did not urge me to write anything in China, unless inspired, but she would just like to think of me in China, as she thought I belonged there.

I did not go with her. But I went out two months after she sailed — every step of the journey, ticket, passport, and people to look after me at each change en route, arranged by her. She was on the jetty at Shanghai to meet me. After three days of visit there, she put me on the train for Peking in the care of a Y.W.C.A. secretary traveling north.

So I came to China.

I

A GUEST

Kuo yu kuo fa; chia yu chia fa.
("Each country has its laws; each family its regulations.")

— CHINESE PROVERB

I

ARRIVAL

1

IT was late in December, 1920, when the waterways of
North China were ice-sealed, that I first came to the homestead
of the Lins on the Grand Canal. Accompanied by her husband, her husband's elder brother and his wife and daughter,
and three serving matrons, Shun-ko journeyed up to Peking to
welcome and escort me to her dwelling place.

Of the serving matrons, — who are called "Bald-the-third,"
"Sweet Rain," and "Faithful Duck," — she presented the
first to me, saying, "This is your woman."

We were carried an hour by train and then boarded the
Lin family boat. We had with us five baskets of provisions.
"Enough for two weeks," Shun-ko explained; "because, although this journey usually occupies only one day, it is
wisest when traveling to provide so as not to be fretted if there
is delay."

The boat was fitted with sledge runners and a sail for use
"when the wind is favorable." But there was no wind, so the
sail was folded. There were two compartments. The men
took the fore, we women the aft. Snug red mattresses, fox-
fur rugs, back rests padded with camel's wool, silk quilts
of duck down, and charcoal foot-braziers made travel comfortable.

The craft was manned by three boatmen. They worked
in single shifts. Each timed his duty by setting an incense
stick alight in the niche before the carved image of Lung-mu

—"the - Dragon - Goddess - ever - listening - to - the - prayers - of-mortals-who-pass-over-water" — at the boat's stern, and continuing until the incense stick burned down.

We were propelled forward with a long metal-tipped staff. So engineered, we left the canal side and turned south on the ice without collision with similar sledge boats that careered by in like manner.   In a nest of soft furs and gay quilts I was cozy between Shun-ko and her niece, Mai-da.   Each held one of my hands under the coverlets.

We kept to the right on the frozen highway.   On our left passed a continuous line of boat sledges piled high with country produce.   Crates of chickens.   Yellow-billed white geese. Brown ducks.   Demure grey pigeons in wicker hampers. Rabbits contentedly nibbling at greens.   Squealing black pigs protesting rancorously against carriage.   Broad-tailed fat sheep.   Heaps of eggs.   Bushels of hulled rice.   Red corn. Golden millet.   Peanuts in hull.   Trays of candied red fruit neatly terraced to a high ridge.   Pickled mushrooms in salt-crusted tubs.   Reed containers with their contents protected from the frost by wadded covers — one, blown off, disclosed celery, another lettuce, and a third beetroot.

Packed amid their produce were farmers and their wives and their children, en route to town for market day; all dressed in clean starched long blue gowns, over wadded coats and trousers, their cheeks like hard rosy pippins, their dark eyes sparkling, and their jolly faces quick to smile.

Small boys and girls darted through the more serious traffic on small sledge boats, pushed forward in the same way as ours, miraculously escaping accident by fractions of an inch.   Skaters pursuing earnest errands glided swiftly up and down the frozen highway.   The leisured amused themselves by skating fancy figures in wayside bays.

With care not to endanger the double-track sledge path, men cut ice for summer use.   They stacked it in flat baskets woven of stout twigs, and hung each basket by its strong

handle from the middle of a carrying pole. A man at each
end of the pole carried the ice to the canal-side earth-mounds,
where they buried it away for summer use, exactly as explained
in the annals of Wei, written thirty centuries ago.

Women wheeled hamper barrows down to the opened water
and exchanged banter with the ice-cutter, while they let their
ducks and geese out to swim. All along the frozen road
fishers made round holes and squatted over them with nets,
waiting for inquisitive fish.

We slid under frequent high-arched stone bridges, many
with legends carved on them, some humped so that the name,
"camel-back," by which they are called, is apt. A few were
perfect granite half-circles that cast a shadow, when the sun
was just right, so that travelers passed through a "good-luck
ring."

In passing, the Lins noted the ice-level against each bridge.
At some places they stopped and a boatman measured with his
hand-span. Mai-da's father recorded his findings in a notebook. Shun-ko saw my interest and explained: "Engineers
constructed the Grand Canal System. Through previous
centuries the best engineers of each generation were detailed by
the throne to tend it. It is a dragon of enormous strength
sprawling through the provinces.

"So long as we keep it in good health we ride on it peacefully.
But when neglected, it is of dangerous temper. History records that it sweeps out, in time of melting snow or summer
rain, devastating fields and cities, taking heavy tribute of
human life, and leaving folk who survive to face famine.
This province is the watershed of the Shansi mountains.

"The canal has been dangerously ignored. Each year of
the Republic, our family have reported to the Capital that
there were silted channels and weakened dykes in our neigh-
borhood. My husband and Mai-da's father have just interviewed the present President. They were received politely,
but their conclusion is that nothing will be done. According

to what they heard in the guildhalls and tea-houses, representatives from canal districts in other provinces and from the Yangtze and Yellow River valleys are of the same conclusion. Their homesteads are also menaced by fear of flood and famine."

There was little snow. The country was beige-colored and appeared barren. One locality was indented by rice paddies roughened by dead stubble. At intervals there were patches of sparse winter wheat on which cattle pastured. A boy whose duty it was to keep the cattle from nipping the wheat too closely sprawled on the back of the largest steer in each herd.

I saw no isolated farmsteads. Worn paths went up from the canal side to walled villages, radiated from the fields to the walled villages, and connected walled village with walled village. Each village had its "asking protection" shrine by the canal, but the people had built their homes well away from the water. "Because it is wiser to carry needed water up and to take the washing down, than to dwell where all sorts of people pass."

The village gates were hostile to travelers, Shun-ko explained. For the accommodation of strangers there were mud-and-wattle inns on the canal side. These served meals, provided sleeping quarters, had mangers for beasts, trestles for boats, and usually a craftsman to do repairs. The rooms in the two at which we stopped to buy hot water for tea were alive with insects and putrid with the stale sour sweat of centuries of travelers.

Men and women rode over the countryside paths, straddling wooden saddles perched high on the backs of little donkeys, and often with a downy-haired baby snuggled in the curve of one arm. The donkeys had tinkling bells sewn to their scarlet collars. Other folk reclined in comfortable-looking litters swung between shaggy ponies. A few traveled in gaudy sedan chairs — green, scarlet, or blue — carried by four bearers, who cleared lesser folk out of the way shouting: "Lend light! Lend light! An important person would pass!" All lesser folk moved aside. They appeared to enjoy the pageantry of the brilliant procession as much as I did.

A goodly number of riders sat in mule carts. These had two high wooden wheels each. These wheels were thickly studded with polished brass nails, and had axles that protruded far beyond the cart on each side. Each cart had a larkspur cloth-covered cabin, in which the occupants sat cross-legged on a sheepskin-padded floor.

PEKING CART

Pedestrians peopled the paths, carrying sometimes a rooster, sometimes a paper image to burn at a family grave; sometimes returning a cooking pot to a next-village neighbor after a wedding, and sometimes just strolling along. But most had shoulder poles loaded with looped-up clouds of threadlike spaghetti or tissue-thin moon cakes of gelatine. Shun-ko told me spaghetti and gelatine were the two staples of the district. The bearers were en route to the town, which has as its chief industry the packing of these products in bright paper containers for sale in the cities.

Lazy white clouds floated overhead, as they do in the season we call "Indian summer" in my native Pennsylvania. The atmosphere lulled me to peaceful dreams, from which I was roused by the voice of Mai-da's father.

"Why," he demanded, staring at me, "has Japan been given Germany's holdings in China?   We were persuaded to interest ourselves in the European War by being told that the rest of the world must teach Germany that present-day civilization is against aggression.   America counseled us to declare ourselves with the Allies.   But, at the end of the war, we were n't freed of Japan's throttle hold on our country.   Instead she got what Germany had seized.   Even putting all consideration of China aside, the Versailles Treaty is the most uncivilized paper written since men knew how to record thought.   It will not only upset the economic balance of the world, but lead to more wars.   Can we Chinese count you civilized since you signed it?"

Shun-ko silenced him. "My daughter by affection cannot be blamed any more than your Mai-da can be blamed because the Republic does not repair the canal!"

Mai-da's father then begged my pardon.

At a bend in the canal the Weary Pagoda graced our journey.   We loitered there to enjoy the music of the wind bells swaying under the pagoda's five-storied eaves.   Shun-ko's husband told the pretty legend of the pagoda's trek from beyond a mountain three thousand miles away.   The pagoda meant to go to Peking, but stopped to rest.   And, when it saw how the people passing along the canal, working in the fields, and living in the villages were made peaceful at heart by its beauty, it decided to stay; reasoning that the Emperor and the Empress at the Capital had already plenty of other pagodas.

The boatmen moved up close to listen.   As Shun-ko's husband spoke, he leaned forward and by accident brushed two oranges from a basket of foodstuffs.   The fruit rolled over the ice.   It crossed the path of a tall skater dressed in a claret-silk gown and a marten-skin cap. The stranger bent gracefully and picked up the oranges.

He returned them with a polite bow, and exchanged a few musical sounds with the men of our party. Then he skated east. We sledged west.

Shun-ko murmured something in a stern manner to Mai-da in Chinese — then said, in the same stern tone, to me: "Girls of a marriageable age are as dangerous to the peace of a family as smuggled salt. Don't ever again, while under my chaperonage, look *at* a man. Direct your gaze modestly to the ground when one is in front of you."

2

Just before midday we sighted the painted ruby, emerald, and sapphire gate-towers rising out of the grey wall of the City of Noonday Rest. Then the stoutest of the boatmen seized the staff out of turn and sped our craft forward to song. The other two kept time to his prods with handclaps. At great speed we circled under the shadow of the east wall, which rose in perpendicular height from the canal, and around to the South Gate wharf, where broad stone steps went down under the transparent ice.

We disembarked and climbed the steps to the sunny area between the wharf and the south wall, where a chatting, merry throng was gathered. Here idle sedan-chair bearers and boatmen from craft at anchor loafed. Young girls, carrying kettles of steaming water, soap, soft towels, and blue basins, sold "Wash your face for a penny!" Barbers had set down their portable barber shops and trimmed the cropped heads of republicans, or combed the queues of the old-fashioned, or jerked out with firm tweezers the stray hairs that marred the faces of their beardless countrymen, or cleaned ears with a multiple of spoon tools. Two letter writers, one at each end of the wharf, and a fortune teller midway between

them, each with a stout oak-stemmed oil-paper umbrella stuck
in the ground behind him and tilted to shade his worktable,
brushed letters for "those who have no leisure to write for
themselves" and gave advice to the anxious.

Here, too, itinerant cooks had wheeled their barrows, built
to combine portable work-board and stove.   The cauldrons
gave off a delicious steam which whetted my hunger.   Thick
meat and vegetable soup, piping hot!   Crusty golden dough-
nut twists!   Sweet steamed yams!   Flaky white rice!   Roasted
chestnuts!   Pork dumplings!   Buns of light steamed bread!
Grain porridge!   Candied red apples!   Nougat-stuffed dates!
Fried noodles!   Bean curd of rich brownness!   As they
worked, the cooks advertised the quality of their food with
songs and gestures which brought laughter and retorts from
the crowd.

As each purchaser received his filled bowl, with chopsticks
laid across the top, he carried it to the communal stone tables,
worn by much use, under an ancient evergreen tree.   A young,
blind minstrel leaned against the tree trunk fingering a three-
stringed guitar.   "He was a soldier in the army of Tuan
Chi-jui, and lost his sight in August 1917, in the battle which
defeated the attempt to restore the Manchus," Shun-ko explained.   "He found his way home and now sings for a living
in public places and at such private social occasions as he can.
He has new ballads of his own rhyming, and the old songs
which made his grandfather famous throughout the tea-
houses of eighteen provinces."

I made the mistake of supposing that we were to supplement
our lunch basket from the wharf restaurateurs.   But we
carried it only for emergency.   It was left in the boat.   Bald-
the-third motioned me into the fifth of a file of nine sedan
chairs, in which the men led and the serving women came last.
The chairs for Shun-ko, her sister-in-law, niece, and me were
closed — so that we "need not be stared at."   Level with my
eyes there was an oblong slit covered with brown gauze.

Through this I saw that we were carried inside the town, up a steep narrow street along which shop signs swung, and then turned to the left, into a narrow passage, between high grey brick walls broken at intervals by tightly closed, heavy vermilion gates. Through one of these gates, which was clankingly unchained to Yang-peng's order, we were put down in the third inner courtyard of a quiet *posada*.

A man, who appeared very slim in a rich dark-blue silk gown, met us here. He bowed us into a small room, and to stools placed two and two around a square table of rosewood. We did not give a special order, but had the restaurateurs' usual "five dishes," which cost one dollar per person.

Chicken and walnuts with sour-sweet gravy. Shrimps, mushrooms, and green onions. Cabbage, pork, and bean curd. Noodles, celery, and pigeon eggs. Fish and bamboo soup. Warm rice wine, served in thimble cups to "aid digestion." And dishes of salted radishes and red fruit jelly, set in the centre of the table.

While we ate a soldier came in. He leaned over Shun-ko's husband and examined our food. He stared at me for what seemed a long time. The others took no notice of him but continued intent on their chopsticks and bowls. I tried to do the same.

Finally he laid his gun, which had a bayonet at one end, across the only other table in the room. The soldier had a stupid heavy face and wore ill-fitting garments of coarse cotton, but our elegantly gowned inn host carried food to him with his own delicate hands. The servants who waited on us were called away to help please him, and he was even given our dish of jelly without any of the Lins seeming to notice his insolence.

He fed quickly, sucking and hiccuping. Having finished, he rose and slapped down a twenty-dollar paper note (which Shun-ko later told me was worthless because printed by a governor who had since gone out of office). Our inn host bowed so that his skirt swept the floor, and told the soldier with soft cadence that he had been the guest of the house for his meal. The soldier did not return the bow. He drew himself up stiffly. In a harsh rumble of sound he replied that he did not accept bribes of food, and wanted his change in silver. Then he thrust the note in the host's face.

Our host took the worthless money. He deducted one dollar as the price of the dinner and gave the soldier nineteen silver dollars. The soldier rang each dollar against his bayonet to test the purity of the coin. All rang true. He dropped them into his purse. Then, picking his teeth as he went, he walked out. As he passed, I saw that his soldier shoes were of cloth like his poor uniform, and badly torn. He had put newspapers in them to keep his feet warm.

A brazier heated the room. When the noise of the soldier's departure had died away, the innkeeper dropped the twenty-dollar bill and the chopsticks that the soldier had used into the fire.

Our meal closed with clean bowls of steaming rice and fragrant tea made in a squat brown pot. Shun-ko explained that all good restaurants and careful homes have teapots for different needs. Our inn host, who had never seen a Western girl before, had asked about me. When he learned that I was to visit in the Lin homestead, he suggested tea from "the pot which prevents misunderstanding."

We were carried back to the wharf. The boatman whose turn it was to work grinned with well-fed content; the other two curled up asleep on the sledge's broad stern. For a time fields and frozen highway were occupied as before. Then we crossed paths with a sledge boat overcrowded with soldiers and propelled by a frightened boatman. Farther on we saw another boat commandeered by half a dozen young boys and an officer. They pushed an old farmer and his "lily foot" wife about ruthlessly, scattering their produce over the ice. One lad speared the old lady's brown rooster with his bayonet and held him high while the others applauded. When she struggled to help the dying bird, the officer clouted her on the head. Half a mile on, we heard a shot and saw a child fall — she had been reluctant to give up the donkey hitched to the mill where she was grinding flour. The soldier who shot her then led the donkey down to the canal for sledge transport to "the war."

Without slackening pace, the Lins conferred in low voices with their boatmen. The serving women took an active part in the discussion. We turned down a branch of the canal to detour trouble. The fields we now passed were deserted. We met no one on the way to the hamlet where the uncle of one of the Lin boatmen lives. The boatman went in to borrow a cart to take us overland to the Lin homestead.

He returned weeping. Five boys from the hamlet, one of them his uncle's only son, had been taken to be made soldiers. All five were between the ages of twelve and fourteen years. Shun-ko said, "If our nation is to be built by soldiers, then this must be, as the only way to brutalize men to soldiering is to take them at the beginning of adolescence."

It was impossible here, or at the four further villages where we tried, to secure assistance. The people were occupied with their own affairs. There had been no soldiers in the district for the previous five months. This foraging raid had come as a surprise in mid-morning, when the gates were open and folk scattered. They had lost carts, animals, food, winter clothing, and all their sons between the ages of twelve and sixteen — excepting those few who had been shrewdly and quickly hidden. One Village Elder had parleyed with the soldiers while three boys had been dropped in a well bucket to a niche in the well wall prepared for such emergencies, and the bucket left to swing empty.

"The soldiers passed too quickly," villagers said. "This was but a survey and they will return in larger numbers." So they were busy tightening walls and gates, taking their

saddles, sedan chairs, and carts apart to hide the pieces separately, driving their cattle in, and sharpening kitchen knives
and farm tools as weapons.

All our party agreed that we were safest to keep off the main
canal. We could not walk, as Shun-ko, Mai-da's mother,
and the serving matrons had "lily" feet. We sledged devious
ways. I saw plentiful supplies of hot food set in cauldrons
before each barred village gate. Twice we saw tired-looking
soldiers feeding on this "peace rice."

It was long after sunset when we came to the Lin homestead
city. The gates are sealed at sunset. The city wall, thick
enough for nine horses to trot abreast on it, rises in perpendicular height from the canal. A boatman beat against the
heavy gate. Finally the gateman was roused.

But he refused to open the gates before sunrise. He acknowledged that he knew all the persons who had gone to
Peking to meet the foreigner. Yes, he had known them since
childhood. And the voices from without were like the voices
of these Lins and their servants. Yet he could not open until
the appointed time.

After much parley, the gateman's son was dispatched to the
Lin homestead. We waited in the eerie green-gold moonlight
a cold and weary while. At last, someone hailed us from
within the gate. The eldest among us replied. There was
another call. The next eldest replied. So on, through all our
number. Lastly Shun-ko told me to shout my name.

The gate creaked open. We walked in. Before greeting us,
the elderly man from the homestead who had identified us by
voice closed the gate again. He secured its locks and pasted
a fresh strip of paper over the paper he had broken, across
the crevices where the two halves of the gate meet. On the
fresh paper he brushed his name with black ink.

He had brought sedan chairs. In them, we followed him
up a steep narrow street, turned to the left through a narrower
passageway between grey walls broken at intervals by closed

vermilion gates, and then down a broader street to a scarlet
gate in which a peephole was slid open at the sound of our
coming.

Camel-back, the Lin gateman, recognized his Family. He
opened the "To and From the World Door," bowing and smiling his joy in their safe return from the perils of travel.
Massed behind him were Lins, young and old. I stood forgotten as my escorts were welcomed home. "*Chia ho fu
tzu shêng,*" they said again and again; repeating the sentence
which I now know means, "Happiness springs up of itself in a
united family."

Thus I entered the Lin homestead, on the Grand Canal, in
Hopei Province, North China — which was once named in
derision, and is now called in affection, the "House of Exile."

II

THE HOUSE OF EXILE

1

FROM the moment of my arrival in China it was as
though, like Alice, I had stepped through a looking-glass into
another world. The world I left behind became a dim, fantastic dream. Only this into which I entered seemed real.

"Glazed brick, white mortar, and blue roof-tiles do not
make a house beautiful; carved rosewood, gold cloth, and clear
green jade do not furnish a house with grace; a man of cultivated mind makes a house of mud and wattle beautiful; a
woman, even with a pock-marked face, if refined of heart,
fills a house with grace," is a literal translation of the carv-
ing on the first stone laid in the building of the Lin homestead.

There are six generations of Lins now living. They dwell
in one-story-high, single-room houses, which are built foursquare about a paved courtyard. The roofs extend well
over the pillared verandahs, which finish the front of each
house, so that one can get into a sedan chair in rainy weather
without exposure to wet; and, after their utilitarian duty is
done, tilt upward in easy curves displaying faëry scenes and
fabulous creatures painted gayly under the eaves.

Here one is ever conscious of the beauty of the heavens;
because to go from one room to another in the homestead one
must always cross a courtyard. The houses have doors and
windows only on one side, the side opening into the court to
which they belong. The homestead is composed of sufficient

courts to house comfortably the Family, who are eighty-three men, women, and children at the time of this writing, and to permit them to entertain in accord with their station in society.

The courtyards are connected by gateways cut in the courtyard walls in the shape of a flower, a fan, a vase, or a full moon. The courts, with their dwelling rooms for the living, cluster around the double-roofed, story-and-a-half Hall of Ancestors, which shelters the life tablets of twenty-nine generations of Lins, and their wives, who have "plucked the flower of life."

A protective grey wall, six feet thick and four times a man's height, surrounds the homestead. The homestead neither overlooks nor is overlooked by its neighbors. From the many times higher city wall above it, only the flamboyant roofs can be seen through the lacery of intertwined trees; or occasionally, before the poplars come into leaf, the flutter of a bright silk gown as someone walks along the path to the summerhouse by the lotus pond.

The "Gate of Compassion," a small window cut in the north wall, where charity is given to the needy, and the "To and From the World Gate," a door of solid planks large enough for a horse and carriage to be driven into the entrance court, are the only openings in the wall connecting with the outside world.

The view in through the Gate of Compassion is closed by a shrine which holds a portrait of the Goddess of Mercy. The view in at the To and From the World Gate is closed by a screen of porcelain tiles. This screen is an arm's length thick, twice as wide as the gate, and as high as the homestead wall. On it a gorgeous green dragon writhes over a blue sea after a scarlet ball of life.

The homestead is called the "House of Exile." Thirty-five generations of the Family have been born inside its stout grey walls. The people of Hopei speak of the Lin Family as the "Kuangtung Lins." The Lins in Canton speak of the Lins resident in the House of Exile as "temporarily from home."

But Lin Fu-yi came from Canton, of Kuangtung province, in the Yuan dynasty, six-and-a-half centuries ago.

His name was in the draft called by the Mongol Emperor, Kublai Khan, to extend the Imperial Grand Canal northward to the Mongol court at Cambuluc, now known as Peiping. Lin Fu-yi was eighteen when the command came from the governor of Canton for him to go north in the service of the Mongol Emperor. He had already made himself conspicuous by building a new kind of canal lock in a local waterway. Since he was the only son of a father who had "plucked the flower of life," his departure was delayed, by the Emperor's permission, to permit the consummation of his betrothal, and extended until it was certain that his bride had conceived.

Then he traveled up to the place on the Imperial Grand Canal where he had been told that he would find Sun Hung-shen, the engineer under whom he was to work. He fell in love at sight with Sun's daughter. Sun Li-la was fourteen. She should have been safely hidden in the "Springtime Bower" of her parents' homestead. But she was a dimpled child of three when her father, drafted north, had taken her along to soften his exile. The years had enlarged his affection for her as well as added to her stature; so he evaded, with plausible excuses, his wife's written demands that he should send their daughter home to Hangchow.

The policy by which the Mongols ruled China was that of peace by sensible compromise. When Lin Fu-yi's bride delivered a girl, a request submitted to the governor of Canton by the Lin Family, who were a power in rebellious Kungtung, resulted in an order from Cambuluc dispatching Lin Fu-yi to his parental homestead. Twice in six years he made this journey, siring a second daughter and then a son.

The country was prosperous. The Imperial Grand Canal was the roadway over which passed the riches of the Empire en route to the Capital. In addition to sending his Homestead

Elders sufficient to satisfy them, Fu-yi built his dwelling, the "Three Eastern Courtyards," and put aside a small fortune by the time Li-la was twenty.

Then, although Fu-yi could not make her his wife and her father refused to consider a proposal for her as a *Ch'ieh*, she climbed over the wall of her father's dwelling and entered the

ENTRANCE TO THE HALL OF ANCESTORS

courts that her lover had made ready for her as a "green-skirt" mate. Fu-yi never went south again until sixty years later, when his clan legally claimed his body after death.

Fu-yi has two life tablets. The one in the Lin homestead at Canton records an unfilial son. The one in Hopei is as tall as the lotus, measuring from root tip to seed pod. It stands

12583

in the shrine Li-la designed for it at the place of first honor
in the Hall of Ancestors of the House of Exile.

"Man and woman in perfect harmony are like the music
of the harp and lute" is what Shun-ko, who told me the story
of the founding of the House of Exile, said.

Li-la's union with Lin Fu-yi was blessed with a son, a daughter, and a son. When the son born to Fu-yi's wife died, his
aged grandfather made the difficult journey north and pleaded
with his grandson to obey the third dispatch from Cambuluc,
which his growing power on the canal made it possible for him
to avoid. Fu-yi turned the old man away with the gruff answer that he would sire no more children except with Li-la.
Then Li-la, in compassion, followed the old grandfather a day's
journey. She quieted his sorrow by giving him her first-born
son, then her only son, to complete the line of succession. This
boy became governor of a province and Elder of the Lin clan.

The daughter married a Wong, of the next-door neighbors.
The passage through the division wall, still in daily use between the Wong and the Lin households, was cut so that she
could visit the home of her parents without ceremony of departure by the To and From the World Gate. It is called
"Mai-lin's Walk."

The second son grew at his father's side. On completion
of the system of canals uniting Cambuluc with the Yangtze
and the eastern and southern waterways of the kingdom, Fu-yi
was appointed supervisor of the transportation of tribute rice.
When he retired, his son (who had brought the joy of seven
grandsons to the House of Exile and for whom the "Sons'
Courtyards" were built) slid into his place.

When he retired, his son came into his place. By then "Col-
lector of Traffic Taxes" had been added to the original title.
The phrase "and in control of canal improvements" was written on with the vermilion pencil before the post was passed to
his son. Thus, in four generations, the House of Exile was
firmly established.

2

The records in the Ancestral Hall of the House of Exile
dovetail into the annals of the Yuan, the Ming, and the Ch'ing
dynasties, and make it obvious that the loyalty of the descendants of the second son of Li-la and Fu-yi has always been to
the Imperial Grand Canal.

The annals also made it obvious that each new Emperor accepted this inland water highway as the most valuable of
China's assets in her century-old policy of "keeping herself
to herself." The records of the lives of the Lins show them
not only intelligent in canal improvement and management
but also astute in adapting themselves to conditions in national
government. The Lins received grants for the use of land,
tax free, as early as the Yuan dynasty, and they have tilled
the same fields through the centuries. But they have never
put even a summerhouse on these acres.

As they have need for more dwelling space, and their finances
permit, they add to the original Three Eastern Courtyards.
The library was built, and the collection of ancient manuscripts begun, by the fifth son of Fu-yi's second son. He won
distinction for the house by securing first place at the Imperial examinations when, in 1315, the Emperor Jen Tsung
restored the "Forest of Pencils," and the system of appointing
the nation's governors from the nation's scholars. The white
marble of which the Wall of Heaven in the Court of Sunrise
is built was brought through the Khyber Pass by a Lin who
traded with India.

"Better establish a branch than cut off a line" was chiseled
over the front gate by his brother's grandson. He did not
come into power as Elder of the Household until he was eighty
years of age. Yet he established the custom of consultation
in family matters by journeying to Canton to confer with the
Elder of the southern homestead. He brought back a four-

year-old Cantonese bride for his favorite great-grandson, who was then a child of five.

This couple are remembered as ideally happy. It is now the custom when a Lin daughter marries to say, "May you be as happy as the maid from Canton." The azalea terraces in the Springtime Bower were planted by a Lin who was magistrate in Chekiang. He brought the roots from that province. The schoolroom court was added by Lin Shih-mo, who disliked children at lessons in the library. The "Garden of Children," with its shallow sand pool, was designed by his son, who was a merchant.

The main garden was begun by Lin Wu-lin. He collected rocks, made pools, built pavilions, and planted bamboos to give his mother pleasure. It was then enlarged by his great-nephew, so that his wife, who was a poetess, could have a private place for meditation. "The Poet's Retreat" is separated from the rest of the garden by a hedge of dwarf pines. Although it is encompassed within a few square yards, he so carved the flat plot of land that the perspective is seemingly one of many miles, as the winding path, provided at intervals with seat and table for her use, goes by a tumbling waterfall, climbs through mountain foliage, passes a flower-perfumed dell, penetrates a forest, comes out at a tea-house by a lake where tall lilies blow, follows a lazy river through a field of restful table-grass, and ends at the door of a rustic cottage. All her verses are treasured in a pretty inlaid chest, kept in the cottage.

The courtyard named the "Place of the Meeting of Winged Friends" was constructed by a Lin wife who loved birds. She carved the feeding boards where rice is scattered, made the baskets which hold suet in zero weather and stuffs for nest-making in mating season, designed the lovely sand and water baths, and planted the seed-bearing shrubs.

In such ways the homestead has grown through six centuries and a half. So it continues to grow. The high grey wall does not run in straight lines, but is stretched out to surround whatever land can be secured as more dwelling space is needed.

3

And as in other homes, in all parts of the world, where a family have dwelt in continuous succession for many generations, legends and supernatural beliefs have collected about the House of Exile. When two grey doves are seen perching silently on the roof of the Hall of Ancestors, the Lins await the immediate death of a member of the Family. When two grey doves moan in the maidenhair fern tree in the Three Eastern Courtyards, they abandon any marriage contemplated for a son or a daughter of the house; even if, as has happened, the daughter has already left the homestead in her bridal chair, or the son's betrothed has been welcomed over the "apple of peace."

III

RECEPTION INSIDE THE ORCHID DOOR

1

THE night of my arrival at the House of Exile, Bald-the-third set up a bust-high screen and pushed me behind it to undress. She reached around the screen and took each garment as I removed it. She examined it, then passed it on to Faithful Duck for examination, and thence to Mai-da, who was undressing behind a similar screen.

Mai-da pantomimed my death from cold and cuddled down cozily in a nest of quilts on the brick bed. Bald-the-third and Faithful Duck brought an earthen jar. They filled it with hot water halfway up and pushed it behind my screen. When I was slow in getting in, Bald came behind and put me in. Then she poured more and hotter water in with me until the bunch of herbs that she had added floated just under my chin.

The jar was of a size that I could just sit in, with my feet tucked under me. I was terribly sleepy. Each time I attempted to get out Bald pushed me down.

She kept me soaking until Faithful Duck brought supper. Then I dried on warm towels and was folded up in quilts on one side of the brick bed. A six-inch-legged table was set between Mai-da's nest and mine. Our supper was served on it.

First two lovely robin's-egg-blue bowls and two pairs of ivory chopsticks with silver handles were laid; then three steaming covered dishes. These contained breasts of chicken, red cabbage and green pepper, and tenderloin of pork with chestnuts — each cooked in such a different and delicious sauce that I was eager to possess the recipes to send home to my sisters. When we had eaten of these three dishes, I managing as best I could with my chopsticks, Bald-the-third took them away. I had dropped bits and spattered sauce on the tray. Faithful Duck removed it and set a clean red lacquer tray in its place. Then she placed two sea-green bowls with porcelain spoons to match. Between the bowls, Faithful Duck set a covered tureen of the same sea-green china. It held fish soup. We ladled the soup into our bowls and ate it with the porcelain spoons. It was good, and, having a spoon, I got more of it than of the previous dishes.

The soup was taken away and steamed rice brought. Again we had clean eating bowls — transparent white ones. The rice was served alone. We had chopsticks to eat it with. I did not manage to convey much to my mouth. Mai-da and the serving matrons laughed merrily at my attempts. We finished our meal with hard white winter pears and cups of jasmine tea. The tea was a pale amber in color and served without milk or sugar.

After the meal we were given hot towels to wipe our faces and hands. Bald-the-third thrust more cornstalks into the fire in the stomach of the bed and snuffed the candles. On the merry music of crackling flames I went to sleep.

I woke to the homely sound of cocks' crowing. The sun shone on my face. Mai-da was asleep. She had a block of wood, similar to the one I had pushed out of my bed, tucked under her neck. Faithful Duck was by the window combing her long black hair.

Mai-da woke. Rubbing her eyes, she sat up and glared at me. Then she spoke to the women. Faithful Duck rolled down the paper curtains, shutting out the morning light, and pushed me back into my bed. We slept again. Bald-the-third wakened us with cups of hot rice-water. We drank, then washed and dressed.

My clothes were gone. Two lacquer chests stood side by

side against the wall under the windows.   Mai-da, who then spoke no English and has always stubbornly refused to learn any since, made me understand by gesture that one was hers and one mine.   The serving matrons took identical outfits from the chests for us to put on.

Following Mai-da's lead, I dressed.   I wound myself from my armpits to my hip-joints with a tight bias binding of strong flesh-colored silk, then put on pyjamas of peach silk.   These were made with trousers that wrapped over in pleats in back and front.   Over the under-pyjamas, I put on a second suit cut to the same pattern, but of heliotrope satin lined with white rabbit fur.   Next I pulled on white socks, tucked the legs of the two pairs of trousers neatly into them, and wrapped my ankles in puttees of apple-green satin.   After this I had a third pyjama suit fashioned exactly as the first two.   It was of wine-red brocade, warmed with an inner lining of grey squirrel fur.   I felt so stiff in all my garments that I was glad to do as Mai-da did — thrust my feet out over the edge of the bed and let Bald-the-third put on my black velvet boots lined with red fox.

Shun-ko came.   She explained that my own clothes were put away because they were not suitable in the House of Exile. She pulled out my hairpins, saying that my hair had best be dressed as Mai-da's.   Otherwise it would cause unnecessary comment, since a girl does not pin up her hair in China until she is married.

It was gummed smooth, parted in the middle, pulled back behind my ears, braided at the nape of my neck into a pigtail that swung to my knees.   My braid was wound, a finger-length from the lower end, with half a finger-reel of scarlet thread.   Bald-the-third wanted to dye the hair black, as it is the color of the yellow gentian of misfortune.   But Shun-ko reminded her that yellow is also the color of the innermost petals of the sacred lotus.

So Bald was content, and took satisfaction in my hands,

which she then discovered measure exactly as Shun-ko's. But a few moments later, when she found that my ears had not been pierced in childhood and I could not wear the sapphire earrings provided to match Mai-da's, her depression was pitiful.

Mai-da took a sleeveless blue jacket, lined with beaver, from "my" chest and told me to put it on. When it was buttoned we took leave of Mai-da and went across several courts to Shun-ko's dwelling, which is in the "Court of the White Jade Rabbit" — so called because the legend of the jade rabbit is told in gay colors on the eaves of the four houses that open into the court.

2

En route, Shun-ko stopped to explain a long spiral burning before a bronze Bird of Dawn: —

"This is the Time Stick. Camel-back, our gateman, makes it each day of well-mixed sawdust and clay. He lights it by the stars. His fathers, for eleven generations, have measured time for the Lins. His young grandson proved last spring, when the old man was sick, that he has inherited the gift. They take the time from the sky and their own intuition. We regulate our Western-made watches by our Time Stick,[1] and we amuse ourselves by setting them when we start to Peking so that we can compare them with the big Western clock there. The

---

[1] The twelve carved divisions on the spiral of the Time Stick represent the hours. There are twelve in one day. Two hours of foreign time correspond to one of Chinese time. The hours are named: rat, ox, tiger, hare, dragon, snake, horse, sheep, monkey, cock, dog, and pig. Usually candle-dips are extinguished and we sleep (all but Camel-back, who carries his lantern through the courts sounding his "I am here, robbers!" rattle during all the hours of the night) from the Hour of the Pig to the rising Hour of the Dragon. Then, after rice water and sweet cakes, the children go to their studies, women to the household tasks which we share in rotation, and men to their duties, until a gong announces the morning meal in the Hour of the Snake.

The afternoons pass according to age, necessity, and inclination until the meal in the Hour of the Cock. Then, after a rest for digestion, each one is occupied until sleep. To make a family prosper is like digging clay with a needle, and each member must do his or her share. Idleness brings ruin to a homestead like water removing a sandbank.

clock is a good timepiece. We have never found it more than a quarter of an hour wrong!"

As in Mai-da's house, Shun-ko's dwelling has a brick bed which is built across the back of the room and touches three walls, occupying three fourths of the floor space. It is used for sleeping at night and as a sofa in the daytime, when the folded quilts are stacked at one side, where they make bright layers of scarlet, gold, leaf-green, lavender, and sapphire.

We removed our shoes and our outer jackets before sitting, with our feet tucked under us, on Shun-ko's bed. She gave me a small mortar and pestle and set me to pounding paint ready for her use on the "chart of the lessening of the cold" which she was preparing.

This is an annual record kept as a help with garden and farm work. Shun-ko drew a plum tree. She gave the tree nine branches. She gave each of the nine branches nine twigs. Then she mixed the pigments I had pounded in daubs on her palette with a thin, round-pointed knife. She selected her brushes with care, and shaded the tree-trunk and the branches realistically. She compounded color for leaf buds of brown, green, and silver, and added a generous number to the sketch. Finally she put in the shadow of a pink blossom on each of the eighty-one twigs, and said that after the Winter Solstice she would paint one blossom each day, according to the weather.

A pair of cabinets, of black wood carved with garden and farm scenes, stood against the west wall of Shun-ko's room. She opened one and took out fifty silk scrolls. A plum tree with eighty-one blossoms was painted on each of the scrolls. But no two trees were exactly alike in shape or arrangement. Shun-ko taught me how to read these pictures, so as to know whether a day had been cold or mild, cloudy or fair, windy or still, rainy or snowy, by the way the paint had been put on the petals of a blossom.

Then from the companion cabinet she took fifty other scrolls. From these she read the harvest of fifty seasons, and showed

me how winter weather has affected summer and autumn crops
in the Lin garden and on their farms.   She said that it is the
custom for the wife resident in the Second House of the White
Rabbit to keep these records, as they were started twenty-two
generations ago by the wife for whom this house was designed.

While we cleaned the mortar, pestle, mixing knife, palette,
and the brushes with evil-smelling kerosene, Shun-ko told me
how my place in the House of Exile had been decided.

"Each dwelling place here is inherited by a person entering
the Family by birth or marriage in accord with customs that
have grown into the family regulations with the generations.
You have no place either by birth or by marriage.   Neither is
there precedent in our knowledge for the entrance of an unmarried woman, without the chaperonage of her mother, as a
guest in a Chinese homestead.   You are also the first foreigner
to enter our To and From the World Gate.

"I am sponsor for you.   I am responsible both for your conduct and for your safety.   I prefer to be in the relationship of
mother to you than of friend.   As my daughter, your place is
in the most carefully guarded court of the homestead — the
Springtime Bower.   I reason that the sheltered Springtime
Bower is the only safe place, in a Chinese homestead, for a
maiden of marriageable age.

"But the Springtime Bower in this house is foolishly in-
adequate for a family of this size.   It has only three houses.
The twins, Ching-mei and La-mei, share the first house.   The
second belongs to Su-ling.   She is studying in France.   But
her room could not even be borrowed.   The rule in the House
of Exile is that each daughter's house is absolutely hers until she
acquires, by marriage, a house in another homestead.   The
third house is Mai-da's, although, but for the slackness of the
Elder, she would have been married last Lotus Moon.   So we
puzzled for two moons about where to put you.

"I happened to remember that you had given me the year,
the month, the day, and the hour of your birth in a letter, so

that I could have a horoscope cast for you, and that they were identical with Mai-da's. Then, as Mai-da was willing to have the test made, the Elder wrote your name and hers, with this information, on a slip of red paper. He put the paper on the altar in the Circle of Ancestors. It lay there for three days. During those days, tranquil weather, and fortune in the repayment of a loan made three generations ago to the Yen Family, were taken as omens of a peaceful double domicile. Mai-da prepared to share her house with you."

Next, Shun-ko drew for my guidance a list of the "Living Generations of the Family." She wrote in the names according to English sound, and left space below each for me to add phrases to aid me in remembering who was who.

After this she drew a map of the homestead to aid me to find my way about. As she worked, she explained, "The general plan of the house in which I was born, and of all the Chinese homes in which I have visited, is the same as this. Homes here are on a similar system, whether of one court or one hundred. This is sensible. One knows on entering a homestead which way to go to find the place of books, the garden, the abode of the Oven God, or the residence of the Family Elder."

3

Mai-da's mother joined us. We three lunched together, waited on by her Swift Needle, Shun-ko's Sweet Rain, and my Bald-the-third. When the meal was ended, the women fussed nervously over my appearance. They added cuffs to my outer coat, recombed my hair, plucked my eyebrows to a high thin arch, rouged my mouth and the lobes of my ears, and perfumed the palms of my hands. They changed my black velvet boots to jade silk slippers embroidered with eglantine.

Shun-ko put on ceremonial garments. She adorned herself with pearl earrings, pearl hair ornaments, pearl coat buttons. She rubbed her polished nails to a high pink gloss. Then she

turned her attention to my appearance again, worrying, until
at last Mai-da's mother teasingly placed my hand in Shun-ko's
and pushed us out to the round of visits which Shun-ko dreaded.
We went first to the Garden of Children. There nine little
boys and girls received us. Shun-yi, who was then ten years
old and had an intelligent face, rose from a game of hedged-in
chess which he was playing with his sister Hsing-mu. He took
her left hand and the right hand of their half-brother, Wen-wu,
and all bowed together. A chubby lad, Tsai-fu, thrust a
shuttlecock into the pocket of his long turquoise gown and
bent so that his forehead tapped the playroom floor. Ming-chi
had boots of yellow-and-black-striped tiger cloth. He saluted
with his feet well placed to display them. The baby brothers,
Chin-shan and Chen-feng, were bright-eyed, rosy satin bundles, held in their nurses' arms. Nan-wei, slim and graceful, assisted by her cousin Mai-lei, — a maid of five summers,
— gave us jasmine tea and saw to it that the boys passed the
salted watermelon seeds frequently.

Next we went to the court adjoining the Springtime Bower,
to which girls graduate from the Garden of Children, and
called on capable Shou-su and shy Li-niang. In the Bower, the
lovely twins, Ching-mei and La-mei, and my house-partner,
Mai-da, greeted us with formal ceremony. Following Shun-
ko's example, I soon learned that when a hostess lifts her tea-
cup to her lips the polite moment to say farewell has arrived,
and that one should then go no matter how much the hostess
begs one to stay.

Li-la, the first mother of the House of Exile, was a "green-
skirt" mate. So in the courtyards of the mates of Lin sons,
Shun-ko was careful to stay as long in the dwellings of those
who wore the green skirts as in the houses of wives. We
visited first with the Fourth Generation, who live in three
courts called the "Favorite Eaves of Nesting Swallows."

In the south court of the Eaves, young Sung-li, the only wife
of Lin Ju-liang, fulfilled the rites of courtesy in the first house,

but made me feel uncomfortable. She is antiforeign, with bitter memories of the invasion of her father's house by Western soldiers following the siege of Peking in 1900, when, at seven years of age, she saw her mother raped.

Ah-chiao, a bride of a year, and Sou-mai, a bride of a month, were married to brothers. Their houses both opened into the same court as Sung-li's. They both asked Shun-ko to tell me I must not be troubled by whatever reception Sung-li had given me. They both said that they wanted me to know that Sung-li is good, and to excuse her because she cannot forget what her beloved parents suffered and so thinks it dangerous to have invited me into the Lin homestead.

In accord with custom, we called next on the women of the Third Generation. Mai-da's mother, who shares the Court of the White Jade Rabbit with Shun-ko and Fu-erh, is a student and needs a study, so has two houses. Fu-erh has one house, which she has made into a comfortable, homey dwelling place. She is a timid wife, afraid to live away from the family homestead, and chose the daughter of a neighbor to accompany her husband to Malay, where he is the manager of the family interests.

In the "Court of the Goldfish" the lake was frozen over. Yu-lin and Chu-kang showed me the fish moving sluggishly about in wooden tubs in a heated paper house, where they rest all winter, without food. They all had descriptive names. "Looking up to Heaven" was a variety with large eyes in the top of the head. "Looking to the Earth" had eyes set the opposite way. "Grey Chiffon Veil" had a filmy fin. "Silver Arrow" was slim-bodied, with a broad head. "Gold Nugget" was almost round. There were seventy-two pairs in all.

The visits to this generation were completed with two calls in the "Court of the Ginkgo Trees" — one on Chao-li, who believes that the golden age was in the past; and the other on Mei-lui, the first Wong mother who did not break her daughter's feet to the "golden lily" fashion.

We went then to the mates of the Second Generation. In the dower court of the "Within the Orchid Door" half of the Sons' Courtyards, the widows of the Elder's first son gave us tea, seasoned by wrapping it in lotus petals, and tiny doughnuts stuffed with chestnuts.

In the court of the Son's Wife, Kou-hsing, the only mate of the financial head of the Family, showed me snapshots of the school she runs for the Daughters of the Village Poor.

In the court of the Meeting Place of Winged Friends, I exchanged smiles with Fan-li, the woman versed in folklore who is the only wife of the Elder's third son; with Mi-ying, whose mating with the Elder's fourth son gave the Family Fou-mu — a wizard in money accumulation and in growing chrysanthemums; and with Kang-nen, the widow of the Elder's fifth son, who is deeply concerned over the stabilization of the Chinese Republic, for which cause her husband gave his life on the battlefield at Lion Hill in 1911.

Shun-ko explained the Elder's sixth son to me as we walked to the courts of his mates, which are called the New Courts. Wen-lieh was born in 1884. In babyhood he selected military toys from the pedlars, and demanded that the candymen make warriors. He was educated by tutors at home, in the Peiyang Military College, and in the Training School for Military Officers in Japan, from which foreign place he graduated with distinction. Since then he has been occupied every year with a war to end war in China. He is wise in politics and gentle to women. He has married seven times.

When the Elder said that he should be careful not to take up more space in the homestead than rightfully belonged to a sixth son, he received the hint with good nature. He bought up about four acres of land which touched at one place on the boundary wall of the House of Exile. This land was occupied by small shops and dwellings, but he had them razed. The homestead wall was stretched out to embrace it. Then it was divided into seven spacious courts with dividing walls of blue glazed tile.   A poetic name was set in colored pebbles over each court gate.

As the winter violets had come into bloom, he asked Hua-li to make him seven bouquets.   He put one of the seven poetic court names in each of the bouquets.   He carried the bouquets in a basket to his mother and asked her to give each of his mates one.   Thus there was no favoritism in deciding just who should have any particular court.

This done, he gave each woman exactly the same generous purse to build whatever house she desired and landscape her ground to her own fancy — and went off to his army.

In the New Courts, each of Wen-lieh's seven mates received me kindly in her own house.   But even on that first day of meeting, I knew that Nuan, whom her husband rescued from the Manchu massacre at Nanking, was drawn to me, as I was drawn to her, by that mutual esteem which is called friendship.

4

"The First Generation will not receive you in their residences in the Three Eastern Courtyards, but in the Guest Hall of the Court of Dignity," Shun-ko said, and took me back to her own dwelling house.

There she anxiously re-tidied me, and rehearsed me for this audience.   When she was satisfied that I could bow "making a curve like a bamboo sapling swept by the wind," that I understood how to take the cup of tea that would be offered to me in the palms of both hands and not to drink it but to offer the cup back as though I felt myself unworthy to drink in such company, then when the tea had been pressed upon me three times to walk backward, in "flowerlike modesty," and seat myself in the most lowly place, "the chair by the table nearest the door," she made me warm myself thoroughly by the charcoal brazier and started out with me again.

The opaque shell lattices at the Orchid Door were drawn

aside by serving matrons. We passed out of the Women's
Quarters and around the Phœnix Screen into the Court of
Dignity.

This court had a slippery ice film frozen over the paving
stones. We had to walk with care and help each other. As we
approached the Guest Hall, blue-clad serving women opened
the cinnabar-velvet door of the Hall of Dignity.

The entire south front of this hall is of carved openwork
rosewood picturing historical legends, just as in the West it is
the custom to picture Biblical stories in stained glass in churches.
The carvings are set off by gold rice paper placed between the
two surfaces of the wood, which are identical whether viewed
from the court or from inside the hall.

The hall occupies the entire north side of the court and runs
back so that its depth takes in all the space of an additional
ordinary court. It is beamed with dark rafters. On the sides
of these beams brilliantly colored scenes from the lives of Lin
men and women are painted. A portrait of Confucius hangs
on the north wall, and on either side of it gilt scrolls on which
are written two of his analects. Portraits of the founders of
the House and other ancestors, mounted on yellow silk, all
dressed in rich silk robes and done in realistic color, decorate the
east and west walls. The floor is of grey tile and uncarpeted.

The furniture is of heavy black wood polished to a mirror
surface. There are small tables, straight-back chairs, and stiff
settees, all set in prim order against the wall. They are so
arranged that Chinese people know exactly which seat is in what
grade of honor. It is here that all receptions are held on Feast
Days.

The only heat to combat the winter chill of the hall, which
Shun-ko whispered to me had not been used since the Autumn
Festival, was one small bronze brazier on the floor in the centre
of the room. Each of the "First Ladies of the Homestead" had
a tiny charcoal-filled hand-warmer, but it would not have been
polite for Shun-ko and me to have so warmed our hands.

There were three of these ladies.   They sat stiffly erect, not touching the backs of their chairs.   Kuei-tzu, the wife of the Elder, was directly under the portrait of the first mother of the homestead.   She is small and delicately made.   Her face is marked by surprisingly few wrinkles.   Her eyes are two bright black crystals.   Her hands taper and are very white.   She wore a fitted gown of black brocade with hairpin, earrings, dress buttons, and finger ring of gold, set with large diamonds.

Ju-i, the Elder's second mate, sat in the same settee, but to the left.   Ju-i is five feet nine inches.   She has a dry yellow skin stretched over her gaunt frame.   Her nose is Hebraic, and she is proud of her birthplace — Sianfu.   She drops her black hair in waxed wings over her ears in defiance of fashion. She heightens her high cheekbones with daubs of carmine.   She paints her thin lips to a carmine line.   She plucks her eyebrows out and draws in short thick eyebrows with a black pencil.   That afternoon she was costumed in green taffeta and had scarlet shoes.   She scared me in our first exchange of glances.   I stayed scared for many years.

The widow of the Elder's Second Brother sat in a chair to the right.   She wore a gown of grey cotton and the white cord of mourning in her hair.   Her wrinkled face is sweet and sad. She is blind to earthly things, but gifted with sight into the future.

I made my three bamboo-sapling bows to each lady.   I took the cup of tea into my palms and then refused it three times. When it had been pressed upon me three times, I did my best to walk modestly backwards to the chair nearest the door.

This over, the First Lady spoke to me.   As I did not understand, Shun-ko changed her sounds into English.   I replied in English.

The First Lady then made sounds that were like ice tinkling in a glass.   Shun-ko told me to bow my head and to withdraw.   Thus I was dismissed.

So Kuei-tzu, Lady of First Authority in the House of Exile,

gave the command that I was not to be presented to audience again until I was sufficiently civilized to hear and to speak for myself, and that no member of the Family was ever again to speak with me in any language except Chinese.

5

Shun-ko took me back to Mai-da's house. Mai-da dropped the lid of her chest as we entered and busied herself with the embroidery of a shoe. By gestures, Shun-ko told me to sew the cuffs of my coat, and left us.

Mai-da barred our door on her departure. With pretty grimaces and signs she dramatized herself and me against all others. Then she put her shoe embroidery away and took out the work she had thrust into her chest on hearing our footsteps.

While I entered the day's activities in my journal, she finished an excellent likeness of the tall skater who had picked up our two oranges on the way down from Peking.

6

Originally it had been arranged that the announcement of my arrival in the House of Exile would be made to the ancestors on the evening of the same day as my introduction to the children and women of the Family. But the First Lady's dismissal of us until I could hear and speak postponed this ceremony for a considerable time.

Eventually, however, my ear, my brain, and my tongue were sufficiently well versed for Shun-ko to present me for examination. Then the Hall of Ancestors was swept. Laurel incense was bought. The Family gathered under the "lamp of continuous life" within the circle of tablets of the Lin generations who have gathered the flower of life.

The Elder announced my arrival in a speech in which he

explained how it happened that I had been invited. As previously instructed, I lit three tapers before the tablets of the Founders, three tapers before the tablets of each of the men and women whose earthly lives are woven into the homestead pattern, nine candles to the memory of Lin Yan-ken, and nine candles before a tablet to the memory of J. S. Waln.

IV

THE FARMER'S CALENDAR

1

TIME in China has no immediacy as in America. Here I find the swift passage of our few earthly years accepted as naturally as the fall of flower and leaf. This philosophical acceptance of the individual life as just a part of the life of the race, which goes on as the life of the tree goes on, makes time limitless. A century past or a century in the future is not considered far off.

I hear and speak a language in which grammar has no tense. Both scholars and illiterates, in ordinary daily speech, tell an event of centuries ago as casually as an incident of the hour. Only as my knowledge has accumulated have I been able to know whether something related happened just then or in some past dynasty. Even now, after twelve years, I often do not know.

"Events that happen," so a rickshaw runner explained as he pulled me to market one morning, "are not put away in books. That would not be fair. Only a few folk have leisure to read, and history belongs to everyone. It flows in every mother's milk and is digested by every babe. Thus it becomes a part of everyone's experience to use when needed. That which happens is not past. It is all a part of our now."

I have always had difficulty in keeping any time schedule. Consequently I slipped more unconsciously into time's easy flow in China than one of different temperament might have done. Hours, days, weeks, and months glided smoothly by in the cycle of seasons, from which serenity we were occasionally summoned by the special festivals. With the fast of Li Chun men prepare to welcome the spring. The fast begins fifty-three sunrises after the winter solstice and requires three days of abstinence from meat and from woman.

On the last day of the fast, Kuei-tzu, Lady of First Authority in the House of Exile, summoned all the maidens, including me, to the Court of Sunrise. The morning was mild. We found her seated in a wicker chair with her back to a sun-warmed wall.

And we promptly knelt as "flowers bent by the nourishing rain," which is the name of the salute due from daughters to the home mother. She had called us to make the things ready for the "Welcome to Spring Procession."

The procession torches are by tradition lit with fire drawn from the sun. This is done with a concave mirror which Mai-da now had to polish with dried corn silk. Seeds of each crop the House intends to plant have to be carried in the procession. Ching-mei put them into blue-green or vermilion silk, according to the season of planting. At the proper time in the ceremony this seed is watered with dew. The Family Elder had set metallic plates on pedestals in the centre of the court. These had already drawn a plentiful supply of dew from the sky, which was now transferred to a white jade bottle.

A craftsman brought a life-sized papier-mâché water buffalo and buffalo driver. Camel-back wheeled in a barrow filled with willow whips. One of us counted them. Each farmer in the procession must have a willow whip to beat the buffalo in the chase that drives winter away.

I had to dust the drum used to call the patrons of the soil. One beat calls the spirits from the water. They come easily. Two beats are needed to summon the timid wood spirits. It takes three loud raps to waken the sluggish spirits that dwell in laziness on the seashore. The spirits of the field, who are busy folk, will not come for less than four beats. It takes five beats to bring the spirits that live within the earth. Their

hearing is not good.   The spirits that live in the sky are proud:
they wait until they have been called by six beats.   The spirits
of the mountain are given seven beats.   They are the most
important.   They disappear after the harvest and must be got
out again in the spring.   They make harmony between man
and nature.   When they are stubborn farming is not successful.

Ancient manuscripts in the House of Exile library cabinets
tell that in olden days maidens took part in the spring rites
celebrating, then, the festival of love.   But Kuei-tzu, First
Lady in Authority now in the homestead, trusts neither ancient
manuscript nor Western custom.   Maids under her protection
do not join in any festival procession which includes men —
except that procession which goes direct to the bridegroom's
door.

On the holiday morning, the wives and girl children went
out with the boys and men to join in the Welcome to Spring
Procession.   We maids of marriageable age were left inside
the homestead.   Kuei-tzu locked the To and From the World
Gate with the special key she uses for such occasions.

Folk go to meet spring in their winter clothes.   They change
to the flowerlike pastel silks worn during spring when they
return home.   These dresses were all ready, but it is the
maidens' duty to take them from the chests; also to finish
the preparation of the Spring Feast.

The other girls had all ridden in sedan chairs in the procession each year until puberty.   As we sat on top of the Wall
of Heaven, with our arms about each other's waists, Mai-da
told me that it is the nicest procession of the Farmer's Calendar.
She said that I must hurry to marry so that I might have a wife's
right to ride in it.

When the Family returned, the young wives made me
envious, chatting elatedly about how they had joined the
tenant-farmer families at the Temple of Agriculture, watched
the Elder draw fire from the sun, applauded the dancers who

waved the pine-faggot torches, admired the lithe vigor of the young farmers who whipped the buffalo into the chase, swayed to the rhythm of the music, watched the seed poured on the earth altar and moistened with dew from the white jade bottle, clapped hands to the drumbeats that summoned the patrons of the soil, joined in the glad chorus when the singers announced that spring had arrived, and enjoyed the Elder's oration, which was a combination of rhetorical welcome to spring and prudent advice to the farmers.

When we had all been given time to change into spring dress, Camel-back played a flute through the courts, calling the Family to feast together in the Hall of Family Gathering. The Lady of First Authority presided at this feast.

The Elder did not break his fast in the homestead. He presided over a feast in the Cantonese Guildhall. By their invitations to the Spring Feast at the Cantonese Guildhall, the House of Exile signify that they are content to continue a farmer's lease. By breaking his fast at this table, the tenant signifies that he is content to continue to farm the land he farmed last year.

2

During this season the Elder explained land to the homestead children and the brides-of-the-year in a talk given in the library court. I was told to attend. I took notes as they did.

From the beginning of history — that is, for about forty-six centuries — there has been no freehold ownership of land here. Ownership has always been vested in the government in power, which holds the earth in trusteeship for the populace. There is no historic mention of the granting of large tracts in return for feudal services; but there is frequent mention of idle families, and even Emperors, forced to give up for cultivation arable soil that they have walled in as private pleasure parks.

Since a country is indeed weak which cannot produce its own food, agriculture in China has rightly been accorded first place among the branches of labor since time immemorial. The occupation of the land by those who are willing to till it is justice so practical that no government has ever yet denied it. The government must give a lease, or "red card," as it is popularly called, to one who is willing to cultivate any idle piece of land.

The holder of a red card can sell his lease to another farmer. But of course the land still belongs to the government. It does not matter how many times the red card has changed hands or whether or not the government that issued it went out of office centuries ago. If the government in power decides that it is for the general good of the populace, for whom they are trustees, to put up a building, cut a canal, make a broad highway, or change the course of a river, they can "call for the land." They have the right to use the land. They can sweep homesteads and crops out of the way. The deed holder has no right to indemnity.

Yet such disaster does not descend on one family in every thousand twice in a hundred generations. Land in China produces the major revenue which makes it possible for governments to function. So land is dealt with carefully. Governments have always been cautious about committing acts which would frighten folk away from land. Instead they have so fostered land that, if a family make some profit in trade or office, land is always considered the wisest investment; even though under the most careful husbandry it brings in only an average of from 3 to 4 per cent interest.

Since property in China is almost always held by a family and not by an individual, the title to possession is not disturbed by the death of any particular individual. A change in the family, such as the succession of a new Elder, is a private matter and does not concern the government so long as the House continues to pay taxes at the time of demand.

Unoccupied land, whether originally waste, or cultivated but abandoned through famine, civil war, or neglect, — even graves become "waste land" if not swept annually, — may be acquired by planting a crop in it, and making application to the government for a red card. The government can see by the planted seed that the applicant is a farmer and not a land speculator. The official must then issue a call to the last cultivators to come and do the work of the season. If they do not respond, the new applicant must be given a red card without paying any purchase money. He in turn must produce a harvest. If he fails to grow crops, then he can be ousted by another farmer who can.

The holder of every red card pays the government a tax on his harvests. This amount varies in accord with fertility of the soil, the ease with which it can be tilled, and the custom that has maintained in that field. When rough or poor land is first brought into cultivation, it is usual for governments to allow the farmer time for a return on capital expended before assessment, as it is to the interest of the government to induce people to till the soil.

Waste land which no one can be induced to farm belongs to the inhabitants of the nearest village, in common, until such time as someone will bring it into cultivation. There are no enclosure acts in China, and no lords of the manor with special rights in the wild game or in wild growth. There can be no private possession without annual sowing and reaping. Anyone can pasture goats, trap or hunt rabbits, pheasants, geese, and duck, or cut firewood, on any unploughed land. The selling of game and firewood from such common land is the only livelihood of some poor people in every settlement.

When a river in flood washes away land under cultivation, the farmer is entitled to follow his soil. When more than one farm has been moved, the new formation must be divided among the claimants in a ratio proportional to their loss. If there are no claimants for such land, which is often carried hundreds of miles, the first person to plant a crop in it has the right to a red card.

The House of Exile is the second largest landowner of their district.   They possess red card titleship to one thousand, five hundred and forty-three acres.   But their fields do not stretch in one continuous plantation.   Their land is made up of small holdings, some as small as one sixth of an acre, scattered over an area which is dotted by the holdings of others.

By homestead labor they farm ten acres, which is called the "Home Farm."   The rest is divided among six hundred tenant-farmers.   The largest lessee farms three acres; the smallest one eighth of an acre.   The tenant rights are for no settled time, but "at will" — meaning the will of both parties.   The longest single lease in the Lins' possession has been renewed with one family for thirty generations.   The tenants do not dwell on the farms.   They live in the same city as the Lin Family or in either of the two villages farther up the canal.

SPRING PLOUGHING

Under the Lin management the tenant provides all the farm implements and the animal or man power — also the seeds, except in cases of special arrangement such as the rice paddies where, as the Lins are Southerners and so wiser in the growing of rice than Northerners, they prefer to control the seed.   The House of Exile pays all government taxes, provides the material for extension or repair of the irrigation system, and names the principal crop to be grown, as the Family is concerned with producing that for which there is a good market and in keeping up the fertility of the soil.

In addition to the principal crop, all tenants can, and most do, produce subsidiary crops. These subsidiary crops belong entirely to the tenant, but they must not encroach upon the principal crop. The rent is a proportion of the principal crop only.

If the agreed crop is fruit or vegetables, it is gathered by the tenant and divided in the village market place. If the crop is grain, it is threshed on the village threshing floor by the labor of the tenant, in the presence of a Lin who superintends the work and measures the grain. The crop is divided when the flailing is finished. Thus a year's rent is settled at the harvest. The tenant is never in arrears in payment. And the landlord and tenant share fortune in good and bad seasons.

3

The Farmer's Calendar is a sun calendar. It traces the sun's path across the heavens by twelve stars. It divides the sun's journey into four sections. These are the four seasons. And the seasons are further divided into periods, each with an indicative name.

In "Rain Water" we had grey weather at sunrise each day, a south wind each morning, and a fine drizzle of rain all day through. The Family were pleased. They greeted each other with, "If this gentle thaw continues we shall have easy ploughing." We all went about in thatched-straw raincoats and peaked thatch hats. Stable dung was hauled and spread around the paper-shell walnut trees that beautify the fields, around the hazel and beech shrubs that grow along the edges of the paths, and around the giant chestnut tree, in which the Lins have only a half interest, as it is on the boundary line dividing their land from the Wongs'.

On "Get-up-Insects" eve we unfurled pennants on the roofs

to greet the bees. Unless the bees assist by carrying the pollen, a harvest is impossible. We rose at dawn and, in accord with an old superstition, washed in water in which the bark of the lilac had been steeped, to make ourselves beautiful.

It is the rule in the House of Exile to sterilize the water jars and fumigate the sleeping rooms on the first day of Get-up-Insects. We were busy with these tasks until long after sunset, as might be expected in a homestead where there are no "modern conveniences."

In mid-afternoon there was a rainbow in the east. Camel-back came through the courts playing a roundelay on his flute. His grandson ran beside him singing that the heavens announced a period of clear, bright weather. Had the rainbow appeared in the west, he caroled, the future would have been wet.

The fortnight of gentle rain had broken the ice in the canal and thawed the frost from the earth. A radiant sun now dried the earth, clearing up mud and dirty mounds of honey-combed snow. The hibernating creatures came out. Frogs croaked a chorus from the ponds. Beetles came up through the crevices of the court paving stones and warmed themselves. The goldfish were suddenly restless and fed greedily when food was offered to them. Wild geese flew over the House of Exile, going north. Wild duck followed them. The swallows came back and fluttered in graceful swoops in and out of the Favorite Eaves.

During this season I heard much concerning the danger of flood. Wei-sung, Elder of the House of Exile, wrote a petition reporting weaknesses in the canal and advising that repairs be completed before the summer rains. This petition was cir-culated until it held the signature of one thousand Family Elders.

In company with representatives from eighteen other clans, Shun-ko's husband took the petition to the President of the Republic. On his return he reported in Family Council that it was as futile this year as it was in other Republican years to expect government attention.

The Family decided that the canal must be mended. Ho-min was sent out to collect what funds he could from the signers of the petition. Uncle Shao-chun called for farmer volunteers to do the repairs under his direction. In the courts beyond the Orchid Door I heard that this was the way that the canal had been kept under control for more than a dozen years.

"It is our duty to prevent flood if we can," Shun-ko said. "Should our efforts fail it is always our duty, as a Big House, to feed and reëstablish the survivors. Big Houses, with wealth placed where the water cannot carry it away, must do all they can for the Little Houses."

Even after his canal mending was done for the season, Uncle Shao-chun continued to go out to the farms each day on errands relating to the spring planting of crops. He took lunch with him. He was accompanied by Camel-back's grandson. The boy drove the grey donkey hitched to the basket cart.

By our diligence in helping to cut the sprouted seed potatoes, Mai-da and I won approbation and permission to drive with Uncle Shao-chun one day. He managed his itinerary so that we picnicked beside the natural spring in the walnut grove.

We were ambitious about the food. We had some difficulty in making the charcoal glow at first, but it burned well after we moved it into a sheltered place under a bank. We had fried meat pasties of chicken breast minced with celery, which we had made ready for cooking at home; then broiled mushrooms, picked by the roadside while Uncle Shao-chun talked with a farmer; next steamed noodles with dried-apricot sauce. These we followed by a dish of cabbage sauced with vinegar, cloves, and paprika. He ate of everything. So did we. We rounded the picnic with dates stuffed with almonds. Uncle Shao-chun said that after feasting on our cooking he felt more like a comfortable sleep than an afternoon of mental activity.

At the vernal equinox, — the first day of "Spring Divided in the Middle," — the Elder put on the ceremonial ploughing coat and opened the ploughing season by cutting three furrows across the Eastern Fields. Then, generation by generation in orderly succession according to birth, each son of the House of Exile ploughed three furrows. Next, in precedence determined by length of service to the Family, each laborer opened three furrows.

After this, day by day until all the land was turned up in brown waves, the ploughmen went out through the To and From the World Gate early so as to be at the city gate when it was unlocked at dawn, and down to the fields — set in small squares among other similar squares to which ploughmen from other families hastened. Each ploughman carried a light plough on his shoulder, and had a teapot with a packet of lunch tied to it swinging from his left hand.

The five oxen went; the three brown donkeys; the white mule; also the dappled goat. Each beast with his lunch on his back. The men and work boys did not ride on the animals. To ride would take some of the creature's strength. It was all needed for the work.

But even with this care, there was not sufficient beast strength to draw all the ploughs. Many of the rich furrows were turned up to the sun by men hitched in the yokes and a man at the plough handles. After the land was ploughed, it was crushed and smoothed by the harrows and the rollers.

The House of Exile does not rest one day in seven. Although many of the Family can read and all know that the official calendar of the Republic is the Gregorian calendar, they have not yet adopted it. In public they give it lip service. In private they explain their not using it by saying that each dynasty must have a calendar — but that no matter how many dynasties come and go, farming must continue serenely. And although there have been nine different official calendars since the dynasty that gave the Farmer's Calendar, crops have continued through the centuries to be planted, tilled, and reaped according to its ancient wisdom.

On the evening of the "Time of Clear and Bright Air" all the people of the House of Exile were called to the Court of Dignity. The Elder read to us from the Farmer's Calendar: —

"All the ploughing, harrowing, and rolling that has tortured the Earth since the vernal equinox shall now stop for three days that the Earth may be rested by undisturbed enjoyment of the Sun's caresses. All the beasts shall have three days to relax their muscles and no person shall even hitch an animal to a light pleasure cart. For three days all the families must cease to give thought to material gain. Tools must be laid down; shops shuttered; offices closed. Men, women, and children must now lift their spirits above mundane concerns and make merry in appreciation of all that the gods give them free."

The winter wheat was a lusty green and high as an ox's hoof. Tender grass had broken through the last year's stubble. Leaf buds on the maples were bright red. Sap was rising in the grape arbors. Wild wistaria hung in lavender curtains from every rocky ledge. The hawthorn and the wild cherry were in bloom, mingling their perfume by every gentle breeze with the fragrance of the orchard blossoms. The magpie, the rook, the robin, and the wren were mating.

On the first day of the festival, we all went out on foot. We wore gowns and shoes of springtime silk in blossom colors. The clothes of the men and boys were as delicately beautiful as the clothes of the women and girls.

We trod on grass. We planted a tree beside a public path. We swept the graves of the ancestors. While some of us tidied the earth that the winter frost had disarranged on the graves, the musicians of the Family piped airs on reed flutes for the pleasure of the Souls. Food and tea were put down on embroidered cloths beside each grave. The Family kowtowed at each grave to show their respect for their forbears, to whom they are grateful for the establishment and continuance of the Family.

The Family sat on crimson cushions and picnicked of the food that had been ceremoniously offered at the graves. There was no mourning. The descendants were happy. They had come in happiness to put in order, as an act of remembrance, the mounds where the earthly bodies of their predecessors had been laid. They spoke of the exact places where they hoped their bodies would be placed. They talked calmly of their descendants a hundred years in the future.

We brought home branches of sweet pine and decorated the courtyards. Kuei-tzu made fire between two willow sticks for the children's delight. Shun-ko brought baskets filled with pigeon, hen, duck, and turkey eggs. These were a gift from the wives to the children. We of the Springtime Bower gave the children packets of bright dye. Assisted by their nurses, they colored the eggs, boiling them in the dyes over the elm-wood fire. When the eggs were cool, they polished them with sweet-perfumed oil, arranged them in woven nests, and presented some to each adult of the home.

The Men's Courts gave the children gay-hued feather shuttles. Everyone in the homestead enjoyed these. Children and adults played a graceful game of skill the object of which was to keep the toy in the air as long as possible, kicking it up, each time it fell, with the backs of one's heels.

Pairs of vermilion wood posts with a crossbar were set up at the east, the south, the west, and the north extremes of the garden. A blue silk rope swing was hung from each crossbar and fitted with a green seat carved like a curved dragon. A green pillar ten feet high was planted firmly in the earth at the centre of the garden. A huge purple wheel was fastened to the top of the pillar. Twelve silk ropes of different colors, one for each star on the sun's road, were hung as swings from the stout wheel spokes. The Elder said that we were like shimmering butterflies in our festival gowns as we swung north and south, east and west, or whirled round and round, on the wheel. All the household enjoyed this sport, which is called "the sport of the immortals" because it gives the sensation of flying.

During the festival, members of the shoemakers' guild, the weavers' guild, the silversmiths' guild, the printers' guild, the wine guild, the jewelers' guild, and the boat-builders' guild knocked at the To and From the World Gate. Each group was given a blue-green dragon purse filled with silver coins, and welcomed into the garden. They were all dressed in fairy costumes, and enacted fox-sprite and fairy-legend plays.

After the festival, work began again. The House of Exile sows in accord with a system of crop rotation — given to the people by an Emperor of the Han dynasty — which they trust will keep the soil ever enriched. Shun-ko was kept busy verifying statements as to what had grown in each ground plot last year, and seven years back, according to her charts. Uncle Shao-chun diligently inspected the seeding of the shifty among the tenants, to make certain that they planted that which should go into the soil.

4

"Ch'in chien fu keui chih pen" ("Diligence and thrift are the roots of wealth and honor") is the song of the vermilion bird — so Camel-back's grandson told me — who comes from the south and rules the agricultural year from the arrival of summer until autumn comes. There were no ceremonies to welcome "Come Summer," as the vermilion bird would be angered if folk stopped their work. The rice plants, now five inches tall, were transplanted into the mud in terraced fields prepared for flooding. Peanuts were hoed in. The sprouted sweet-potato tubers were cut into small pieces and planted in sandy soil. Peas were brushed, so that they could climb up toward the sun; gourds poled. Cucumbers and melons were moved, set in groups of four plants, and covered with bamboo

frames that had coarsely woven cotton cloth stretched across to keep out the melon bugs. Turnips, leeks, carrots, onions, parsnips, chili peppers, celery, cabbage, lettuce, ginger, and artichokes were thinned. The plucked-out seedlings were planted in other places. Beets and eggplant were sown.

Mai-da's brother, Peng-wen, came home. After much hesitation and doubt the tiny green peaches were thinned in accord with a new theory to which he had been converted by the Nanking School of Agriculture. He was enthusiastic about Sun Yat-sen's ideas, ardent in his belief that a government for the people and of the people and by the people was possible in China, and convinced that Nanking should be the capital of the Republic.

Everyone agreed that Nanking was a beautiful city and a central location, and that one capital for the country was more economical than the present situation of one capital at Peking, one at Canton, and the people in every province left to the mercy of whatever man seized district power. The homestead family also agreed that the only reason, ever, that any government exists is "for the benefit of the people."

They said that "of the people" helped to make a sonorous triple rhyme. The courtyards rang with argument each time he attempted to make converts to "by the people." That, they considered, was absurd. Since time immemorial people were entirely occupied with their own affairs, and paid willingly, or even gave one or two sons to the service of the government, to be relieved of such responsibility.

Sun Yat-sen was called a "donkey" so repeatedly that the Elder forbade the use of the word, as it upset Peng-wen and took his thoughts away from the care of the fruit orchards. The reason Sun Yat-sen was called a donkey was because, after appointment to the presidency of the newborn Republic ten years earlier, he resigned in favor of his bitter enemy, Yuan Shih-kai, hoping thus to make peace in the land, "when even the barbers knew that Yuan Shih-kai was a reptile."

The Springtime Bower found all this occupation with politics tiresome. The other maids scolded Mai-da because she did not keep her brother quiet. But they all encouraged him when he told of serious, young, pretty Mrs. Sun Yat-sen, the second daughter of the Shanghai House of Soong. No one was tired when he described her dresses on the different occasions he had seen her. He could remember each detail of her costume, as he had found them intriguingly individual in design — sometimes of Western pattern, sometimes of the simplicity of the early Ming period, and often combining the best features of many fashions. He had a photograph of her and delighted us by having copies made for each of Mai-da's special friends.

The Family liked especially to hear about her foreign house in the French Concession at Shanghai. I had told them numbers of times of homes where one does not have to draw water up from a well, carry it across courtyards in wooden buckets, heat it in iron cauldrons from which it must be dipped and carried to the place where it is needed — but where one just turns a tap with thumb and finger, and it gushes out hot or cold in any place where one wants to put in a tap. But they never believed me until Peng-wen told us that Mrs. Sun Yat-sen had such taps.

All the Family encouraged Peng-wen to tell about the handsome and intelligent young man whom he had met at Fenghua, while visiting a maternal cousin. He had dined at the homestead of this young man, who was named Chiang Kai-shek and had formerly been secretary to Sun Yat-sen. Peng-wen said that his cousin had told him that a friendly Russian, then visiting China, had told Sun Yat-sen that his former secretary, Chiang Kai-shek, would be welcome at Moscow any time that it would be a help to the Republic to have a representative study the Soviet method of putting ideals into workable government form.

Mai-da's mother interrupted this talk of Russia to ask her son if, since he found this young man so admirable, he had remembered that a suitable marriage had yet to be arranged for his sister. He murmured that an acquaintance could not mention such a matter to Chiang Kai-shek. His mother reminded him that the Lins, as well as her own father's House of Tong, were equal to any in the hundred names. Peng-wen said that the younger Republicans disapproved of family-arranged marriages.

She retorted, "Ah! Yah! Then when this Republic gets itself established, girls will have to go out and hunt for their mates? If their families cannot help them get married, then they will have to become bold and deceitful, preying on any man they can get, yet pretending that they are not wanting one. Only the most artful will mate! Shy, plain, good maids will wither into a fruitless age!"

5

In "Small Fullness," men's backs were bent to weeding in every plantation. Soil was loosened around each stalk of the winter wheat, now heavy with swelling grain, with fine one-toothed hoes. The red cherries ripened. The crop of the district was so abundant that few could be sold in the local market place. The profit in cherries was decidedly too small to warrant taking them to Peking by hired boat, and the homestead boatmen were already occupied hoeing the more important winter wheat. So what could not be eaten were made into cherry vinegar, compotes, and jellies.

Each afternoon the homestead mother dispatched Camelback's grandson through the To and From the World Gate out to the Home Farm, driving the grey donkey hitched to the basket cart; he carried refreshments to the men toiling in the dusty fields — tender pickled lotus roots, plump red cherries, freshly picked and each on its own stem, and brown earthen teapots filled with refreshing green tea.

In "Sprouting Plants" we had three sunrises of rain and then

sudden heat, bringing everything on almost too rapidly.   The
tutors voluntarily picked strawberries, enjoying the days in
the south meadows as much as the children — whom the
Family Elder released from lessons to help gather the fruit,
when it ripened faster than the men, even though ably assisted
by the women, could harvest it.

Packed in leaf-lined trays, nine boatloads of the strawberries
were dispatched to the Peking market.   A good sale was expected, as many foreigners resided then in Peking, "and
foreigners like strawberries."   But the strawberries were
brought home next day and sold, at less than half the expected
price, in the village square.   It had been impossible to get to
either Peking or Tientsin, as a war of unprecedented fierceness
was raging between Wu Pei-fu and Chang Tso-lin, who were
attempting to settle which of them had the right to appoint the
President and other servants of the Republic.

In "Summer Divided in the Middle" raspberries were de-
liciously juicy.   Straw was heaped under the tiger-apple trees
and the fruit picked up each evening, as these apples are tastiest
if left to drop off of their own ripeness and then to lie for a few
hours in the sun.   The vibrating *thu-ing* of whetstone on
scythe echoed with the rolling tattoo of the grey-headed green
woodpecker as the winter wheat was cut.   Tied in sheaves, the
wheat was carted to stacks safe inside the city wall.

The reaping on the Home Farm was finished; but the tenants
to the northeast, where the crop is always seven or eight days
later in ripening, had just begun to harvest when a contingent
of Chang Tso-lin's army came across country.   The soldiers
were circling homewards in high spirits at a safe arc outside the
war area, foraging a fat living from the farm crops, com-
mandeering men and beasts to carry them and their loot in
comfort to Manchuria.

They had missed the opportunity to return by rail, because of
their placement in the war.   But they held no resentment

against their comrades who had commandeered all the trains and made off quickly with them. They told how, when he felt the retreat behind him, General Chang Tso-lin had come back from the front to persuade his men to continue the war. He had distributed silver; also displayed his coffin and declared that he intended to win or be carried back through the Wall in it. Yet everyone had continued his preparations for departure. The soldiers said that the opponent, General Wu Pei-fu, had not played fair in bringing to war Feng Yu-hsiang, the Christian General, whose men were savages. They came into battle singing bloody songs! They possessed neither umbrellas nor teapots! So the Northerners would not fight.

As soon as the alarm "Soldiers!" spread, farmers ran from their farms to their villages. Gates were quickly close-barred. Only five men of the district were taken. Camel-back's grandson, with the lunch-laden basket cart and the pet grey donkey, was among them.

The crops were not tended again until three sunrises after the soldiers had passed.

In "Small Heat" lentils were sown; the second crop of sweet potatoes planted; the peaches and summer plums harvested; the winter wheat threshed. The buckwheat was sweet with blossom, the corn knee-high. Wild iris unfurled purple banners beside the trickling irrigation streams and on the canal side. Young kingfishers learned to fly.

In "Big Heat," although there were rumors of terrible famine to the east, the south, and the west, and despite the prophecy of the "Welcome to Spring" buffalo, there was a fall of rain. This welcome but heavy downpour damaged the summer pears; but it left sufficient pears for the homestead table, and pears are of no value compared with grain. It increased the height of the summer wheat, the rye, the oats, the millet, the buckwheat, the alfalfa, the soya beans, and the corn so rapidly that Uncle Shao-chun said he could hear them grow.

6

"Come Autumn" arrived the first week in August. Camelback's grandson was gone, so he could not explain it to me. But young Shao-yi, heir-in-line for the Family Eldership and of the fifth generation, told me that the white tiger from the west is monarch of the agricultural year from the arrival of autumn until the coming of winter. He is the hardest master of all. If men do not get their crops harvested industriously enough to please him, he reaps it for them with the white frost. He is to be feared particularly because he comes in so quietly that it seems that summer is going on forever.

Black beans were gathered; rosy-cheeked golden apricots carefully picked, so as not to bruise them, into trayed baskets; ripe chili peppers and capsicums pulled, dried, roasted, and ground to a fine spice. The men brought the tender ears of the corn, now in yellow and red tassel, home to boil for each evening meal.

In "Go Heat" fleecy white clouds drifted lazily across the sky. The sun continued to coax the crops and set the crickets singing. Millet and oats were reaped; sweet potatoes taken up; sunflowers mulched.

Chang Tso-lin had followed his men home to Manchuria. President Hsu Shih-ch'ang had left the presidential palace and returned quietly to his private residence in Tientsin. After considerable delay, President Li Yuan-hung, who had been residing in Tientsin since his resignation in 1917, had returned to Peking and re-assumed the Presidency. The road to the Capital was decided safe. Peng-wen went up with three boatloads of grain, vegetables, and fruit. He found the produce in much demand, because of the shortage in other districts, and sold it for three times the price Uncle Shao-chun told him he should get.

In "White Dew" soya beans were gathered and rhubarb dug, peeled, threaded, and hung to dry. Corn was cut, the ears stripped from the stalks, the stalks laid away for fuel; the ear sheaths were turned back to expose the kernels, and the cobs suspended in rows of orange, red, and yellow under the eaves of the courtyard.

The sound of the flail hummed through all the daylight hours. Harvest had called home every available Lin man. Daily they visited the village threshing floors, to measure the harvests of the tenant-farmers. The Lin women supervised the crop division and where tenants were reputed to be cunning, as women are most capable in material matters.

A new group of tax collectors came through the district assessing the farms. The House of Exile had already paid taxes one year in advance. But the departed officials of the Republic had taken away the government treasury, and the new officials, who assumed responsibility, must have finances to be able to serve the people. The tax collectors were feasted at the Cantonese Guildhall. The first course was melon; and when each guest opened his fruit he found one hundred dollars inside. The taxes had to be paid — but just half what had been demanded.

As a reward for committing to memory the first book of Confucius, young Tsai-fu was taken to Peking by Uncle Yang-peng. He attended the ceremonies at which China accepted an airplane from the French Caudron Aircraft Company, and on returning home he resolved to be an aviator.

He brought back a prospectus of the Nanyuan School of Aviation, also pictures of the new French plane and of an Italian plane, six Handley-Page passenger planes, forty Vickers-Vimy commercial planes, forty Vimy training machines, and sixty-five Avro planes. He said that all this craft had been received within the last three years for the use of Chinese students, and that, although it had all been seized by militarists to use in their wars against each other, he was not distressed — as there were plenty more machines where these came from.

He was not depressed, either, by the fact that the School of Aviation was not functioning just then, nor by the fact that all the American, French, Italian, and British instructors had either gone home or were working for one of China's war lords. He had faith that when he was of age to start his career the time would be propitious for the carrying of mail, passengers, and goods in the air over the old trade routes of China.

At "Autumn Divided in the Middle," the Farmer's Calendar devotes three days of festival to "Thank the Harvest." All work stopped. The storehouses were already well filled, and field and orchard still held the promise of further abundance. Goldenrod and gentian were in flower on every bank and in every hedge nook. Larks sang above the meadows.

At dawn on the first morning of the festival, the men, women, and children of the House of Exile met the tenant-farmers at the Temple of Agriculture and went together to the Eastern Fields. While music was played for the Earth Mother's delight, they offered a part from each crop and burned yellow scrolls on which they had written their prayers of gratitude.

They returned along the detour — worn smooth by processions through the centuries — by way of the hillside spring, where they knelt in a circle of thanks to Water for nourishing their seed.

Then came three days of pleasuring, during which the village Elders boasted that there was not one empty food basin in the village. On the third day, the House of Exile gave a great banquet, in the Cantonese Guildhall, to their tenant-farmers. After the feast the Elder gave each tenant's little boy a packet of seed.

Every absent member of the homestead who could possibly get home had returned to help thank the harvest. There were games, two feasts daily, generous plates of juicy white walnut meats, which are the special mid-autumn delicacy, and pretty gifts for everyone.   But the young wives, the maids, and the girl children were sulky.

The village was in carnival; but the Elder's wife, Lady of First Authority, forbade the young wives, the maids, and the girl children to go outside the Orchid Door.   She said that the village, and even the masculine side of the homestead, were rowdy with too much barley wine.

The men, the youths, and the boys — over whom she had no control — joined in the village gayety.   The young women of the adjoining House of Wong went out at will through their To and From the World Door.   It was they who told us of the theatricals, arranged by the village Elders, in the courtyard of the City Temple, also of the three rival troupes of lion dancers that the festival attracted.   Each troupe consisted of three or four mountebanks who manipulated their blue and yellow lion, made of cloth and wire, in an agile dance after a scarlet ball bounced by a fifth mountebank.   The beast's eyeballs, tongue, jaw, ears, and tail wiggled in accompaniment to bells, as the lion pursued the ball through open doorways, onto low roofs, pushed a pedestrian forward and jumped over his back, or peered under a fat man's skirts in search of it — indulging in capers that made everyone laugh except the person who happened to be the butt of the joke.

In addition there were the Stilt Walkers, some of whom were professionals and some of whom were sons of the House of Exile, the House of Wong, or other village families.   They wore humorous make-up and exaggerated dress; they pranced, minced, strode, and anticked in a parody of life and manners — as a fashionable lady, a bold bad man, a hunchback pawnbroker, a simpering girl, an ugly wife and her husband, a pious priest, or a shortsighted farmer — for the amusement of themselves and the crowd, who rewarded them with coin when pleased.

In "Cold Dew" all crops were lifted from the soil.   Then ploughs, harrows, and tiny stone rollers were busy again breaking the land to pulverized fineness. Soon men swayed back and forth, sowing the winter grains in the plots where the summer crops had grown.

Winter pears were picked and packed in sawdust to keep until the New Year festivities. Grapes were brought in and sent to Peking and Tientsin markets. Threshing was finished. Stone mills in every homestead one passed creaked out the song of flour as women ground from the grain that had been spread out on their roofs to dry in golden sheets.

In "Frost's Descent" plump speckled pheasants were disturbed while the red persimmons were gathered from the hillside orchards. Sunflowers were cut. Hazelnuts, beechnuts, and walnuts were brought in. Chestnuts were harvested in competition with the industrious squirrels. Nuts in excess of homestead needs were sold to the dealers who came through the district, buying what they could. The ripe walnuts, halved and picked from the shell, brought a good price from an export merchant who caters to trade with America.

Frost turned oak shrub and maple tree, lichen and grass, to burgundy and crimson, russet and amber. The shortening days were filled with the plaintive melody of the lingering song sparrow and the blithe call of the katydid. The wild geese passed over, going south. Lastly the black dates ripened. Then folk said that winter was near. Tools were brought in. The homestead roses, shrubs, and vines were wrapped in straw. The House of Exile was tightened against blizzard.

7

"*Tung pu t'ui wu*" ("Stay in your house in winter") is the law of the sombre black tortoise from the north, who is king from the arrival of winter until the coming of spring, as Shao-yi said. At "Come Winter" the homestead gave up hope of ever seeing Camel-back's grandson again on earth. Until then, they had sent scouts hither and yon to follow every clue. Now they ceased to try to find him, and said: "The sombre black tortoise has got him."

When the Milky Way drooped, summer clothes were packed in cedar and everyone dressed in fur-lined garments. When the tail of the Great Bear was directly to the north, windows were sealed and fires lit in the beds.

"Small Snow" and "Big Snow" passed. Then came "Winter Divided in the Middle." We had "Little Cold" and "Big Cold" to pass before the weather would grow slowly warmer and it would be time to welcome spring again. Within doors we were plaiting the cured wheat straw into hat braid for sale to the Western world.

Most afternoons, young Shao-yi read aloud to his sister and little cousins as they worked. I liked the stories they liked, and his manner of reading. I formed the habit of sitting in the west room of the Garden of Children.

One afternoon he was in a teasing mood. He said that he had searched diligently, but he could find nothing suitable for feminine understanding. Dressed in a long gown of pearl-grey satin, lined with grey squirrel fur, he sprawled at ease among the cushions on the east side of the brick bed.

"It is right that I should be idle while you toil," he drawled. "In spring, when the blue-green dragon is king, men are pushed out to labor in the fields. In summer, when the vermilion bird reigns, we are forced to the limit of our endurance. In autumn, when the white tiger is dominant, we have to fight to gather our harvest before the frost destroys what we have grown.

"But in winter the black tortoise is emperor. Then we rest. Then we enjoy the peace and the comfort of our homestead. Then we take satisfaction in watching our womenfolk toil. We are luxuriously idle. We dress ourselves in beautiful garments — which our women relatives must make for us. We fill our stomachs with good food — which our women relatives must garnish and season to our capricious appetites.

"The house is woman's sphere.   Here she reigns supreme.
As man's authority is confined to the outside world, so he need
have no responsibility about the work inside the courtyard
walls.   The female must cook, and spin, weave, braid, and sew
all of the stuffs — the hemp, the jute, the flax, the silk, the
straw, and the cotton that the male has brought to her."

The dimples began to dance in his twin sister's cheeks, but
she kept her head down modestly as she addressed Shao-yi in
a quiet voice.   "Brother, take this straw in your strong hands
that I may stretch it tight for the braiding — there; hold it
just so!"

When she had imprisoned his hands with the straw, which
she could just as efficiently have stretched over the leg of a
table as we were all doing, she said demurely, "Now, dear
Brother, please do continue your enlightening discourse."

And he complacently continued.

V

THREE BIRTHDAYS

1

F ROM the time I left America, kind relatives and friends
sent me frequent letters, current magazines, new books, the
Friends' Intelligencer, and the *Philadelphia Ledger*. They
wanted to keep me in close touch with home. But I was too
entranced with China to read much from these. When I made
attempts, I found their contents too far away to hold my attention.

While resident in China, I had no intention of insulting my
own countrymen, but when I met them I was sometimes unconsciously rude. My nature is slow. In each new experience, my thought must germinate alone before I can share it.
I resent having others, even those most closely associated with
me, probe into my mind. I avoided both contact and corre-
spondence. I could not answer the kind-hearted attempts
made for my "good" to warn me against "going native."

It was not that China and the Chinese people charmed me
more than America and Americans do. I think I am sin-
cerely devoted to the land of my birth. But I find the earth
so entrancing that I can never stretch myself to encompass
more than the part that has captured my attention at the
time. From my babyhood it has always been so. Listening
to a bird sing, I never hear a band pass.

Mr. Charles Crane was American Minister to Peking during
the early part of my residence in China. I did not forget the
generous, thoughtful hospitality that his wife and he had

given me in New York three years earlier, when I was asked to join the Armenian Relief Committee staff of which he was an executive officer. But on arrival in China I neither registered at the Legation nor called.

One winter morning as I rode down Hatamen, in a glass-windowed carriage with Shun-ko, Mr. Crane saw and remembered me. He signaled me to stop, and invited me to the Legation; saying that he wanted me to meet some other young people at supper on Sunday night. But I could not go, because I shrank away, then, from social contact with other Westerners.

As my stay in China lengthened, more people than I had ever realized, although all my life I have been surrounded by loving care, seemed anxious about my future. Especially when Grace Coppock, who had sponsored me, died. I was of legal age. No one could command me to return. But urgent letters, and then cables, advised me to do so.

My answers only created more alarm. I could not say that I had come to teach the Chinese people anything. Neither could I say that I had definite intent to learn anything from them. Three dear people felt such concern that they made the long journey from Pennsylvania to persuade me to return. I was made unhappy by their uneasy concern for me. Yet I was charmed by a spell I could not break. So I did not go.

If I could have told them that I was writing verse or story, it might have given comfort. But I have always been evasive and shy about writing. Pressed about it, I usually surprise even my own ears with the stoutness of the lie asserting that I am not doing any. Writing is something that I am ever driven to do, and concerning which I am never satisfied.

In my childhood I hid my verse and story in a box buried under a tree in my grandfather's wood lot. The urge to put down what flowed through my imagination stayed with me as I grew older. But I never mentioned it to parent, school friend, or teacher. I am one of seven brothers and sisters.

We all wrote, and what we had written we shared with each other, although we kept it carefully concealed from our elders.

Now that I have a daughter, I know about her when she comes to meals with that evasively reserved face and listens without answer to her governess's stern reproof for absence from lessons in piano or geography. I do not tell that I know. I am sorry that she also must be ever driven by a creative imagination, and I pray that she will find satisfactory mastery of the craft of words.

When we were pressed for funds, in my teens, I sent things out to be printed, even syndicating my lore about flowers and birds. I felt no elation that they were accepted; only an unexplainable shame because of their inadequacy. But they brought me friendship with John Burroughs and the welcome at Slabsides, where I was privileged to listen to his other guests, Henry Ford, Thomas Edison, and Roosevelt among them.

One of my brothers and one of my sisters also sacrificed some secret things to our monetary need. Among them *Conquests of Peace*, a pageant we had enacted over and over again, as its parts were revised, in the dell within our own wood. Meg was still dissatisfied with it when she posted it in answer to the widely published Chautauqua quest for a pageant. It won first place and was enacted all over the United States. When the letter came announcing that it was chosen, she wanted to get it back so that she could do it all over. She was kept from demanding it back only by the cash prize, which happened to be the exact amount needed for our youngest sister's fee at George School.

But our writing not only supplied needed money. As we matured, it gave satisfaction to our elder relatives and friends. We are bred of generations of Quakers. Perhaps too closely bred to be quite fitted for daily life. We were entirely nurtured among Quakers — not in public but in Quaker schools. Quakers are people of careful life purpose — serious, gentle, loving people, who educate their young to listen to the voice of

God and apply themselves to practical usefulness in life. Generous people, always glad to find reason combined with spirit in anyone's action.

In my verse and story, printed in my teens, my relatives and elder friends found sensible excuse for my absent-minded childhood truancy from schoolroom lessons. It was the same about China.

My first group of nine Chinese poems appeared in a December issue of *Scribner's*. The Woman's Press of the Y.W.C.A. bound my short novel, *The Street of Precious Pearls*, in a holly-red jacket, lettered in gold, and put it in the bookshops at Christmas. The *Pictorial Review* announced my story "Beyond the Orchid Door" on their January cover with a star next my name. Then I received cables and letters from my relatives and friends assuring me that all who had been troubled in spirit concerning me were now at peace.

2

"We know not the beginning nor the end of life." So Sou-mai's mother spoke on the day it was known that her daughter carried a new life under her heart. "Philosophers in China have been busy for centuries divining truth to satisfy the intellect. Doubtless philosophers in all the other lands have been busy in the same way. There are many creeds and many religions. But we do not know what is really helpful to the soul about to be born. So it is best to use all the advised methods to safeguard a child's entry into the world."

Then she took from a basket she had brought on her arm all the things that had safeguarded her when she carried Sou-mai.

She placed a long sharp knife, blade upward, under Sou-mai's bed and laid a sword, fashioned of cash strung together with red cord, beside it. She pinned two pairs of scissors, cut from red paper, on the bed curtains, and stretched a tiger skin in her mattress. Pictures of fierce wild animals were pasted on the surrounding walls, on the doors, on the windows, and above the courtyard gate. She purchased two sets of charms against evil, one prepared by the Buddhist and the other by the Taoist priests, and hung them under the eaves of Sou-mai's dwelling.

During the time of waiting, each mother in the House of Lin went to the Temple of Motherhood by the South Gate of the city, and prayed for Sou-mai's child. Sou-mai made sweetmeats of pure honey, white rice flour, and jasmine petals for the God of One Hundred Happy Children, whose image has always a great knapsack on its back from which adorable children are peeping. She stitched a pair of tiny baby shoes of bright red satin and laid them on the lap of the Goddess of Mercy. She lit tall tapers, in holders made from the root of the sacred lotus, at sunset each evening before the portraits of the Mother of Heaven, of her Lady of the Compassionate Heart, and of the friendly Madonna of the Chair (which Shunko bought in Rome when on her world tour).

The child entered the world at dawn on the Birthday of the Sun, after distress, alarm, and delay so prolonged that the Family Elders had met in the Hall of Ancestors to consider the wisdom of sending to Peking for a Western-educated woman doctor to assist.

For a day and a night of Sou-mai's pain, her husband waited before her door. As Mai-da and I were dispatched here and there to various parts of the homestead on errands for the women who attended Sou-mai, we were awed by his stillness. He stood hour after hour, refusing to sit or to partake of refreshment, clutching a fold of his grey gown in the fingers of one hand.

Then when Sou-mai's mother came to the door, just as the sun rose, and announced, "A man is born," he disappeared. He returned some time later dressed in his ceremonial robes. After another long wait at the door *his* mother opened it and told him to come in.

Sou-mai was wrapped in the robe of apple-blossom silk which was her marriage-bed nightdress. She held the child against her breast. I saw her smile as her husband came near to her. Before he took the child she offered, or looked on its face, he put on her pillow, as thanks-gift, a gold hairpin such as each mother of a son wears in her nape knot. In his wife's pin he had had set an oblong of clear green jade.

Then he took the child in its warm wrappings of rosy satin in the palms of his two hands. He knelt to his own mother. He knelt to his wife's mother. He carried his son through every court in the homestead, making the new Lin's arrival known, with ceremony, to all the Family — men, women, and children — and to the God of the Hearth. Standing under the lamp of continuous life, he told the glad tidings in the Hall of the Ancestors.

Then he gave his son back into his wife's keeping for the "three days of quietness," when her own mother and her serving woman, Little Tiger, were the only persons permitted to enter the court of her dwelling.

When the sun was high overhead, the Family Elder dispatched couriers to the relatives and family friends with small boxes of fruit, thus without words announcing the arrival of a son in the House of Lin. The relatives and family friends responded with gifts of millet, eggs, brown sugar, and walnut meats, which are the only foods a mother in the Lin clan is permitted to eat during the days that a carpet of sawdust stills the sound of footfalls on the stone-paved courts.

On the morning of the fourth day, Little Tiger brought me a red card brushed with gold characters and translated it as the invitation to attend the "Bath in the Hour of the Sheep." She explained to whom each of the similar cards she carried was addressed, and how difficult it had been for Sou-mai to make selection of a "good-fortune eight" from her host of loved relatives and friends. We eight were the baby's two grandmothers, the Family Elder's wife, his pretty five-year-old girl cousin, two boy cousins of five and three, a maternal aunt, and I.

As gifts we took white eggs, symbols of long life; red eggs, symbols of happiness; bunches of acacia incense, symbols of health; bowls of uncooked rice, symbols of prosperity; and flower seeds, symbols of lovely children. Sou-mai sat propped up on her bed with a heap of lavender and blue silk cushions behind her, and was dressed in a pale pink gown embroidered all over with plum blossoms. The black wings of her hair were brushed to a gloss. She wore no jewels except the gold and jade pin in her nape knot. The dimples danced in her flushed cheeks as she unfolded the quilt to show us the little son who slept at her side on his own tiny mattress.

We placed our eggs in a chip basket which stood ready to receive them. We laid our flower seeds on the little boy's bed, asking his mother to plant a garden for him. We thrust our acacia incense into our bowls of rice and brought them to the child. Sou-mai took the torch that Little Tiger had ready, guided the baby's hand to light them, bid us carry them to the Hall of Ancestors and there to leave them on the altar.

The maternal grandmother boiled water for the bath, putting locust leaves in as a disinfectant and artemis flowers to give a pleasant perfume. Little Tiger brought the polished copper basin, which had been turned upside down and used as a table for Sou-mai and her husband's marriage-night supper, and poured the bath water in. Sou-mai tested the water with her finger and let the little children help to take away the baby's wrappings.

He kicked his fat legs and wrinkled his round face, but did not cry, when Little Tiger held him over the water. His mother told us that his milk-name was Shao-jo. She bade each of us put a handful of water over his chubby pink body. The bath was but a ceremony, quickly finished. After it,

Little Tiger rubbed him with sweet-smelling oil, and we helped
to robe him in a soft vest, a "tummy" binding, a napkin, and a
quilted robe of scarlet silk filled with duck down. Then he
was put away to sleep at the back of the great bed, on his own
mattress, with a tiny screen placed around him to shut out the
light.

Then we arranged a papier-mâché sedan chair, with its eight
bearers and its attendant phœnix, unicorn, tortoise, and tiger,
outside Sou-mai's door, so that she could see the Mother of
Heaven go back into the sky. The two grandmothers put a
trunk filled with gold and silver imitation money under the
seat of the sedan chair. Little Tiger took the portrait of the
Mother of Heaven from the niche in the wall, whence it
had watched over the child during the nine months of germina-
tion and the ordeal of separation, and placed it in the chair.

Sou-mai said, "Thank you, Heavenly Mother, for much
kindness."

And we each lit the fuse assigned to us. I had the one in
the tail of the unicorn. The heavy procession, built in full life-
size papier-mâché, started slowly, gaining momentum as the
fire spread its wings.

3

The pear trees were in ivory flower. It was Mai-da's quarter
moon of kitchen service, but before she went to help prepare
the evening meal she had rolled up our bamboo-paper windows. Tired, I stretched out on our bed to rest for a few minutes before bathing and changing.

With three wives and four serving women, I had been down
by the lotus pond helping to rub, blue, and bleach the family
wash since sunup, with an interval for only a brief basket
lunch at midday.

Three courts away Sou-mai was singing to her baby. The
contralto lullaby drifted on the perfumed air: —

T'ien wan liao, hsiao hai-tzu,
Shui chiao nin k'an, hung ku lu chiao ch'ê, pai lo la,
Li t'ao tao'rh chih i ko.
Ch'iao jen chia, tai ssŭ ho pao, hsiao chih'rh cha,
Hui ch'uan p'i ao yin shu kua.
Hsiao hai-tzu, pa chih ch'ê yuan'rh.
Wen a ko, "A ko!   A ko!   Nin shang na'rh?"

(The day is gone, little son,
Sleep and you will see, inside a red-wheeled cart drawn by a white
   mule,
An aged man who rides alone.
He wears trousers of fine silk embroidered with gay threads,
And he wears a coat of squirrel skin over a coat of white rabbit.
   Little son, lean on the shaft and look inside.
Ask the aged man, "Aged sire!   Aged sire!   Where do you go?")

It was the eve of the eightieth birthday of Wei-sung, the
Family Elder.   Invitations had not been sent out, as it would
be bad taste to ask folk to come with congratulations, but the
homestead had hummed with activity since the new moon.

Wei-sung was an official of the government during the
Ch'ing dynasty, having won the position by excellence in the
literary examinations under the system of the "Forest of
Pencils."   But his posts were always minor ones, in places far
distant from the Capital.   Posts of exile, to which he was appointed with the flowery words of sham honor — as the House
of Lin, of Canton origin, was continuously under unproven
suspicion of disloyalty to the throne for the last century of the
dynasty.   He succeeded to the Eldership of the Family when
his father plucked the flower of life; but he had to wait three
years before he was permitted to resign his government appointment.

On coming home, he settled into the routine of the House of
Exile in quiet contentment, although he had spent only a few
days at home since the time he first went to Peking, at eighteen,
to sit for his examination.

He was sixty when he came home.   In the years since then,

so he told me, he had passed the To and From the World Gate only to perform the Family Elder's duties at the spring and autumn services; and he planned never to go out for other purpose until his body was carried to its final resting place in the Eastern Fields.   Unless it happened that he survived the Elder of Wong.   In which case he would of course escort the funeral procession of his loved friend.

Once, when his wife urged him to travel, I heard him say: "Go and see the world if you like.   You will soon come home again.   I was abroad for forty-two years, and I know that the best of the world is inside our own homestead wall."

He is sorry for anyone who must go from home, and slow to complete marriage contracts for the family daughters, as he is sad to break the home circle.   It is Mai-da's duty to receive for distribution and to collect for dispatch the letters which come and go by government post.   So I know that he receives fat letters frequently from the places where daughters have gone in marriage or where members of the Family are staying for study or work; and that he always sends a fat letter in prompt return.

In the weeks preceding his birthday, letters with the same postmarks as those he usually receives came addressed to his wife, who seldom has letters.   Mai-da lingered with each to learn its contents.   Thus we shared in the secrets: that Su-ling had decided not to accept the scholarship for further study at the Sorbonne, but was returning from Paris in time for the Elder's birthday; that the husband of Fu-erh and the companion she had chosen to accompany him to Malay were coming home, bringing two young sons who had not yet bowed to the ancestors; that a great-grandnephew would come from San Francisco, leaving a maternal cousin in charge of his business there; that Wen-lieh had been granted leave of absence from his army command to honor his Elder; that the grand-daughter, married away to far Szechuan, would come, accompanied by her husband; that Wei-chun was arriving in time from Canton, flying home by airplane; and so on with each day's mail, until the personnel was more than I could remember.

Consequently, we were not surprised when orders were given to clean the homestead, to cook foods for the lunch baskets of those who went to meet the voyagers, to prepare the boatmen for travel, to ask Hua-li for "welcome" flowers from the hothouses, and to launder all the family linen.

As members of the Family arrived, they joined in the preparations for celebration. The courts echoed with the swish of brooms, the beat of flays on dusty shutters, the tap of hammers. By the birthday eve, the interior of every dwelling house had reached a perfection of tidiness. Pillars and eaves shone with new paint. The sand-scoured court paving stones reflected a white radiance. Even the goldfish in the cleaned pools seemed brighter. The hothouses were filled with an abundance of plants ready to distribute through the dwelling at sunrise the next morning. The carpenters had built a stage for the birthday actors, opposite the Hall of Ancestors.

The birthday dawned bright and clear. The children of the family, dressed in lovely new birthday clothes, accompanied the Elder's breakfast tray caroling greetings, each dragging a red carpet piled high with cards of birthday greeting. When he had breakfasted, the Elder opened his gifts in the Court of Sunrise, where all the maidens of the Springtime Bower helped him to arrange them on satin-covered tables in front of the Wall of Heaven.

Usually in the House of Exile we dined in small groups, each in our own court. But on the Elder's birthday, and by his request, his wife gave the order that the meal in the Hour of the Snake was to be a joint family meal. As the weather was unusually mild, the table was not set in the Hall but in the court, where the pear trees were in ivory flower and the orioles were making a silken hammock nest.

We could all sit down, because the Elder had thoughtfully

arranged for a restaurant keeper to take charge of the homestead kitchens from sunrise until sunset on his birthday, as
he said he wanted the women of his family to be free that
day from domestic concern.

Shortly after this meal, guests began to arrive. The eldest
grandson received all callers first in the Hall of Dignity, acting
as proxy for the Elder and in this way saving the honored one
much fatigue, as the ceremony of congratulation includes the
exchange of three kowtows. The guests then passed on
through the intervening courts to the Three Eastern, where
they talked with the Elder as though they had already greeted
him.

Before long the Elder, who always keeps the children of
the Family clustered about him, asked, "Where is my daughter
Sou-mai? Is the baby Shao-jo's birth-month not yet full?"

His favorite, Mai-lei, answered, "To-day is the day of his
full month, but his mother says that it is a day short of a
month because she does not want anyone to consider anything
except the fullness of your eighty years."

"I am the first-born now in the House of Exile. Shao-jo,
five generations below me, is the last-born," the Elder responded. "What more perfect arrangement could Heaven
make than that we be congratulated together?"

He sent the baby's father to stand proxy beside his proxy
in the Hall of Dignity, and he dispatched Mai-lei to bring
Sou-mai and her son. When they came he kept them beside
him until all the guests had praised the mother and admired
the child.

Family and guests had put away the heavy garments of
winter and wore the elegantly fitted gowns of springtime silk,
which are without embroidery and as delicate in color as the
springtime blossoms. They wandered at will through the
courts. Some lingered in conversation by the waters of the
pool. Others renewed friendships in quiet corners on seats
in the bamboo grove, or listened to the minstrel from the City

of Noonday Rest who sang in the Poet's Retreat. Many admired Uncle Keng-lin's birds in the Well of Heaven aviary. All accepted refreshments at the tables and gave attention to the theatricals on the stage opposite the Hall of Ancestors.

The players were from Peking. They were all men. But they filled the women's parts with such skill that I did not know until long afterwards that they were men. The plays were given on a stage without scenery, as plays were given in Shakespeare's time. But so vivid was the acting that it created the impression of background.

The theatricals charmed me. I sat listening most of the day. The actors did not speak their parts. They gave them in poetic beaten measure to which an orchestra kept time. The principal guests, as they seated themselves at the refreshment tables, were requested to name a play which they would like the actors to perform. Then the man in charge of the troupe was given the guest's preference, and as soon as the play in progress was finished the new play began. The guests were of course politely considerate. If they saw that a play had just started, they said that it was their favorite play, as they knew that the day was too short for the actors to perform a tragedy or a comedy for every guest.

There was never any hesitation or demur from the players. They seemed to have all the plays in their heads and all the necessary costumes in their boxes. With slight intervals for refreshment, the players went on until the star Canopus was clear in the heavens. After sunset the stage was lit by flaming pine knots in iron baskets, held high at each end of the stage, and tended by Camel-back.

We had *The Siege of the Empty City, The Death of Chu-ho, The Filial Daughter, The Naughty Wife, Love in a Fishing Boat, The Two Cousins, The Black Donkey's Complaint,* and *The Dance in a Jade Bowl.*

In the civic plays the orchestra led off with a single skin drum, followed in succession by the castanets, the flutes, the pipe flageolets, the balloon guitar, the reed organ, the two-stringed violins, the chiming gongs, and the small kettledrum. The military plays were announced by a march played on the large drum and the small gongs, followed by the cymbals and the clarionets. When the actors played sad parts, the orchestra was slow, low, and plaintive. When humor was acted, then the accompaniment was a quick, laughing rhythm. And when justice triumphed over wrong, the musicians made their instruments sing the victory.

The two plays which caused the most merriment were *The Naughty Wife* and *The Black Donkey's Complaint*. I liked best the Elder's own choice, *The Filial Daughter*.

The story of this play is: —

"At Peking, in the Flower Quarter, lived a young girl who supported her sick father. One day she heard that a matron was going on a pilgrimage to Mount Ya-chi, and she went to her and asked, 'If I went on such a pilgrimage, would my father get well?'

"The matron replied, 'Those who go there and pray with sincere hearts receive all that they ask.'

" 'How far is it?' the girl wanted to know.

" 'Two hundred and fifty thousand steps,' was the answer.

"That evening, after she had finished her work in her flower garden and seen that her father was comfortably asleep, the girl went to her courtyard. With lighted incense in her hand she walked up and down until she could not force her weary feet to do more. Then she knelt and prayed with her face turned toward the mountain, 'Please excuse me for not coming to your temple, but I have to care for my father and to tend the flowers here, as we depend upon them for the money to live.'

"She continued to do this every night. At the end of a fortnight she had walked two hundred and fifty thousand steps.

"At this same time pilgrims were arriving at the mountain from every province to venerate the Goddess of Dawn. There was a great crowd of wealthy and of poor people elbowing each other on the mountain road all day and all night. At each cockcrow there was a struggle as to who should enter the temple first, for tradition said that he or she who first offered incense would most surely have his or her prayer answered promptly.

"On the very same evening on which the little Flower Girl completed her two hundred and fifty thousand steps, a rich man arrived at the Temple and blocked the door in order to be the first to enter next morning. And at the first cock-crow he hastened to the altar.

"He found a glowing incense stick in the censer at the feet of the Goddess, and in a raging temper sought the temple guardian, to whom he had given a large bribe. 'The door was closed all night,' said the priest. 'I do not know who could have offered this incense.'

" 'I will return to-morrow,' said the rich man, and gave the guardian another piece of gold. 'Search the temple at nightfall and attend to it that none approach the Goddess before I have prayed.'

"The priest stood guard all night. At dawn he let the rich man in, well ahead of the surging throng. He ran to the altar. But a stick of incense already glowed there. And on the kneeling stone, worn by many prayers, lay the shadow of a prostrate young girl.

" 'Who is this?' cried the rich man; but as he approached the shadow vanished.

"The priest turned pale, but did not know. The rich man persisted, 'Do Spirits offer incense to this Goddess?'

"The priest could not answer. So the rich man turned and asked the opinion of the other pilgrims.

" 'Ah!' suddenly remembered the matron who had been questioned by the Flower Girl. 'Could it be the pious daughter who, unable to come herself, has sent her soul to beg the healing of her father?'

"The rich man forgot to light his incense or to make his petition. He drew the matron from the crowd and questioned her. Then he ordered his servant to saddle his fleetest horse and rode away at once to the Flower Quarter of Peking.

"He found the girl and her father. He secured a famous doctor who cured the father. But even after the father was well, the rich man continued his visits. The more he went

A PRIEST

to the house of the father and daughter, the better he liked them. He no longer enjoyed the pleasures he had formerly enjoyed, and his friends chaffed him because his face was no longer seen in the theatres or the tea-houses. He spent his evenings helping the girl to water her flowers and assuring her that he would be pleased to have her father live in his homestead, where the air was fresher than in the lower Flower Quarter. And in the last scene they were married with magnificent colorful ceremony."

When Canopus was clear in the heavens, a table was arranged in the Court of Sunrise. It was covered with a vermilion altar cloth which fell to the paving stones on all sides, and the portrait [1] of the God of Longevity was put on it. Six plates of apples, symbols of peace, and six candles, in symbol of the six generations it was hoped the Elder would remain on earth to count, were placed before the portrait. And a satin kneeling cushion was laid before the table.

The Elder knelt first. He burned incense and gave thanks for eighty years of life. Then each member of his family knelt and thanked Heaven for permitting the homestead the blessing of his Eldership, and petitioned that it should continue for another decade. Then the guests — of whom only the most loved had been asked to remain — prayed, and departed.

When the last guest had gone, and the To and From the World Gate had been closed, the Elder examined his gifts. Each caller had brought something, in addition to what had arrived by post; and three long tables were loaded with presents. Each had an attached card on which was written the donor's name and an appropriate greeting.

It happened that from among the jewelry, scrolls, pictures, books, gown-lengths of silk, embroidered slippers, handkerchiefs, fans, vases, silver plates, cut-glass bowls and such, he was attracted by a huge peach made of satin and painted in realistic colors.

" 'Prince Erh-sung,' " he read aloud, from its card. "I do not remember that I have a friend of that name. It is a Manchu name. There was one of that name stationed with

[1] This portrait is one of the homestead treasures. It was painted four hundred years ago by an artist who knocked at the Gate of Compassion in a bitter blizzard. When the news of his call was brought to the lady who was the wife of the Family Elder of that time, she had him welcomed in, through the To and From the World Gate, and ordered that his rags be destroyed and fur garments, food, and shelter be given him. He painted the picture in return for his entertainment. The god is riding a stag. A purple bat is flying over his head. He has a ripe peach in one hand, a staff in the other, and a gourd and a scroll attached to his golden girdle.

me at my first government post.   But we were not friends.
I heard that he was stoned out of this world at the Manchu
massacre at Nanking.   It might not have been true; but
surely, if he is here, still he would not have sent me the Peach
of Long Life."

He pressed the satin fruit and it sprang open.   A frightened
bird nested inside on a heap of fluffy silk waste.   The bird
was one of the species whose familiar name is the same as
Mai-da's pet name.   The Elder took the bird on his hand;
and, as he thoughtfully let it fly away over the homestead
wall, he said: "Ah — now I understand.   This gift is perhaps more a symbol of request than a symbol of long life."

And Shun-ko, who stood near him, said: "It is years past
the time at which Mai-da should have married.   In my father's
house daughters are arranged for at eighteen."

4

In the House of Exile the birthdays of childhood are the
Fullness of the Month, the Rounding of the Year, and the
Cycle of Ten.   After these the only birthday celebrated,
until after the half-century is past, is the bride's first birthday
after marriage.   The birthdays of childhood and the bride's
day are family affairs.

The twins, Shao-yi and his sister Ching-o, and the cousins Nan-wei and Ming-chi were all four born in full moon
of Chrysanthemums and completed the Cycle of Ten in
the autumn of the same year as the Elder filled his eighth
decade.

So when the moon was round in Chrysanthemums, the birthday awnings were spread over the Garden of Children and
their courts were decorated with picturesque lanterns, happiness banners, and crimson joy characters.   Their dwelling
houses were filled with lovely flowers and the model ships were
set afloat on the shallow sand pool with all flags flying.

The relatives sent gifts. The birthday children were dressed in festival gowns and received congratulations from all the Family, who bowed to them in turn. The Family Elders permitted each birthday child to choose an entertainment for the combined party.

Shao-yi asked for the marionette players. A tiny stage was put up for them, and the same plays given as are given in the theatres. The troupe responded to every request. They did *The Women Robbers, A Visit to the Moon, Submission to the T'ang Emperor,* and Shao-yi's favorite, *The Battle of the Red Cliff,* which had to be repeated three times for his special benefit.

Shao's twin asked for the juggler. He came. He was a child not much larger than Hsing-mu; but he threw plates above his head and caught them on a twirling stick balanced on his nose, danced between sharp swords, turned handsprings while he tossed eggs about and yet did not break one, and finally took a live rabbit out of Ching-o's pocket and gave it to her as a birthday present.

Nan-wei asked for the candy maker and was laughed at for wanting this ordinary old man, who comes by the To and From the World Gate every day, as a special treat on a feast day. But he was invited in, and was one of the most popular features of the birthday. He made nests of birds, ladies' fans, three-sailed fishing craft, prancing horses, a cat with kittens, the God of Happiness, a monkey eating an orange, and whatever was asked for, from syrup which he boiled — on a little charcoal stove that he carried with him — and blew deftly into shape through a hollow reed.

Ming-chi asked for the fortune teller from the Street of the Sound of Thunder. He found signs of good omen in the palms of all the children, and foretold marvelous adventures to come to them all in the future.

At evening the birthday feast, for which the birthday children chose the menu, was served on a long table in the open courtyard. The table was lighted by forty candles arranged in four groups of ten each, and held in bronze holders made in the likeness of the tortoise. After dark, old Camel-back set off a bevy of skyrocketing stars — one for each child to wish on.

VI

HOMESTEAD HERITAGE

1

MY life in China was broken by a brief visit to America. I traveled home on the *Empress of Asia* with Mr. and Mrs. Arthur Scribner. They had an Englishman, then seventeen years in the Chinese Government Service, to sit at the same table. He had just been stationed at Peking.

After introducing us, Mrs. Scribner told him that I had been resident for some time in North China. When he turned his fierce attention down on me, from his more than six feet height, and said, "It is strange that if you have been in North China I have not known it," I knew that if he next said that I had not been there, I should not be certain that I had.

The only Englishmen I had previously met were English Quakers who had come over to Philadelphia for Yearly Meeting. They are so different! This was my first encounter with the type that England educates for foreign service — that is, the class she imbues with the idea that a man must make and keep himself physically fit and to whom she teaches endurance on special playing fields, whom she drills to quiet command of self and others, and impregnates, generation by generation, with a tender love for England; then dispatches abroad to positions of responsibility and authority — posts where sometimes for years on end they must live far from their kind, and where they must make their decisions alone, affecting not only the future of the Service but the lives of others of different race.

These men, no matter where they are, are England. The
majority of them are abroad from twenty to about sixty,
with "home leave" to break their exile about once every five
years.   They do not take on any of the native ways of the
countries to which they go.   Their food, their dress, their habit,
and their speech is as of "home."   When one of them says
the word "home," he does not mean the place where he may
have resided for the past thirty years. He means England.
England is the place that keeps warm in his heart, the place
to which he will retire when his life's work is done.

To others unacquainted with this kind of Englishman, as
I was then, the manner, when met for the first time, must also
seem alarmingly self-assured regarding all the details of life.

I had a premonition, from the first moment I saw this one,
that he would marry me.   I accepted the fact that one would
eventually marry.   It seemed to be what happened to the
majority.   But I had always prayed that I should marry a
mild man.

This man was disturbing.   He never raised his voice, yet
when he spoke people listened.   Servants did his bidding almost without need for him to utter a word.   He seemed to
win at games without effort.   When asked, he sat at a piano
and played or sang well what was requested, and just as though
that was a usual accomplishment which everyone had.   Also,
he was too handsome.   I distrusted handsome men, even if they
acted unconscious of their looks.

I avoided him with diligence.   But I could not avoid meals
by the excuse of seasickness, as the sea makes me feel well.
I did get my place moved so that I was not opposite him, and
did not have to meet his eyes every time I took a spoonful of
soup.   But he could not be entirely avoided, even on deck.
I had just to be careful never to get left alone with him.   He
was very polite.   He did not pursue me in any way.   It was
just that the more information he gathered about me, the
more he treated me as one who should have a keeper.

After I reached Swarthmore, I received a brief letter from

him. It hoped that I had arrived safely, trusted that I would not go to China again, and assured me that my going had been more dangerous than I had worldly knowledge to realize.

I spent the month of August with my six brothers and sisters at camp in the Pocono Mountains. I woke on the morning of the eighth remembering that I had heard the disturbing Englishman say his birthday was that day and ashamed that I had not answered his kind letter. I found my youngest brother already up and saddling a horse for a morning canter. I told him that I wanted to cable a birthday greeting.

The nearest telegraph was twelve miles away. Jim said that he would go with me. We saddled a second horse. We had a fine ride into the sunrise through wooded trails, down a ravine, and over meadow daisies wet with dew.

My brother eased the saddles and rubbed the horses while I went in to write my message. When I had the telegraph blanks before me, I realized that sending a birthday greeting to a stranger was a foolish idea. I could not disappoint the telegraph man, so I sent love to one of my aunts.

Some months after I had returned to China, I received another letter from England. It was addressed care of *Scribner's Magazine* and presumed that the first had failed to reach me. It hoped that I was well, stated that the writer had received and accepted an invitation to visit in the States on his way back to China, so was not going via Suez, and trusted that he would again see me at the house where he was to stay. It closed by setting me right regarding a conclusion on China that he had read in one of my recently published stories. I am not a competent letter writer, and I did not accomplish a reply. Neither did I ever mention him to anyone in China or America.

2

When persimmons were ripe, Shun-ko sent me through Mai-lin's Walk, which tunnels the wall between the houses of Lin and Wong, with a basket of gold fruit, and the request to

borrow a set of drying racks. I found the women of the
Wong homestead in tearful agitation because their Elder had
given the order for his burial clothes to be stitched. While
I waited for the racks, he came in through the Orchid Door,
followed by a merchant with materials from the big shop in
the Street of the Sound of Thunder on the Flat Ground.

On the approach of the Elder, his wife motioned the two
young women of the Family, who were pregnant, to leave the
court where we were gathered, as women concerned with the
beginning of life must not loiter where consideration is given
to the end of life's pilgrimage.

The merchant and the elder wives exchanged greetings.
Tea was brought. Two lads, who came close on the merchant's
heels, set down the bamboo pole over which they carried his
pack. The lads unknotted the twists in the blue pack-cloth
and spread it out as a carpet on the flat stones. The merchant
then gave attention to the display of his silks.

Squatting on his satin-clad feet, with his long dark cash-
mere gown folded neatly under his knees, the merchant rever-
ently undid the dull gold wrapper around each bale. Reds
for the coffin-bed curtains came first. Red is the color of joy.
When a man or woman has conscientiously filled seventy years
and leaves as fruit of his or her life a numerous, well-behaved
posterity, there can be no grief concerning the completion of
this life and the beginning of a new existence.

Hues of pink, rose, damask, coral, carnation, flame, scarlet,
cherry, ruby, claret, crimson, magenta, and carmine were
passed from woman to woman and laid aside in a heap of flowing color. Each length had its name: "Dawn over the Mountain of Eternal Peace"; "Springtime in an Orchard"; "Wings
of a Singing Bird." But the women of Wong looked without
interest on all the merchant could show. One of his lads was
dispatched to the shop to bring further treasure.

The racks that I had been commissioned to borrow were
wanted for work in progress. As I lingered, Shun-ko came to

tell me so.   She stayed and helped to examine the blue silks for the inner trousers and short jacket of the Elder's Heavenly costume.   When the women found nothing to their liking, the Elder indicated a length called "Sky in the Late Summer" from the heap of bluebell, columbine, flax, cornflower, hyacinth, larkspur, and gentian which, by then, lay in a mass. Swathing of raw silk was selected and the merchant commissioned to tint it a delicate pink.   A fine white fillet for the head was chosen.   Then the yellow silks for the winding sheet were opened.   When we left, Wong Mai-su politely walked back with us to the gate in the dividing wall, discussing with Shun-ko the cut of sleeves in the Ming period.   When I asked why the garments would be fashioned as in the Ming dynasty, she answered, "Because we always enter Heaven dressed that way."

In a dream two days earlier the Elder of Wong had seen his Soul stand beside him, dressed in traveling clothes and carrying a scroll.   So he knew that his earthly scroll was filled. Through a circle of seasons, in which he continued in robust health, he made ready.

Of clothes he had five complete changes, in addition to the riding jacket and cap for the journey, as he desired to be suitably garbed for whatever occasion he must meet.   His wife took the pearls from her dowry earrings and sewed them into the lining of his money pocket for emergency, should his cash be insufficient to satisfy the gatemen on the toll road through Hell.   His eldest daughter embroidered and filled a tobacco pouch, and her husband sent an amber-stemmed pipe.

In the House of Lin we bought stuffs and made a quilt on which we stitched appropriate sentiments.   The House of Chow sent a quilt of jade-green crêpe de Chine filled with thistledown.   Other houses sent "Warmth of Affection" coverlets until there was sufficient for the coffin bed and a great heap laid on a table in the Guest Hall.

The sons prepared the coffin for their father.   When it was

made, priests from both the Buddhist and the Taoist temples
came to bless it.   Then it stood ready in the Hall of Ancestors.
The Houses of Lin and Wong believe that Li-hua, the blind
widow of Lin, is more gifted than any other seer of their
knowledge.   She chose the soil under the redbeam tree, in the
southeast corner of the land the Wongs farm, as the place where
the Elder of Wong should give his body to the earth.   From
the day of choice he labored to build there a place of pleasant
dalliance, where the living members of his family would be
happy to spend leisure hours.   "I want the music of their
laughter and the ripple of their talk," he said to me.

He planted three poplars, a scarlet maple, a walnut, and a
cutting our Elder gave him from the maidenhair fern tree.
He brought builders from Peking to construct a pavilion.   He
set wistaria to climb over it, and put forsythia before the
door.

Winter was late that year.   But on the Second of the Pepper
Moon, thirteen months after the Elder of Wong's dream, we
had a fall of wet snow.   Mai-da and I were in Yu-lin's dwelling, learning to do seed-stitch embroidery, when the Elder
of Wong's Third Green Skirt came to ask if she might look
down the road through the telescope, as she was anxious because he had set out, by sedan chair, at dawn and had not yet
returned.

The shrine in which the telescope is housed is kept locked.
Su-ling, who brought it home when she returned from the
Sorbonne, feared that the children might be tempted to
tamper with it.   I was sent to unlock and dust the instrument.
But it had no power to open a road of light through falling
snow.   When the Elder of Wong's Third Green Skirt had
tried in vain to find her man, she put her head down on the
table and sobbed.

Bald-the-third came to us with umbrellas.   She took us
back to my dwelling place, where she made the woman drink
tea laced with corn-spirit and then escorted her home.

She told us that the Elder of Wong had arrived some time before and gone to his bed, where he lay alternating between chill and fever, but stubbornly refusing to swallow either the beef tea his wife had made, or the physic his granddaughter pressed upon him.

He did not get up again. On the evening of the fourth day, the daughters of the homestead knelt in the circle of prayer (the cries of virgin daughters are the most audible to Heaven's ear) asking that Heaven's gate be unlatched for the earth-departing Soul. But the Soul did not leave until the light of a new day illuminated the sky, and this is a good omen that the homestead family will continue to eat three meals daily.

According to local proverb, "In the canal, water is driven onward by water behind; in the world, newcomers take the places of those who pass." The instant the Soul of the Elder of Wong became unconscious of earthly details, the next heir in line became the Elder of Wong and took control of proceedings. He climbed to the roof of the late Elder's dwelling and begged the departing Soul to tarry yet a little longer with the homestead family. The Family, gathered in mass in the courtyard below, echoed his pleas. When all efforts failed to bring the Soul back, the new Elder ordered the males of the homestead to unravel their queues, the females to twist white cotton in their hair, and candles to be lit before the God of the Hearth.

The body was washed with water from the temple, then dressed for the journey and placed comfortably on the coffin bed, with the changes of clothes, the pipe and tobacco pouch, a book to read, and the necessary passports and money conveniently near to the hands. Warmth of Affection quilts were tucked around. The curtain of joy, on which the wives of the homestead had stitched wishes for a long and prosperous life in the Western Sky, was hung in the Court of Dignity, where the coffin stood.

The new Elder of Wong set a table at the coffin head. On it he put a tablet carved with the late Elder of Wong's personal name in gold lettering. This is the life tablet now cherished in the Wong Hall of Ancestors as the symbol of the Spirit in Heaven. He replenished the sesame oil in the basin of the pagoda-shaped Lanthorn of Heaven. Before the tablet he stood the Lanthorn; on its left an incense burner sending forth fragrant purity; on its right a vase of blue "virtue flowers."

In the street, to the left of the To and From the World Gate, a red pole was set to announce to all passers-by that a man in

THE WONG GATEKEEPER

a coffin lay within. The Wong gatekeeper went to summon the musicians and priests who had been engaged to chant.

These home details attended to, the males of the House of Wong dressed in gowns and head fillets of coarse white cloth, put on straw sandals, and walked to the Temple of Agriculture to announce to the Lord of the Soil that their ancestor now had need of a place in the earth for his body.

The scribes of the Wong Family brought large sheets of yellow paper into the Lin library, which the Elder of Lin offered, as there was need of a quiet place in which to write the funeral invitations. Wei-sung, who is versed in the phraseology of officialdom, prepared the copy for all government servants; Su-ling, experienced in modern ways by three years in Europe, wrote out what should go to the Wong maternal cousins in the port of Tientsin. Although different in phrasing, the invitations were essentially the same, in that they recorded briefly the life of the late Elder of Wong from birth until death, listed the honors he had won, and stated the days appointed for the reception of guests.

The Lin twins and I worked much of the day helping the children of Wong fold the yellow envelopes to hold the invitations. On each we pasted a stripe of blue and of red. Mai-da attended to the posting, carefully accounting the cost of the stamps, and moderately tipping the green-coated postman.

On guest days, a young priest beat a drum in the entrance court to let the Family know of each arrival. The Family then knelt beside the coffin in order, but the visitor did not address them until after honoring the departed man by kowtowing three times to his coffin and his spirit tablet. Each time the visitor bowed, the Family bowed in unison with him, and the courts were filled with the music of instruments and the chanting of priests.

Serving folk then politely conducted the guests from the hall to the banqueting room, and set food before them. Men and women of the House then thanked the guests for honoring their ancestor, and for the Heavenly gift that each brought. In this exchange of greeting no word of sorrow or consolation was spoken, as such would be a slur on the departed one's chances of preferment in Heaven.

The funeral catafalque was covered with a heavy white satin cloth, and was carried by seventy-two bearers dressed in green embroidered with red characters, meaning long life in the Western Sky. The order of the procession was: the deceased's sedan chair; the boat on which he traveled the canals; his portrait on an easel; the chanting priests, eighteen of them Taoists, eighteen Buddhists, and seven Lamas; a stringed band; one hundred and eight bearers carrying Heavenly gifts; twenty-one bearers of white paper brooms to sweep the road to the Western Sky; the sons on foot, the eldest carrying the spirit tablet, the second the lighted Lanthorn of Heaven; the time-beater with his wooden clappers; the catafalque; the wives, wearing white cotton and riding in carts drawn by mules in white trappings; the married daughters in blue carts; friends in their own conveyances; more bearers with Heavenly gifts; more chanting priests; and at the rear another band of musicians.

At intervals silver paper cash was thrown to right and left by the sons to bribe the devils who might be wandering about. Along the route friendly families had erected little houses to honor the Wong ancestor. The procession stopped when the coffin came opposite these, a white mat was spread across the road, and the sons knelt to thank the donors. There was a tablet to the late Wong in each house.

When the procession reached the grave, the beater called relatives and friends to a circle. Then, to the throb of eerie music, each of us threw earth on the coffin. When it was covered, the priests sent the Heavenly gifts to the sky by fire. Some of the gifts were life-size papier-mâché servants, each with his or her name attached; banner-men with scrolls of grey, blue, or black silk; papier-mâché horses, carriages, and grooms, and a motor car with uniformed chauffeur; pots of cypress bent to animal shapes; silver and gold; a chest of books; a table lute; a set of chess; a three-sailed boat manned by a boatman and his wife; a hen with chicks, and a basket of ripe peaches.

Then the House of Wong took home their spirit tablet, symbol of the ancestor who had plucked the flower of life, and set it in their Ancestral Hall.

Never in the House of Lin or of Wong have I heard anyone speak of the late Elder of Wong (or of any ancestor) as dead. On all feast days they send him, by fire, gifts symbolic of wishes for good fortune in Heaven. On all days he is very much alive on the lips of his family, who speak of him as having a keen interest in all of their affairs.

During the first sixty days following his departure, they expressed concern for his travail on the road through Hades by wearing coarse cotton gowns, white shoes, and a white knot in their hair. In this time no one went abroad, except by necessity, when the dress was changed to one of black with a white girdle, white cap button, and white shoes. After sixty days they wore grey gowns with black shoes and blue hair strings. The women used no ornaments until one hundred days were passed, when they put on silver. Until three years had gone they did not wear either silk or satin.

3

The late Elder of Wong spent thirty years in toil away from his homestead, and accumulated more money than is recorded of any other of their family, but his decease gave no member of the House concern about his wealth. As Shun-ko explained, the power of bequeathing by secret document, which the West calls a "will," does not exist in China. No member of a House, on plucking the flower of life, can make disposal of any material thing which he has accumulated, thus advancing the fortune of one relative more than another, or preferring a friend above Family.

The Family is a unit. And, as a unit, it is heir to all the

credits and all the liabilities of each and every member. When a person leaves the homestead, arrangement must be made at the time of departure as to whether or not he will be held as "separately established."

If separately established, his earnings do not fall into the common fund, nor will his fortune ever be enhanced by any inheritance from the homestead. He goes forth to brave fortune with an empty pocket, and he has neither voice nor liability concerning members of the Family.

But if he decides to continue "of the homestead," then his dwelling place is kept ready to welcome him, even if he is absent from youth until old age. And his successes or failures are of common concern.

"The debt of one is the debt of all" is not an idle proverb. Neither is the saying, "When anyone in a Family breaks the law, the head of the Family is to blame." By the rule of immediate succession there is always an Elder to every Family.

Intention of separate domicile must be told in the Hall of Ancestors, with all the Family gathered to hear; and published abroad for all the world to know, so that no one deals with the separately established under false pretenses. Should a man go abroad without making such an announcement, it is understood that he continues of the homestead. On leaving home in youth, the late Elder of Wong elected to remain of his House, so his success belonged to his House and his fortune was just a part of the common fortune of the homestead.

His second son found Family membership irksome, and chose to be separately established. So he received nothing from his father's prudent industry, nor from the fortune of the thirty-four earlier generations. Property cannot go to an heir, except the House dissolve by mutual consent of its members. An heir must come to the property. One separately established has made a life decision, and may not return.

On the day following the Star Festival, Chu Lu-mai came to stay in the House of Exile, as the House of Chu was dissolving by mutual consent of its members.

She is the daughter of the late sister of Su-ling's mother. Tall and graceful as the willow, with skin soft as the petals of the golden peony, brows arched like the butterfly's spread wings, and temples as the cicada, she is gentle of manner and speech, unselfish in daily consideration for others, skilled with the needle and the table lute, quick at hedged-in chess, and gifted in cookery.

And there were then sons of the House of Lin of age to marry for whom betrothal arrangements had yet to be made.

Because the House of Chu was thus brought close to us, our courts were filled with gossip of the partition of their worldly goods. I heard the Lin Elder say, "Sons are heirs to material wealth in equality, regardless of the order of their birth or whether born of wives or green-skirt mates; but on the first-born of each father falls the responsibility of the care of his ancestral tablets and other insignia of his existence, as well as the father's place in concern for the welfare of the younger brothers and sisters."

"In a Family living in compound, the Family Eldership descends from the homestead founder through the eldest son. So a man may be Family Elder in a household where he has uncles of greater age belonging to an earlier generation. But a Family Elder is a priest, not a civil ruler. He leads the ceremonies in the Ancestral Hall, but in Family Council his power is checked by the fact that each member has voice according to generation, beginning with the generation nearest the founder, and decreasing in strength in descent. In Family division all shares are equal, but he who inherits the care of tablets and tombs is heir to an extra share to cover extra expenses.

"Daughters inherit shares as sons only when the agnate line is extinct. They cannot continue the line, but they can

claim the property by sweeping their parents' tombs." **So**
Chu Lu-mai told me one day, as we sat shelling beans. She
continued: "Each daughter of a homestead, whether from a
wife or a woman entitled only to wear the green skirt, has the
right of maintenance until marriage, and power to demand
that the Family arrange a suitable marriage. She cannot be
kept at home unmated even on excuse that she is necessary
to care for ill or aged parents, nor can she be forced to work
in order to help support her birth home. She has the right
to the exchange, between her father's household and the
homestead she is to 'complete' as a bride, of betrothal presents
in accord with her position, and to a wedding ceremony with
music and a procession. Her dowry should contain clothes
for four seasons and adequate household furniture. Whether
or not her equipment includes jewels depends upon the
wealth of her birth home, and the love of its members for
her."

Chu Lu-mai lived in the House of Exile under the care of
Shun-ko, who was made her patron at her first birthday.
The other unmarried daughters of Chu lived under the
care of other guardians in other homesteads until marriage.
The inheritance money for Chu Lu-mai's living, dowry, and
wedding celebrations was sufficient to provide her more lavishly
than any daughter of Lin who has been married in my time.
Yet the House of Lin did not propose marriage for either son
to her.

Wei-sung, Lin Family Elder, said quietly, " 'You cannot take
ivory from the mouth of a rat.' She is a charming, lovable
girl, but she is of the House of Chu, and the House of Chu
has dissolved twice in three hundred years."

It was while Chu Lu-mai was still with us that Mai-da, Su-
ling, Lu-mai and I were working under Hua-li's direction.
We had unwrapped the winter coat of straw from the roses,
spaded the earth around dwarf plums, and were sweeping the
blanket of leaves from the violet beds, when we heard the

voice of the hot-cake vendor, and sent Camel-back to purchase refreshment.

So we were his deputies at the To and From the World Gate when the brass knocker clanged. In bravado, Mai-da called in deep-voiced imitation of Camel-back, "Who knocks there?"

And a high feminine voice answered, "It is I. The wife of Lin Chien-lu, with his son and his daughter on either hand."

Then Su-ling took charge. "The wife of Lin Chien-lu is within, and sitting now by the window in her dwelling in the Court of the Ginkgo Tree. The daughter of Lin Chien-lu is married and lives in Peking. The son of Lin Chien-lu is a grown man. Fly away, evil spirit. Fly away."

"Call the Elder of our House," the voice continued. "I am weary and cannot stand here. Tell him I am the woman Lin Chien-lu mated at Shanghai. I have the clothes he wore on leaving this homestead and his likeness in the faces of our daughter and our son."

When Camel-back returned with the cakes he was consulted. He recognized the garments of Lin Chien-lu and the Lin brow and nose. So the woman came into the Hall of Ancestors where the Family were assembled in Council, and convinced the House of her rights.

Although Lin Chien-lu had not communicated with his homestead since the day, nine years previously, when he departed for Canton; although the woman had not known his whereabouts for seven years, she was entitled to shelter, food, and raiment in accord with the family fortune from the homestead treasury for life; to a funeral with banners and music; to have her spirit tablet set in the Circle of Ancestors. She must do her share of cooking, cleaning, and sewing. But she cannot be forced to earn for the common fund, and she must be nursed in sickness.

His first wife, married with music and ceremony twenty-two years before his departure, had to give the newcomer living space in the Court of Nesting Swallows. The children he

sired at Shanghai have inheritance in their father's House equal
to the rights of his children born here.

In the event of the death of the first wife, the newcomer
would speak with the authority of Lin Chien-lu in his absence, in matters concerning the property and concerning *all*
his children. Even if a woman's husband has deserted her,
as Chien-lu appears to have done, the homestead cannot frown
upon her as an extra rice bowl. Even though her husband be
expelled from the homestead for misdemeanor, she can continue in her full rights.

Should a woman become a widow at the end of the breath
which announced her in the Hall of Ancestors and before her
husband has cohabited with her, she cannot be forced to leave
the homestead, and make a second marriage. If a woman
mates twice it must be for her own pleasure or by her own
choice. A woman need not ever be anxious about material
things so long as the fortune of the homestead with which she
mates is good. A mother is never subject to the child to whom
she gave the privilege of life. Public opinion is such that no
purchaser would venture to take transfer of property which
a son offered for sale without his mother's approval.

One day, in the midst of the turmoil about the admittance
of the woman and the two children, Shun-ko said, "On my
world tour I heard much concerning woman's rights. I even
heard folk, in comparing their condition with ours, pity us
Chinese women. But I have returned home to the customs
in force in China, for centuries, well content with my rights
as a daughter of the House of Ho and a wife of the House
of Lin. And I trust that civil war will so occupy the country
during my lifetime that there will be no time for a new code
of law modernizing our privileges."

4

Just as the rice was in grain, the Family knew that Ko-nen
was with child. She had failed to conceive on her marriage

bed, and her husband had since been away on business at Canton, where he had mated and bred three sons.

A wife may be returned to her father's house for insubordination, as harmony is the keynote of courtyard life. But if a bride goes forth from her father's care as a virgin, then unchastity is her husband's fault, and it is his duty to inflict the punishment for adultery, which is death by strangulation.

The Elder of the House of Exile sent for Ko-nen's husband. He came. He saw his wife. And he astonished the homestead by calling a Council in the Hall of Ancestors and declaring that he was willing to accept the child in Ko-nen's womb as his own. But this the Homestead refused to permit.

A woman may not be punished in China while she carries a new life in her body. From the day of his speech in Council, her husband, who could not leave the homestead until after the birth, refused to take part in family life and took no food except rice water.

Suspicion pointed to her husband's cousin, a youth of twenty-two years, whose marriage had been arranged with a daughter of Ho, Shun-ko's niece, for the Harvest Moon. The House of Ho immediately withdrew their red card of agreement and returned the betrothal bracelets.

Ko-nen had been married at seventeen. She was now twenty-two. I had always considered her exceedingly plain. So had the Lins. But in gestation she did not grow grotesque, as most women do. She came into health. Her dull eyes brightened and her hair had gloss. Her sallowness cleared to rose-petal creaminess. Her breasts swelled in lovely curves under gowns that had once hung slack.

Despite ostracism, she was in radiant beauty, and in the fullness of time she delivered a boy without much pain. At breakfast call next day, when her serving woman took her gruel, Ko-nen had swallowed gold and given gold to her child. Beautiful, as all love children seem to be, he rested in the curve of his mother's arm.

Sin in a son can rot the foundation of a homestead and bring a family to corruption.   The most insidious of sins is trespass beyond the Orchid Door.

He who was suspected of knowing the wife of his cousin was brought to audience with his assembled kindred, including three representatives from the Lin clan at Canton.   Within the circle of tablets symbolizing his ancestors, he was denounced by his nearest of kin — his own mother.   For his guilt was beyond doubt.   He had been a well-loved lad.   But among all the Lins there was not one dissenting voice, from man, woman, or child.   One dissenting voice could have saved him.   That, or the appearance of the two grey doves.

Disinherited, he was sent from the homestead, doomed forever to use only the name "outcast," with no place to lay his body in the earth among kindred, or to set his spirit tablet — and no rights in the patrimony, either for himself or for his descendants, beyond the cotton gown and straw sandals ir which he was dressed and the packet of rice, food for three days, tied to his shoulder.

VII

MARRIAGE

1

I T was the afternoon of Feast of Lanterns Eve, in 1922.

"You are," said Su-ling, as Mai-da cut another bias ruffle from the shell-pink velvet, "about to cause us all to be memorized, by our Family Elders in Council, on the degeneracy to which the Occident has sunk, during the last century, in having been converted to a trust in propinquity and the biological urge for the continuance of their race. Also to cause us to be reminded that marriage is not a relation for personal pleasure, but a contract involving the ancestors, the descendants, and the property. A contract not to be emotionally entered into, in our land, where we pride ourselves on a continuous procession of prudent generations."

"It might also," added Ching-mei as she bit off a thread, "be wise to remember that while negligent farming brings temporary poverty, a mistake in marriage brings poverty for life."

Immediately after the meal in the Hour of the Snake, the wives of the homestead had gone out to burn incense at the Temple of the Hill of Eternal Greenness. We knew that they would not return until after dusk. Their chair bearers would detour home by way of the Washing Horse Pond, and loiter so that they and the women might enjoy the ice lanterns. These are chiseled in the image of flowering trees, giant frogs, ferocious tigers, scaled dragons, historic courtesans, renowned warriors, happiness sprites, and such, in accord with the fancy of the icemen. On every Feast of Lanterns Eve they are set up in competitive pairs on each side of the avenues leading to the pond. They are lit at dusk. Then the Village Elders judge them, presenting prizes to the three best, and giving tags of honor to three others.

Above her sewing table Mai-da had tacked a color sketch of the Pearl Fairy, holding open her oyster-shell home, as a pattern from which to create her costume for the Lanterns Eve masque. She had shaped an oyster shell of whalebone, in size to close comfortably about herself, covered it with grey cotton cloth touched up realistically with white and green paint, and lined it with a fine shirring of pink gauze. It lay finished on her bed. She had fringed the pale pink chiffon veil that makes the fairy invisible, cleaned her best satin slippers, and completed the basque waist of the shell-pink velvet dress. It awaited the attachment of a wide *bouffant* ruffled skirt.

But she had found the task of hemming and attaching the tiers of tiny ruffles more than she was equal to in the time remaining before the masque. This circumstance had forced her to trust her cousins concerning her intent to dance in the street masquerade at which guilds frolic.

She told of the note she had received from Erh-sung, the Manchu Prince, asking her to come as the Pearl Fairy to meet him, who would be disguised as the Fisherman's Son. Also how she had put her consenting answer under the loose stone behind the shrine of the Old Man in the Moon, in the Street of the Purple Bamboo Forest, which had been her letter box for communication with him for many months.

So, as the wives were all safely out, Su-ling and Ching-mei lectured Mai-da wisely on marriage while they sewed with diligence. I polished the jade earrings Mai-da had promised to give her servant Faithful Duck, if she got safely out through the Gate of Compassion and in again. Mai-da cut ruffles from the roll of exquisite fragile tissue velvet which her great-aunt had given her for her bridal gown.

When the stitching was finished, Mai-da donned the costume and showed us how she could dance the pageant in her pink satin slippers. She held the shell in her hands and mischievously closed its dullness around her dainty beauty.

We had tidied the room before the pat-pat of the chair bearers' feet sounded at the Orchid Door. The wives found Mai-da in the kitchen, assisting at the preparation of the evening meal.

Clouds covered the moon in the early night. Mai-da squeezed her slim loveliness through the Gate of Compassion and handed one earring to Faithful Duck. A Fisherman's Son kept tryst with her at the homestead wall. He flirted in a dance all down the mystic lantern-decorated streets, returning her frolic with quick response. She was puzzled, thrilled, and half frightened.

She knew that he was not Erh-sung. Yet he enchanted her with his charm. They dined with other masqueraders at the Abode of Orchids. He brought her safely back to the Gate of Compassion just before dawn.

Faithful Duck awaited her there. When she was again under the shadow of the Goddess of Mercy and had lit a tall taper of thanksgiving, her escort recalled her to the door with a low whistle. Then he lifted his mask — and she knew that the gay companion of her escapade was her favorite uncle, Keng-lin.

Next day, when the Elder's Wife sent Mai-da to polish the brasses in the Hall of Ancestors, Uncle Keng-lin followed her and told her how her letter had come into his possession. An itinerant priest had seen her put it under the shrine in the Street of the Purple Bamboo Forest; secured it; followed her home; and sat down at the To and From the World Gate to sell it to the first man of the Family who came out.

He had demanded five hundred dollars.   Keng-lin had got
the letter for three hundred, and sealed the priest's lips against
gossiping Mai-da's name all along his holy pilgrimage to Wu
Tai Shan in Shansi.

Two days after the Feast of Lanterns, Wei-sung, the Family
Elder, called Mai-da to the library.   Five cards proposing
marriage were laid face down on his writing table.   He told
her to take up one.   Thus she, who over a period of many
years had managed to avoid betrothal, selected her husband.
And Wei-sung, reluctant to break his family circle by giving
any girl in marriage, was saved from making a choice for her
beyond giving his sanction to the Family-in-Council's decision
that any one of the five was suitable.

From then on Mai-da, who is bred of centuries of folk who
accept marriage as a duty, accepted her fate with philosophy,
and seemingly without undue curiosity concerning her future
husband.

Uncle Keng-lin carried a red card, identical in size and shape
with the proposal, and containing, similarly, the record of her
year, month, day, and hour of birth, to the man's homestead,
which is but three streets away.

When he had gone, the Family Elder put the proposed
groom's name with Mai-da's on the altar in the Hall of Ancestors, between the life tablets of the founder of the House
of Exile and his mate.

"Marriage," Shun-ko explained to me, "is a contract between two families and must be made with the free consent
of both families.   A maid is wed in accord with the wisdom
of her clan.   In mating we are careful to have our descendants mate well.   The name of Mai-da's proposed husband will
lie with her name for three days on our family altar.   Mai-da's
name will lie with his name for three days on his homestead
family altar.   Only if there is peace in both households during this time will the considered alliance go further.   If criticism of their union be spoken in either homestead, the matter

will be dropped. But as the cards are on the altars, no person will speak without real concern."

Late on the third day, Mai-da and I were in the central room of the Three Eastern Courtyards. We were searching for a volume of Li Tai Po's poems, from which her mother had promised to read to us, when the Elder's servant came in and put down a padded wicker tea-basket. We realized that a visitor had been announced at the gate. Reasoning that we could not avoid being met in the courtyard if we went, we stayed behind a lacquer screen. The Elder entered, pulling his ceremonial robe about him. The servant left off flipping his duster to help fasten the neck buttons.

This room was the Hall of Dignity of the original homestead and is the place where especially honored callers are received. The doors were flung open. From our peep-crack, we saw that the Family Elder had ordered the visitor's sedan chair to be carried to this inner court. We recognized it as the chair of the Elder of the House of Mai-da's proposed husband.

An uncle of that House descended from it. He was dressed in a richly ornamented gown of many colors. A servant accompanied him. The servant spread a red mat. The master knelt before the Elder of Lin, despite the latter's polite attempt to stop him. He presented a betrothal contract. This, he announced, was signed by his Family Elder and the four heirs-in-succession to the Family Eldership. "I am the voice of our homestead," he ended, "who are united in eagerness to welcome the daughter of Lin."

The men drank tea. They talked of crops; of weather; of political conditions. We grew weary in our cramped closeness. Finally, when the call had stretched to proper politeness, the visitor asked to pay his respects to the First Lady of the homestead. The servant preceding them with the red mat, they left to go to Kuei-tzu's apartment. Then we slipped back to the Springtime Bower.

After the caller had gone from the homestead, Kuei-tzu sent
for Mai-da.   She gave her the betrothal gift from the Lady in
First Authority in her future husband's homestead — a gold
bracelet set with three rubies.

Next morning Uncle Keng-lin rode out in the Elder's chair.
He was accompanied by Camel-back.   Camel-back carried a
red mat.   Uncle Keng-lin had a contract signed by the Elder
of Lin and four heirs-in-succession, also a gift of jade coat
buttons from the First Lady of Lin to the betrothed bridegroom.

In the afternoon, the Elder of the groom's homestead came
to the House of Lin to ask for the wedding date.

The nineteenth day of the Peony Moon, and the birthday of
the Protectress of Blossoms, was chosen.   This is Mai-da's
favorite day.

As soon as they could be baked, and while they were still
warm from the oven, the groom's mother sent sweet cookies
in a red basket to Mai-da.   These cookies are called "phœnix-
and-dragon cakes."   Two servants, garbed in wedding coats
of green and red, brought the basket.   They carried it on a
red pole by way of the principal streets of the village.   So it
was made public that the betrothal between the two houses
was complete and the wedding day named.

Mai-da had to present to Kuei-tzu a list of the homesteads
to which she wished to intimate her approaching marriage
so that they might help with preparations.   Kuei-tzu vetoed
two names and reminded Mai-da to include a lady patron of
her birth who had married a second time and was now domiciled in Shantung.   Each phœnix-and-dragon cake had the
wedding date stamped into it with red sugar.   The cakes were
divided into packets of five.   The packets were wrapped in
wedding paper, then nestled around with red cotton and sealed
up in lacquer wedding-cake boxes, and dispatched by messenger or by post to each household on the approved list.

These homesteads responded with gifts appropriate to the

bride's dowry. They included garments suitable for addition to the trousseau, household furniture, bedding, crockery,
silverware, kitchen utensils, and jewelry.

Seamstresses helped the women of the family sew gowns of
flowered silk for all the family, as well as fashion the wedding
garments for the bride. Luckily Mai-da received three rolls
of shell-pink tissue velvet. In the confusion of the preparations no one appeared to remember that she should now have
four rolls.

Mai-da was teased about her husband. She was laugh-
ingly told that he had flat feet, a terrible temper, a pock-
marked face, a beard, untidy habits, a finicky appetite, a weak
digestion, the body of a giant, and the mind of a simpleton.
She met this jesting with admirable self-control. But she
bartered away her birthday camera to her boy cousin, Tsai-fu,
in return for half a dozen snapshots of her betrothed. So she
satisfied herself that he was the man whom she had seen two
years previously, worshiping the God of Knowledge at the
City Temple.

Red cards of invitation to the "Maid's Feast" were sent to
friends and relatives, so timed as to reach them ten days before
the feast. They responded with many more gifts. Among
them four gowns, one for each season; in these every woman
resident in the homestead of Mai-da's betrothed had put stitches
of welcome.

Hua-li was busy in court and garden coaxing the peonies
with pruning knife, liquid fertilizers, and sprinkling basin.
Mai-da and I thought that the showing of flowers and buds
was perfect. In varieties of every size, from the round of
a summer fan to the rim of a humming bird's nest, they gave
dignity and fragrance to the House of Exile. They rose, on
glazed tile terraces facing the south side of the lapis-lazuli
pond, in a luxurious hill of color shading through dark plum,
wine red, sunset rose, sunrise pink, apple bloom, and cloud
white. Beyond the wistaria arbor, pale yellow peonies unfurled

their beauty against feathery bamboo saplings. In the library court, the plant called "Maiden Asleep in the Moonlight," brought by a bride from the city of Loyang one hundred years ago, proudly lifted purple buds beyond counting on sturdy stalks.

' Reed awnings were put up to shade the courts; crimson carpets laid in brilliant pattern on the tiles. Rosy banners were fastened to float on the spring breezes over the courtyard walls. The house pillars were wrapped in bindings of silk. Vermilion curtains were hung in doorways. All the decorative treasures of ivory, porcelain, bronze, and jade were brought from chests and set where their antiquity showed best. Scrolls of red and gold were pasted on either side of the To and From the World Gate, announcing to all who passed that Mai-da, daughter of the House of Lin, would go out to complete the House of Tseng, as wife to Tseng Huai-ching, on the birthday of the Protectress of Blossoms.

Friends from a distance, and women relatives and friends who desired to assist in the preparation, began to arrive four days before the wedding day. Courtesy demands that feast food be ready to welcome these guests, so there was continuous bustle and stir in the kitchens a week before the wedding.

With thoughtful consideration, the groom's household sent to the bride's household gifts of wine, cakes, roast geese, braised duck, pickled pork, spiced mutton, sugared nuts, candied fruit, and sweetmeats prepared by their recipes. With equally thoughtful consideration, the bride's family, realizing that early guests would be arriving at the groom's house too, sent gifts of wine, cakes, roast geese, braised duck, pickled pork, spiced mutton, sugared nuts, candied fruits, and sweetmeats made by their recipes. There was a delightful confusion of servants carrying baskets between the two households — in itself a source of happiness, as carriers are tipped each time they deliver a parcel in Chinese homes.

In the forenoon of the day before the bride was sent, bearers

in brilliant wedding garments carried Mai-da's dowry to her
new home.   Musicians played wind, string, and hand instruments at the front and at the rear of this procession.   It was
ninety-one carrying poles long.   Each pole was loaded with
what two men could carry.   The large furniture was wrapped
in red covers.   The smaller articles and the wearing apparel
were packed in chests.   But a Swiss clock with a bird that
sang the hour was carried uncovered so that the village might
enjoy it.

Camel-back walked behind the procession.   He was entrusted with Mai-da's jewel box and with the inventory of
her possessions.

On the marriage eve, the "Maid's Feast" was held in the
Hall of Hospitality.   The hall was decorated with the symbols of happiness and illuminated with scarlet candles.
Mai-da's mother presided.   Mai-da came to the hall when the
first course had been served and poured wine into each guest's
cup.

She was dressed, for the last time, in the costume of girlhood.
Her hair had been brushed to a blue-black gloss.   It hung in
a thick plait far below her waist.   Faithful Duck had tinted
her lips with ruby.   Her eyes were bright with excitement.
She was exquisite in the straight bamboo-green dress made for
the occasion.

On the evening before she leaves home, each girl of the
House of Exile dines alone with the First Lady of Authority.
Mai-da dined with Kuei-tzu.   Then she burned the incense of
farewell in the Hall of Ancestors, and was sent to bed.

The pad-pad of cloth shoes on the dusty road heralded the
approach of the bridal chair before dawn.   At sunrise the
flutes played the "Call for the Bride" and the To and From
the World Gate creaked open.

Faithful Duck hurried out.   She returned to our room to
say that the groom's musicians numbered thirty-two.   That
the bridal chair had eight bearers.   That there were two green

chairs, each with four bearers: one which had held the groom's aunt, who had the bridal cloak and red handkerchief, and had gone to drink tea with Mai-da's mother; the other to carry herself, Faithful Duck, the bride's good serving matron. Also more banner-men than she had been able to count, as they moved about so much.   Bearers, musicians, banner-men, all in new wedding coats of scarlet satin, with heavy thread-of-gold embroidery.

Shun-ko came.   She ordered Faithful Duck to stop her chatter and fetch bath water for her mistress.   She laid out Mai-da's lotus-perfumed wedding undergarments.   She hid her emotion by scolding Mai-da for being too lenient with her servant.   Another aunt came and painted Mai-da's alarming pallor with a liquid lotion.   Then Ching-mei used her lip rouge on the bride's mouth, saying that it was absolutely proof against coming off on the nuptial cup.

A cousin came to say that the bridegroom had arrived, and was now kneeling before the Elders, making formal request for their daughter to "complete himself," and would soon return to his homestead to await Mai-da.

The wedding dress was slipped over Mai-da's head, adjusted. It was admired by all the women and children who were now clustered in the room, in the doorway, and around the window. Mai-da had been a quiet doll to paint and dress, but suddenly she began to laugh with shrill hysteria.   No one could stop her. The Elder's wife sent word that everyone, excepting Shun-ko, who "has sense," and Faithful Duck, was to leave the Spring-time Bower.   Uncle Keng-lin came with his table lute and played lullabies to quiet Mai-da's nerves.

It was noon when Mai-da came to the Hall of Dignity.   She bowed to the guests.   She knelt in farewell to the Elders and to her parents.   Her father fastened the groom's cloak about her shoulders.   Her mother dropped his handkerchief as a veil over her face.   The Family cried, "May you be as happy as the

maid from Canton!"   Crackers were fired in loud explosion.
Mai-da was lifted into the bride's chair.   The chair was closed.
The sealing papers were fastened.

Kuei-tzu, Lady of First Authority in the Lin homestead,
put her name on the seals.   The drums rapped the call to start.
The cymbals clanged assent.   Flutes gave the "Wail of De-

THE BRIDE'S CHAIR

parture."   The groom's aunt and Faithful Duck got into the
two green chairs.   Lifting poles creaked.   The bride's procession passed out of the House of her girlhood.   The To and
From the World Gate was locked behind her.

The clan of Lin, gathered from far and near, feasting and
talking and playing table games to pass the time, waited until
the invitation should come from the clan of Tseng inviting the
bride's mother to the "After the Rites of the Marriage Bed
Breakfast," which is assurance that the groom's family are
satisfied.

Thus Mai-da went to her husband.

2

It was the last day of the Dragon Moon, several weeks after Mai-da had gone. The weather was uncomfortably warm and the Elder's wife had told La-mei and me to put big kettles of jasmine tea on the shelf of the Gate of Compassion, that the poor might refresh themselves and not be tempted to drink canal water. Ching-mei came running into the kitchen where we were boiling water, chanting: —

> "*Yu chia ts'ung ch'in*
> *Tsai chia yu shen*
> *T'ien yao hsia yu*
> *Niang yao chia jen*
> *Wu fa k'o chih.*"

> ("A maid weds to please her clan,
> But a widow pleases only herself.
> And if Heaven wants to rain
> Or your mother marry again,
> Nothing can prevent them.")

"Whatever has happened?" La-mei demanded of her twin.

"Chao-li has just told her son that she intends to marry the proprietor of the Abode of Orchids Restaurant," Ching-mei answered. "And he has retorted that 'She who has been wife to one man does not go to eat the rice of another.'"

"Hot boiled sweet potato!" La-mei exclaimed.

Chao-li was then thirty-six and had been a widow for three years. The Family Elder's wife showed her disapproval of this step by hiring craftsmen to regild the Memorial Arch to Virtuous Widows which spans the Big Horse Road and records the women who, although widowed in youth, have upheld village virtue by chastely refusing to "drink the tea of two families." The Family Elder reminded Chao-li that a widow goes out through the gate with empty hands — except that her daughters may accompany her, but that if they do they lose all rights in their birth home. Sons and whatever property the woman brought to the homestead belong to her husband's family. The widow who marries again loses all rights and all voice in the family.

Despite these things, Chao-li continued in her desire to marry Kwong Ching-lei. A widow can demand that her husband's family, to whom she is as a daughter, negotiate her marriage. The Lin Family Elders had to receive the jolly proprietor of the Abode of Orchids in the Hall of Dignity with all the courtesy which custom demands shall be accorded an honorable suitor for a bride. The House had to accept his proffered wedding gifts, and give Chao-li to him.

A woman may not ride twice in a bride's chair, or have the music of union played a second time. She takes only what she wears, and servants carrying the happiness banners may not make a procession for her through the streets. Chao-li walked out of the House of Exile with her second husband in the afternoon of the Tenth Day of the Lotus Moon. Two hours later, the serving woman Big Splash, who had been Chao-li's childhood nurse and had come to the House of Exile in her wedding procession, followed her out of the gate.

Big Splash was accompanied by ten coolies hired from the streets to carry what appeared to me an enormous amount of luggage for a servant to possess. But no one of the Lin household took any interest in this. Shun-ko and Sou-mai were just returning from a visit to the Goddess of Many Children. Their chair bearers had to wait for Big Splash and her luggage to pass before they could come in through the To and From the World Gate. But both declared that they had not noticed her.

3

"Marriage," so I hear often in China, "is the most important act in life. It is the seed of all future existence. If the seed is unhealthy the harvest will be misery." And just as often

I hear, "Marriage involves rights and duties, both for the parties wed and for the children born of their union.   But the rights of the child stand first, as the purpose of marriage is creation.   No matter how blest with happiness the man and the woman are in their relation, the marriage is a failure if it is childless.   This failure is a misfortune to be remedied by adoption, or by the taking of a handmaiden into the marriage to make it fruitful."

From girlhood Mai-da's mother has been interested in the history of marriage in China.   She has a notebook in which she writes extracts from what she reads, touching the customs and the regulations that govern the present-day wedding. From her notebook, I have copied the following, changing the Chinese dates to Western time: —

At the dawn of history, about 2852 B.C., Fu Hsi, First of the Five Virtuous Rulers, lived near the present city of Kaifeng and correlated the customs of mating which had already been evolved from the laws of nature.   From them Fu Hsi instituted the first national code of marriage laws for the people of his domain.

The *Calendar of the Hsia Dynasty*, 2205 B.C., of which part of a copy was found buried in the tomb of Confucius, contains the announcement that at the advent of the middle month of spring youths and maidens shall be made happy in love and set up house.

According to the *Book of Royal Habits*, compiled two centuries before Christ, the ancient Emperors of China made tours of inspection through their domains every five years; then held an audience for their people on Mount Tai, in western Shantung.   After the sacrifices to Heaven and to Earth, after the petitions had been read and attention paid to the aged, the Emperor commanded the Master of Music to bring him all the poems written in all the States during the interval since the last review, so that by studying them he might come to closer understanding with his people.   The *Book of Poetry* is a collection of three hundred and five of these ballads, odes, and hymns that sing of war, labor, and love.   They were written by folk of all classes and make a vivid, many-sided picture of life in the period of about 1719 to 585 B.C.   The songs of love show that even then the Chinese people were sensible and had discovered that mating contrary to convention leads only to unhappiness.

The *Annals of the State of Lu,* 722–481 B.C., which was a section of the Chow domain, record: "Both husband-beating and wife-beating are illegal, and serious offenses."

The *Books of Decorum,* compiled in the Han dynasty, 206 B.C.– 221 A.D., state that a person must not mate with another person of the same surname, or a person of maternal relationship within the five degrees of mourning, and that this edict must be remembered in taking a handmaiden to bear children to a fruitless union as well as in marrying a wife. The tenth volume of the Decorums places the patriarchal Family at the base of society, as it was at the dawn of history in China and has continued to be until to-day. It exhorts all the people to practise exogamy and avoid incest with the maternal line.

The *General Summary of the Laws of the Chinese Empire,* about 1700 A.D., records: "Carrying off or forcing a maid or a widow to marriage is to be punished by strangulation, whether the abductor marries the woman himself or gives her to another man. The woman must be returned to her home. If the abductor has confederates to assist him, then they shall be strangled, but he shall suffer the greater punishment of having his head severed by the executioner's knife."

The Law Code of the last dynasty, 1644–1912 A.D., incorporated the regulations of the past and added qualifying edicts from time to time.

Section 101 reads: "If when one of the sons of a family is away from home, either on official duty or for the purpose of trade, the Seniors of his House — *i.e.,* his grandparents, parents, paternal uncle or aunt, or elder brother — contract a marriage for him in his absence, he shall be bound to fulfill the contract notwithstanding that he may have himself entered into another contract. But if he has actually got married when abroad, such marriage shall stand good, and the contract entered into by his seniors shall be void.

"A woman, whether maid or widow, cannot contract her own marriage, except she has separated from the homestead and is neither receiving her livelihood from it nor claiming a daughter's dowry. But she can in all conditions demand that the Elders of her homestead negotiate a suitable marriage for her. Any Family Elder who neglects to find a husband for a daughter, a sister, a niece, a female slave, or any girl of his household, thus condemning her to an unfulfilled life, is liable to eighty public blows with the bamboo."

Section 101 also includes, "The practice of betrothing unborn children, by cutting off the lapel of the coat, is now declared illegal." (The present Elder of Lin and his wife were betrothed in this way.)

Section 102: "A man cannot mate again with scarlet banners and a procession during the life of his first wife. If there is need of a handmaiden to bear children, she shall be taken into the homestead quietly. A wife cannot be degraded to the position of a Green Skirt, nor the Green Skirt raised to the position of wife, so long as the wife is alive. If committed, these crimes are to be punished with a hundred and ninety blows respectively, and things rearranged as they were."

Section 107: "If any marriage takes place between persons of the same surname, the principals negotiating the marriage on each side shall each receive sixty blows and the marriage shall be null. The woman shall return to her family and the marriage presents be forfeit to the government."

Section 109: "Mating with a woman who has ever been either wife or Green Skirt to another of the same surname is forbidden. If a man takes either his grandfather's or his father's wife or Green Skirt, the penalty is the first degree — death by beheading. For marrying the widow of an elder or younger brother, the penalty is one degree less — death by strangulation; but for marrying the Green Skirt the penalty is one more degree less — perpetual banishment for one thousand miles." And so on.

In every case where there has been intercourse previous to the marriage in one of these incestuous unions, the man and the woman shall both suffer death.

Section 113: "No officer of the government can take a professional prostitute, either as Green Skirt or as wife. If he does, he shall be given sixty blows, the girl sent to her relatives, not returned to her profession, and the marriage presents forfeit to the government. No man can force his wife to accept a prostitute as a Green Skirt with the position or the rights of such in the homestead."

Section 114: "Any priest who takes either a wife or a Green Skirt shall receive eight blows and be required to quit the priesthood. If any priest get a relative or friend to ask for a woman and then take her for himself, it shall be deemed ordinary criminal intercourse. But the penalty shall in every case be two degrees more severe than in the case where the guilty man is a layman. And the woman shall be returned whence she came."

Section 116: "Divorce ends all relationship with the House into which the woman married. Except that she can never again marry a man of that surname. If a man and a woman are incompatible of temperament they may separate, with the mutual consent of their two homesteads, and the woman return to her father's House. In such cases there is no need to refer the matter to the civil authorities. It is a family affair, arranged by mutual good will on the part of the only parties concerned."

But as a woman's parental ancestors are responsible for her breeding and her education, her husband's Family Elders can force the Family Elders of her birth home to take her back for any one of the "seven rights" — *i.e.*, barrenness, wanton conduct, discourtesy, gossip, theft, discontented envy of others, or an infirmity misrepresented in the betrothal contract. Even if a man dearly and passionately loves his mate, his Family Elders may return her to her birthplace, if they so decide in solemn Council; marriage is a family, not a personal, affair, in which the happiness of the group is paramount and not the happiness of the individual.

Three compensatory rights are the principles of justice which prevent a woman from being divorced: *i.e.*, if she has kept the three years of mourning for either of her husband's parents, if her husband's homestead is now more wealthy than when she entered it, or if her birth home has been broken up since her marriage and she now has no place to go. In case of adultery, however, they are inoperative. The penalty for adultery is death by strangulation.

Mai-da's mother has added the following note to this section: "Adultery is only a feminine vice. Copulation on the man's part is not his wife's concern, unless he sires a child. Then she must accept the child as one of her household. All a man's offspring inherit equal rights in his homestead. It is his wife's duty to have all his children fed, clothed, and educated in accord with his property. She must stand sponsor for all of them in his clan and to the world. In the event of his death or his absence, she must assume custody of all his children's shares in the property and speak as his voice to defend their rights. No child in China can ever suffer bastardy, as no man's offspring is an illegitimate child."

4

Born in 1904, Tai-chun was married in the Chrysanthemum
Moon, when he was eighteen.   The present Elder of Lin is
industrious in keeping the admonition of the sages: "Marry
your sons as soon as they are grown."   By the marriage of a
son he can bring into his homestead yet another charming
young woman, descendant of one of his friends, and also fill
the homestead courtyards still more full with beautiful Lin
children.

The messenger delivering the announcements of the birth
of Lin Tai-chun, great-grandnephew of the Lin Family Elder,
crossed paths with the messenger delivering announcements
of the birth of Pien Wei-ling, great-granddaughter of the
Pien Family Elder.   Stopping to gossip, the messengers agreed
that the newborn boy and girl would certainly marry.   This
supposition was also voiced in every House which received the
birth announcements.

Before the "Rounding of the Year," Tai-chun's mother
received and accepted an invitation to spend a moon in the
Pien courtyards, during which the babies shared the same
cradle.   Some time later, Wei-ling's mother returned the
visit.   The children sat in a double pushcart and each had a
hand string to the kite that old Camel-back made and flew
for them.

From then until the "Cycle of Ten" they were together a
month or two every year, staying with their nurses in the
Garden of Children either of the Lin or of the Pien homestead.   The year that they were twelve, Tai-chun wove Wei-
ling a sewing basket of rice straw (the one she still uses) and
equipped it, spending his own pocket money.   And Wei-
ling, helped by her younger brother, made Tai-chun a boat to
sail on the shallow pond.

After that, of course, Tai-chun was too old to play with
girls.   He lived on the male side of his homestead.   He had a

tutor who was gruff with him if he even so much as mentioned them. The tutor punished such idleness by obliging him to commit to memory pages from Confucius's books, to cleanse his mind.

Naturally Wei-ling also was no longer permitted the license of a child. Promoted to the Springtime Bower, she was chaperoned in maidenly seclusion. While kept from man, yet, as marriage was to be her career, her educators seldom permitted her thoughts to stray away from man or the arts by which to please him.

The clans of Lin and Pien are both exceedingly cautious. Both received invitations to betrothal from other clans as the years passed. Neither entirely rebuffed any one of these queries. Then, at New Year 1919, the House of Lin included a pair of embroidered pockets in the usual friendly gifts to the House of Pien. One pocket held a red card on which Tai-chun's name, birth hour, day, moon, and year were brushed in gold. The other was empty. The House of Pien returned the empty pocket filled with a red card on which was brushed Wei-ling's name, birth hour, day, moon, and year.

At the Dragon, the Harvest, and the New Year Festivals for three years after this, the House of Lin sent sweetmeats and flowers to Wei-ling. On the third Dragon Festival they included a pink flowered silk of the shade used only by a bride, thus indicating that they but waited for her to name the day to make everything ready to receive her. She announced the day by sending the wife of the Lin Family Elder a square of the bride's silk on which she had painted seven chrysanthemums, thus indicating the seventh day of the Chrysanthemum Moon as her choice.

Dragon and phœnix cookies, in addition to those sent to the promised bride, were baked for the betrothed groom. Accompanied only by Camel-back to carry the red kneeling mat, he called in each homestead within visiting distance and gave his wedding invitation to the Elder and his wife.   Others were sent by post.

Horn moon lanterns (symbolic of marriage, because each month the pale lady Moon throws herself into the embrace of her lover, the radiant Sun, leaving him only when he has kindled new light in her) were hung outside the To and From the World Gate and were lit each sunset.   Red and gold scrolls below them announced that the great-granddaughter of Pien was soon coming to complete the House of Exile by union with the great-grandnephew of Lin.

The family portraits, even the most ancient and fragile, were unrolled and hung in the halls.   Silk hangings, awnings, banners, carpets, and candelabra were arranged with even more elaborateness than for Mai-da's marriage.   A daughter's marriage holds the sadness of departure, but a son's marriage holds only the joy of arrival.

The Family shared rooms, so that, in addition to the usual guest courts, there were three courts in the men's quarters and three in the women's vacated.   These were prepared for "sleeping guests."   Guests began to arrive ten days before the date.   Food in abundance was ready for them.

They also all brought hampers of cooked meats, cakes, and fruit.   There was so much that even the children rose from the tables replete after each meal.   Trays were heaped with rich dishes for all the needy who knocked at the Gate of Compassion.

Gifts were displayed at one end of the Hall of Family Gathering.   There were fans, furs, gown-lengths of brocade and heavy washing silk, and jeweled coat buttons; books, furniture, bedquilts, pillows, tapestries, rugs, porcelain, mirrors; money in the form of gold and silver bars; ducks, geese, turkeys, and goats (which were taken to the stable); rice, barley, wheat, millet, corn, rose trees, and a canoe.   Each gift was accompanied by a large red card brushed with the name of the donor and the gift.

The magnificent Lin bride's chair, for which the gold lacquer was made at Foochow and whose tapestry occupied the wives of Lin ten years, is of such workmanship that two centuries of use have but enriched its elegance. At dawn on the marriage eve, the groom knelt in the circle of his ancestral tablets, on the hearth of his homestead, and before his elders. In each place he told that he intended now to take the bride's chair to a worthy maid. Firecrackers were set off as he departed. He was attended by musicians, banner bearers, and his aunt. She carried the cloak and the veil for the bride. The House of Pien is three villages up the canal. Giant crackers, exploded at the wharf, were heard in the Lin homestead as Taichun embarked with his escort in four rowboats.

The bride's house in the Lin homestead was waiting when the Pien servants came with her dowry at midday. The Lin Elder's wife, as Lady of First Authority, superintended the placing of her tulipwood bed. Half a dozen wives assisted in the arranging of things. The rosewood chest, carved with one hundred laughing chubby babies, which by custom contains the bedding the bride desires to use on her marriage night, was opened and unpacked. The pink silk bed curtains were hung under the four-posted canopy. The mattress was spread. Coverlets of peach blossom, primrose, and heliotrope were put in place. The copper "baby's first bath basin" was found to need no polishing. It was turned upside down to be used as a table on which to serve the bride and groom's nuptial supper.

The lacquer chest, holding the bride's garments for the festivities, was put against one wall. The table, with its dwarf pine tree, symbol of long life, and the tapers of red wax, was placed against the opposite wall with a straight-back chair on either side of it. "Our Lady of Five Sons and Two Daughters," a lovely tinted ivory figure with a sweet Madonna face, was unwound from her wrappings and stood in her niche above the bed.

The groom returned next day, an hour before the arrival of

his bride, and in ample time to dress.   The Family Elder bade her procession welcome at the To and From the World Gate. The Lin women took the carrying poles from the servants and lifted the bride's chair in, over the apple of peace.   The seals were broken and she descended.   She placed an apple, pledge of peace, beside the string of cash, pledge of fortune, that lay on a grain measure in the centre of the court.

Her husband welcomed her by offering her refreshment after her journey, from the "cup of the perfect circle," which necessitated the lifting of her veil before they could share the wine. Then he led her to kneel with him in the Hall of Ancestors, at his homestead hearth, and before his Elders; which observance is a symbol that henceforth they are one in rights and responsibilities, as though she had been born in his clan.

Then the Lin Family stood at the end of their Hall of Dignity to receive the congratulations of their guests.   To the Elders, each guest said, "May you soon have another descendant on your knee."   To the grooms' parents, "May you embrace grandchildren and great-grandchildren."   To the bride and groom, "May you live together five generations."   To all other Lins, "Good! Good! Good!"

The women's feast was served that evening in the Court of the Favorite Eaves of Nesting Swallows; the men's feast in the Court of the Happy Waterfall.   The groom passed from man to man, pouring wine and pressing some special dish on each.   The bride passed from woman to woman, pouring wine and pressing some special dish on each.   Little girl children sat at table with the women, and little boys with the men.   The courtesy to them was identical to that shown to their elders.

When the wedding couple had accomplished "wine and food politeness," they went to the bride's house, where their supper had been placed on the upturned copper basin.   The bride and groom shared the "son and daughter dumplings," the "bread of long life," and the "wine of sympathy."   While they ate, the Family Elder and his wife sat together on the bench under the cherry tree, outside the bride's window, and sang the "Mating Song." This song may be sung only by a man and a woman who have loved each other for more than five decades.

The bride's mother came to breakfast. The sulky chrysanthemums had refused to bloom earlier despite all coaxing. But they opened their silken petals that morning to welcome the young wife. She was dressed in that stiff silk named by its weavers "roses at dawn." Seamstresses had fashioned it into bell-legged trousers and a collarless but very graceful short coat. It had been embroidered with the flowers of every season in threads so fine that they appeared to be painted on. Her husband's gift, a sapphire like a bit of the China sky at night, sparkled as she patted her anxious parent reassuringly before she sat down.

5

Ching-mei, one of the Lin twins, betrothed at birth, was married to Kui Wen-chow at the end of Chrysanthemums. She had been ill with typhoid when he won the scholarship which took him to America for five years, so could not be wed before he sailed. Both she and her twin La-mei accepted marriage as an inevitable event.

Yet they were heartbroken at the thought of separation, as they had never been apart for an hour in their lives. La-mei had learned some English from me and was keenly interested in foreign thought. Ching-mei believes Chinese the only medium for self-expression. She has her mind shut against all other civilizations, naming them barbaric. She was dumb with fear concerning the Occidentalisms that her husband might have acquired. Yet the contract had to be completed. So La-mei went with her. Of course La-mei could not ride in a bride's chair, nor bow to the Kui ancestors.

But all children born to her have equal rights with those

of her sister and the two trousseaus were similar in every detail.

6

Three weddings within a year, with one of them requiring a double dowry, had strained the resources of the House of Exile. It was decided that the consummation of Su-ling's betrothal be put forward another year. She advanced this suggestion herself in the Family Council. As reward for her thoughtfulness, she went south with an uncle and aunt to visit in the homestead of the clan at Canton for six months.

Two weeks after her arrival at Canton she slipped over the wall of the House of Lin one night and married a young Chinese lawyer named Lui. They had met when they were students in Paris. Their marriage was in the way advocated by the radicals of the rising Nationalist Party. That is, they repudiated the marriages contracted for them by their Family Elders. They mated together. Then announced their act in the newspapers next morning.

Su-ling had dishonored her House by ignoring a contract signed by her birth-home Elder. She received no dowry. She was officially censured. But wayward, independent, winsome Su-ling has never been long in disgrace.

Seven months after her mating, she was heavy with child. She knocked at the To and From the World Gate of the house of Lin at Canton. It was the birthday of the gentle, gracious god Ti Tang, the Redeemer who descends into Hell to secure release for all in trouble. Su-ling saw the Lady First in Authority.

Thereafter she wore that lady's famous pearls in public token of her favor. Su-ling's husband was received for conversation with the Elder of Lin. The Elder of Lin wrote a letter to the Elder of the House of Exile. I heard no further criticism of Su-ling. Nor was it long before she was properly acknowledged by her husband's family.

7

The Englishman whom I met on the *Empress of Asia* was given my China address during his stay in America. In the Peony Moon, he returned to China a fortnight before the expiration of his "leave," and sent his sister-in-law to call upon me. She is nice. I liked her at first meeting.

The second time that she came to see me, he came with her. He said that he had been appointed to Nanking. Mai-da had accompanied her husband to Nanking three months previously. The residence the government provided for him was just five minutes' walk from the residence provided for Mai-da's husband. Aside from giving me this information, the rest of the time of the call was taken up with telling me gravely that I made a mistake in staying on in China.

Twice in the Dragon Moon he kindly took the trouble to explain to me that I ought not to do what I was doing. He came three times in the Lotus Moon. On the fifth day of the Harvest Moon he asked me in marriage.

He was found suitable, on investigation, by both the Chinese and American people who had concern for me. This was well. It made everything much more pleasant.

I was most confusedly in love. I dreaded speaking about it, if he asked me. But he did n't ask. From the first meeting, he had distracted my mind. Even though I resolved not to think of him, his face would keep appearing between me and a book I tried to read, or his voice would suddenly sound instead of the words I tried to write on a page. This still happens even now. I found love annoying and uncomfortable, like fetters, until I got used to it.

From the time our marriage was agreed upon, every practical and material detail of my life has been competently arranged. I wanted to keep my American citizenship. My people have had it a long time. Nicholas Waln's house is in the first plan drawn for the city of Philadelphia, of which I have an old copy.

James and Robert Waln have their names on the brass plate at the second landing of the stairs in Independence Hall. One of my grandmother Nicholson's forefathers signed the Declaration of Independence.

My husband-to-be made arrangements with Mr. Cunningham, the Senior American Consul-General for China. I signed a paper declaring my intent to remain a citizen of the United States despite my marriage with a British subject. According to British regulations, a British subject in China is not legally married unless there is a civil service in a British Consulate. My betrothed's intent to marry me had to be posted on a public notice board. Then, after some weeks, as no one came forward to object, I was asked to present myself before Sir Sidney Barton at ten o'clock.

It was the last day of the Kindly Moon. I wore the brown dress and coat I had worn on the *Empress of Asia*.

This ceremony was brief. When it was done, I found that England does not recognize a woman's right to remain a citizen of her own country after marriage with a British subject. Regardless of my protests, my name was written under my husband's name in the count of British subjects in China.

Ever since then I have been counted twice in each consular district in which I have lived. I am recorded at the American Consulate. The British Consulate takes no notice of this but serves me with the annual notice to register as a British subject. I annually reply stating that I am an American citizen. My name is then written in the British registry. In time of danger I always receive two sets of instructions, one from the American and one from the British Government, telling me what I am to do.

During the weeks that my betrothed's intent to marry me was publicly posted at his country's consulate, it was also read out each Sunday morning in the Church of England: "If any of you know cause or just impediment why these two persons should not be joined together in holy matrimony, ye are to declare it."

No one declared anything, so after the ten o'clock service at the British Consulate, I changed my dress and then was married at twelve o'clock in the Church of England. This very nearly did not happen. Shortly before the service was to begin, the aged Dean of the Cathedral comprehended that I was a Quaker and that, if such was true, then I had never been baptized.

I had n't. Neither had any of my progenitors within my memory. The Dean explained that marriage is a Christian sacrament, which he considered it wrong to administer to one who had not been christened. The Quakers present from Philadelphia were drawn into the matter. Joseph Swain said that words spoken over water did not make it holy, nor could the touch of such water make one more Christian. The aged Dean had a long answer to that. It began to seem to me that my marriage was not to be. Then it flashed into my mind that all water which falls from heaven is holy and words spoken over it could not change it.

I mentioned this quietly to one of my Quaker relatives, an elderly woman whose judgment I have always found sound. She agreed, and quietly told the others.

My betrothed, the Dean, and I went into a side chapel. The Dean asked me some questions. I answered them. He was really a very kindly man. My answers seemed to comfort him. I asked him some questions. I found him not unlike a Quaker. He sprinkled some water on my head. My husband-to-be was written in a book as my godfather.

Previous to my own wedding, I had never seen a wedding other than Quaker and Chinese weddings. Neither had I ever been in a place built for worship other than Chinese temples and Quaker Meeting-Houses. The Cathedral, where I was married, has stained-glass windows depicting scenes from the Bible in color. There were white flowers, tall lighted candles, and a sonorous organ on which one of my husband's friends played music that bade one yield obedience to supernatural powers.

We go to Quaker Meetings with or without hats as we choose. It is the same in Chinese temples. But a woman has to have her head covered to enter here. I had a matron of honor to attend me and prompt me when to walk to the music, when to kneel, and when to rise. She had covered me with a lovely filmy white veil of handmade lace, fashioned it into a cap with a wreath of orange blossoms, and spread it over my white dress so that it trailed far behind. I had also something old, something blue, and something new.

The aged Dean did not conduct the service. A young clergyman, surpliced in white, possessed of the most lyrical voice I have heard, read it from the church prayer book in cadenced solemnity. Hearing this marriage sacrament for the first time, I was surprised at it. During one part I was panicky and thought: "What am I doing here?" I had regret that I had trusted so naïvely. I observed the solemn man beside me. I felt as though some awful trap were closing around me. As word followed word, I had a desire to get away quickly. It was late autumn, but the day was warm. A window had been opened. When I turned from the altar I faced this window.

A wren sat on the inside sill. She was arranging her feathers. The sight of the little bird, sitting inside the Cathedral casually preening herself, restored me. Through ten happy years I have been grateful for her sweet naturalness.

I turned again to the altar. Although Quakers are not wedded with rings, I reassured the startled young clergyman by putting back on the fourth finger of my left hand the ring I had pulled off, and knelt again beside my quietly waiting husband.

II

A BRIDE

"There are Five Relationships: Citizen and state, parent and child, husband and wife, brother and brother, friend and friend; but that of husband and wife is first." — From the *Summary of the Rules of Propriety,* which is Volume I of the *Books of Decorum* of the Han Dynasty (206 B.C. — 221 A.D.).

I

MY HUSBAND'S COURTYARDS

1

OUR honeymoon journey to Hongkong completed, we came to Nanking at evening. My heart was warmed by the kindness of the Chinese officials of the city and about fifty of the Western men and women residents. They were on the platform to welcome us when our train drew in. Massed behind them was a band of Chinese musicians, dressed in scarlet and gold, playing "Here Comes the Bride." Our friends brought champagne.

I tasted the wine for the first time, finding it both sour and dry. It prickled as I swallowed it. But when I had emptied my glass, I felt light and gay. Mai-da was there with her husband. She gave me a pearl friendship pin.

We went home by motor car. The area from the railway station to the city entrance gate was then built over closely by shops and small dwellings, many with overhanging balconies. These pressed in upon the roadway, which was congested by horse carriages, man-drawn trucks, rickshaws, itinerant vendors, and strolling pedestrians. The chauffeur honking the horn continuously, we moved up these two miles at a snail's pace.

Presently, when we had entered the city, through the gate called "Phœnix" the moonlight displayed a fair and open countryside. A panorama of rolling green hills, fertile plains, pleasant valleys, bamboo groves, blue lakes, and furrowed fields, jeweled with an occasional temple, pagoda, or elegant residence, stretched out before us.

The road was white and empty. It ran straight down a hill; then curved and dipped into a further valley to reappear again going up a distant knoll. On this knoll a magnificent Drum Tower was dark against the pale sky.

We rode towards this Drum Tower at a great pace. But it was still in the distance when gates set in a red wall opened. The driveway within was prettily arched with closely set

NANKING GATE

willow saplings lit with welcome-to-the-husband's-courtyard lanterns. It was also thickly paved with warn-devils-away fireworks, which exploded under us.

The chauffeur brought the car to a halt at the open house doors. The Chinese household helpers had themselves ready there, in two rows, to welcome us. Chang the House Steward, Lin-yun the deputy House Steward. Chou the Cook. Chou's wife, standing in the Nurse's Place, because motherhood of ten sons gave her the unquestionable right to present herself as nurse to my first-born. Pu, the Master of Steam Heat. Liu the Elder and Liu the Son, Gardeners; Old Man, the Gatekeeper. Ho and Kê the House Cleaners. Ma the Night Watchman. Sun, the Make-Clothes-Clean. Wives of the above and their children, in sizes from tall as the grown-ups down through toddlers to a babe in arms. And last of all Small Heart, the Kitchen Hand.

Bald-the-third, who accompanied me from the House of Exile, had put on her best garments for arrival, and bought fresh flowers for her hair from the train window. The Household Helpers bowed to her first, saying in unison, "Greetings, Old Matron, may your road here be the road of peace."

To me, they said: "May you find here the five blessings: prosperity, tranquillity, health, long life, and seven children."

Thus I came to live beside the Big Horse Road in Nanking, in a house set in three acres of lovely walled garden. The house was provided for my husband's residence by the Chinese government and had been built, as had the near-by residence of Mai-da's husband, to command respect.

It had electricity, steam heat, and Occidental plumbing, which are not usual attributes of a residence in China. The roof tiles were tight against rain. The entrance had dignity. The lawns were generous. The shrubbery had been well chosen. The flower beds were well drained. It had a large conservatory filled with a variety of ferns, an excellent tennis court, a marquee for garden parties, a garage, stabling for four horses, a wired yard for chickens.

The court for the household staff was to the west. A lilachedged grass walk led to a kitchen garden. This garden had fruit trees trained against its four walls, grapevines, strawberry and asparagus beds, gooseberry, raspberry, blackberry, and currant bushes. It also provided, under the gardeners' careful husbandry, an abundance of every kind of vegetable, including potatoes, sufficient for the entire year.

The kitchen, the pantry, the laundry, and the bathrooms, of which there was one to each bedroom, were white-tiled and fitted with modern appliances. There was always plenty of running hot and cold water in these, in the servants' court, and in the stable. As assurance against shortage of water in time of drought, the boundary wall of the property held five wells within its embrace, in addition to an enormous sunken tank which collected rain water from a system of roof drains.

All the woodwork of the house was of seasoned oak. The floors, parquet. The walls plaster, tinted in quiet colors. Every room had not only steam radiators but a fireplace; concealed thermometers assisted the "master of the heat" to regulate the temperature.

On measuring the smallest room, Bald-the-third and I found that it was thirty feet in length by twenty feet in width. The ceilings were fourteen feet high. There were three floors below the attics. The stairs came down in a grand sweep.

Sliding doors pushed back and threw the ground floor into one room for receptions. Glass doors on to the wide verandah, which ran across the entire south side of the house, folded away at command. The furnishings were suitable and of sound quality.

The service was efficient and silent. I rose at seven o'clock each morning. I always found that the floors had been polished, fresh flowers arranged in the vases, new fires laid in the grates; and there was never even a suspicion of dust when I ran my fingers under chairs or along a shelf at the back of books. We walked on garden paths previously swept. We came in to a breakfast table covered each day with a freshly laundered linen cloth, set with shining silver, glittering china, and sparkling glass.

At each meal plates that should be hot were hot. Plates that should be cold were cold. Candles with shades to match the flowers of that day illuminated the dinner table each night. Chang started the evening coffee percolating when he had put the port on the table. His deputy followed me into the drawing-room, after just the right interval, with the coffee tray. If I poured out immediately, I had always just finished putting in the cream and sugar when my husband joined me.

If at any time during the day I disarranged things, they were quietly and quickly rearranged as soon as I vacated a room for a minute or two. When I left a book open on a table it was put into its exact place inside the glass-doored cases — but always with a marker at the place where I had been reading. A cushion against which I had leaned was plumped out. A shifted chair was returned to its proper position. Sewing was picked up; I learned that I could always find it again in my dressing-table drawer — neatly folded, with the needle and the thimble plainly visible.

And the midday soup was put on the lunch table when my husband came in through the front door.

The house was handsome. The service perfect. But I was soon dissatisfied.

2

There were plenty of rooms. I chose the smallest in the house. It had its own balcony without a roof. This balcony commanded a view of the Purple Mountain where the illustrious Ming kings are laid to rest, and of the hill where the fabled palace of four thousand courts paved with gold, built for the founder of the Liang dynasty, is reported to have stood. From it I could survey the happenings on the Big Horse Road; also look off to the west, toward what was once the country estate of the immortal Li Tai Po, romantic poet of the Tang dynasty.

The room was fitted up as a guest room for persons of lesser importance. But the house had more than enough guest rooms. So I pressed its electric bell. Chang the House Steward came up to me in his noiseless velvet slippers. He listened with civility to my desires. He went downstairs.

With happy excitement I waited for him to bring his assistants. I was eager to move the bedroom furniture into the attic; then to fetch my wedding furniture from the attic where it had been stored away before my arrival. I waited five minutes. Ten minutes. Half an hour.

I planned to use the rug Shun-ko had made in her girlhood on her hand loom. To screw up my rosewood shelves on their copper brackets in a low circle around the walls for my books. To heap my bright cushions on the floor. To have no chairs except three — the long low sofa, the little red cherry rocker, and the big chair especially made by Camel-back the size for my husband. I planned to do it all in haste and surprise my husband with tea there when he came home.

Forty-five minutes passed. I remembered my brown tea-pot and my cups with pleasure. Also my copper coal scuttle.

When an hour and five minutes had gone and yet Chang did not return, I went to investigate. On the lower landing of the back stairs, I found a congregation of all the Chinese members of the household, including the babe in arms. I said, "Why do you not begin the work?"

Chang moved respectfully toward me and bowed. All the others bowed. The pigtails of the children waggled impressively ceilingward. Every face was solemn. Chang spoke. "Honored mistress, does our master know that you would make this change in the homestead arrangement?"

I had to acknowledge that "our master" did not.

No furniture was shifted until he returned and gave the order. When I went upstairs again to do what I could myself, I found that both the attic door and the door of the room I wanted had been locked. When "our master" came home, it was too late to do anything that day.

3

Next day, my room, in which I intended to be comfortably disorderly, was arranged to my complete satisfaction — except that I had no stuff for curtains. After my husband had enjoyed toasted crumpets with his tea in my curtainless retreat, I drew his attention to this matter. He gave me the key to a cedar box, in which he said I might find something suitable.

As soon after breakfast as he had gone to his office, Bald-the-third and I opened the cedar box. It was packed to the lid with curtains of many textures and colors. We had scarcely begun to discover what it did contain, when Cook's wife joined us. I fingered some creamy net reflectively.

"You cannot take that," Cook's wife said, and sat on it. "It is too new to cut. We only bought it when we were in Szechuan, the year of the fall of the Manchu dynasty. It has scarcely been used, as we have not been in a house since that its length would fit."

It was not exactly what I wanted, so I said nothing. I turned my attention to some filmy silk with an all-over design of tiny jasmine blossoms which I saw had charmed Bald-the-third. Cook's wife promptly took that and put it under her too. It had been secured in Mukden and used but one moon when a telegram came transferring the household to another province.

It was the same with some green brocade from Kaifeng. Again with something imprisoning butterflies used in the drawing-room at Hankow. And something printed with apple blossoms from Shantung. Cook's wife, a queen on a rising throne, sat on them all.

I did not care, because I did not really covet any of them. But eventually we did come to something I wanted — a roll of sunshine gauze. I sat on that myself.

I was informed that its thirty yards had never been cut. Also that it had been put in the cedar box just four years after the Boxer trouble, and that it was being saved until the master happened to be appointed to just the right house for it. I did not answer. I carried it away to my balcony room. Cook's wife did not follow me.

Bald-the-third does not trust either my needle or my scissors in fine material when I am in an enthusiastic mood. When I had measured my windows, she tactfully suggested that I arrange books while she made the curtains. I agreed. She then said that she could not cut the stuff straight except in her own room where the light was exactly right. So she took the gauze and went away.

Half an hour later I was reading *Northanger Abbey* on my balcony, and happened to see her in a rickshaw on the Big Horse Road. "I go to purchase matching thread," she shouted up to me.

Within reasonable time Bald finished the curtains. We hung them. I mentioned that the material seemed thicker made up than in the roll, but she drew my attention to how perfectly the color went with the gold woof in the rug. I agreed with her, acknowledging that they suited even better than I had anticipated. They were an everlasting joy to me as long as I lived there.

It was not until nine years later, when I happened to find the roll of thirty yards of sunshine gauze in the cedar chest, that Bald-the-third confessed. As soon as she got away from me she went to a Nanking shop and bought material as near like it as possible for my curtains. She paid for this material with her own money and returned the gauze to Cook's wife uncut. Otherwise, so she gravely told me, "I should not have been able to make a road of peace here for you and me."

4

I had been married seventeen days when I decided to take the motor car and meet my husband at his office without the chauffeur. I asked Bald-the-third to fetch me the garage key, which I knew hung in the kitchen on a certain nail. But she made excuse that her feet, bound to three-inch "golden lilies" in her babyhood, hurt her when she climbed up and down stairs. So I went myself.

"Good morning, Cook," I said, on entering the kitchen, as I walked toward the key.

"Good morning, mistress. Is the bell in mistress's room out of order that mistress did not ring?"

As he spoke I thought that his face was more like a sheep's face than any face I had ever noticed before, and that it was a nuisance that he was making pastry on a table between me and the key.

"It is nothing. I only want the garage key."

"You wish to go out in the car. Ah, yes, I will summon the chauffeur."

"I do not have need of the chauffeur," I answered just as Chang the House Steward glided into the kitchen from behind me.

But Chang addressed me in his suave voice, using pidgin English. "Missy no can go alone through the city streets. Missy no savvee way of China people. Lookee very bad all neighbors see official man's wife drive car. Missy have got motorman with plenty gold trim uniform."

By some agile magic Chang stood beside Cook at the pastry board, and the kitchen filled with the household staff, who crept in one by one until they faced me in a loyal group. The night watchman, the gateman, the gardeners, the house cleaners, the chauffeur, the laundryman, the deputy house steward, the cook's assistant, the wives, and the children. Argument failed to get the key from the nail on the wall behind them. Even Bald-the-third came and added herself to the opposition, saying, "It is not good manners, mistress, for you to drive the motor car."

I went into the yard and ordered a mechanic who was working at the gasoline pump to smash the garage lock. He labored only for the day and owed no allegiance to Chang and his clan. He had raised his hammer when Chang slid forward and undid it with the key. Others of the household staff pushed the garage doors wide open.

I got into the car and drove away.

I honked gloriously, noisily, freely, under my husband's

office windows. I played a concert with both hands on the
electric and the rubber horns while I watched for his astonished
face at an upper window. But while I craned expectantly
upward, he came through the exit gates, hat and stick in hand,
ready for departure, and touched my shoulder.

"Chang feared that you might not get the 'fire-wagon' down
here safely, so he telephoned when you left the house," he said.

5

Although the month was December, the weather was mild.
I had taken my sewing into the sunshine on the balcony outside
my room. As I had need of lace for the pillow slip I was
making, I sent Bald-the-third down to fetch the Lace Seller
when I heard him calling his wares in the Big Horse Road.

I had made my selection and agreed to a price, when I was
startled by the voice of Chang the House Steward, speaking to
me not in Mandarin, but in the pidgin English.

"Missy mean well but missy no savvee China custom. Missy
talkee bargain — missy throw master's money out of the top-
side window by the handful."

Neat, complaisant, courteous, self-satisfied, he stood before
me with a grieved air of suave reproach. I had seen him go
through the courtyard gates and turn to the south an hour ago.
I thought him out of the house for the afternoon. As he
stood before me with his head clean-shaven in accord with the
new fashion, his black silk trousers bound at the ankles with
bands of purple satin, his uniform of white linen snugly fitted,
and fastened with tiny cloth buttons, the sleeves touching his
wrists, and the hem of his skirt touching his black velvet
slippers, he made me feel both guilty and resentful. I was
filled with a defiance as I observed him.

A desire to accomplish an orgy of purchasing possessed me.
If the Lace Seller had not sufficient to empty my purse,
thoughts of running away to a distant street and squandering

my cash in a joyous splurge flashed through my mind. But Chang's smooth voice broke in upon my dream.

"Missy choose what pieces she likee. Put all one heap. Merchant-man drink tea bottom side. I take lace missy want catchee and go talkee bargain."

Without answering I turned to where the Lace Seller had been. He was no longer there. I was just in time to see his coat tail disappear down the back stairs. I thought that Bald would support me. But she, too, was gone. Suddenly I was hot with rage. The money in my purse was money I had brought into the house.

"I have made my bargain," I said firmly in my best Chinese.

With patient deliberation Chang addressed me again in pidgin English. "What money laceman talkee?"

As suddenly as my anger had flamed, it died out. Before I had heard the end of his query I was hopeless with defeat. I knew that Occidental temper is not the artillery with which to battle with Oriental patience. I told him what I had said I would pay.

He took my selection of laces and departed to the kitchen court. Ten minutes later he returned to tell me that he had saved fifty cents. I put the money away, feeling that I had no reasonable excuse for complaint to "our master."

6

That same day, after dinner, in return for a practical joke my husband had played on me, I wrapped his shaving brush in green paper, tied it with Christmas ribbon, and secreted it in his shoe.

Next morning, at the usual time, he came from his dressing room to ask if I was ready to go down to breakfast. I was puzzled. My curiosity got the better of me. I demanded, "How did you get shaved?"

"Shaved?" He was plainly puzzled.

"But your shaving brush?"

"My shaving brush? What is queer about my shaving brush? It was beside the hot water as usual, and did its work very well."

Just then I opened a drawer to get more hairpins, and discovered the green paper, beautifully folded, with the Christmas ribbon beside it. My husband denied ever having seen either the paper or the ribbon. Just then I heard Chang's almost inaudible movement through the adjoining room.

"What about the paper?" my husband asked.

"Nothing," I responded, "I was just surprised to find it here. I usually put paper in another place."

Three more attempts at practical jokes convinced me that it was useless. My husband achieved many against me, but Chang guarded him with invulnerable diligence.

Domestically my early years were controlled by a Quaker grandmother and a Swedish mother. My later girlhood was influenced by Shun-ko, my Chinese "mother by affection."

Grandmother did not frown on the study of Latin or Greek. Neither did she condemn the reading of Jane Austen's novels, provided one's household duties were decently accomplished first. But she did make it her concern that her nine granddaughters bake good bread before the age of ten. She believed that a house which offered its folk or its guests stuff from a bakeshop had fallen to a low condition.

Mother stirred our young minds with Scandinavian legends and the songs of her father's land, but she had behind her a housekeeping tradition as staunch as my grandmother's. She had scant sympathy for any daughter slow at domestic tasks. She taught us that a woman who could not herself do all that she need ever ask a servant to do was incompetent to be mistress of a home. Mother was keen that her children excel in book-learning, yet diligent that her daughters learn to launder linen and to make butter and cheese.

Shun-ko is akin to them.

So by inheritance, example, and education, I approached my husband's house with the presumption that a woman's place is in the home, not as an ornament, but as superintendent of the comfort and the diet of the household. The day after my arrival I began the formula of housekeeping. I made out duties and menus.

But when I ordered fruit jelly, I got peach pie. Pie with a crust that melted in my mouth. I suggested lamb with mint sauce. I had beef with Yorkshire pudding. I said biscuits and I was given rolls. Crisp, exquisite rolls. If I should order a house cleaning of the west rooms the work was almost sure to begin in the east. But my house was spotlessly clean.

7

My husband informed me that after a polite interval the foreign community would call. Mai-da, who had five months' experience previous to my arrival at Nanking, warned me that, when they had given what they considered sufficient time for me to settle into my husband's courts, the ladies of Nanking families related or in any way connected with the House of Exile and the wives of the Chinese officials would visit me.

One morning I came from my bath to find that Bald-the-third had taken away the wool dress I intended to wear and laid out my best silk. She announced that Chang had told her to have me properly gowned, as the wives of the Chinese governor would come at eleven.

They came just after eleven, opening the Chinese visits. Three days later, in mid-afternoon, Bald came up to my balcony room to tell me that I must prepare myself. Chang had just learned, from her house steward, that the doyenne of the Western community would start my Western calls by leaving her cards at four-thirty that afternoon.

So for a goodly number of days I had Chinese lady guests

from eleven on until one each morning; and foreign lady and gentlemen guests from four-thirty on until seven each afternoon. I found both the Chinese and the foreigners of Nanking exceptional in their friendliness, wit, and charm. I enjoyed myself. Among my callers were two who are now my friends.

I had nothing to do but to sit, to listen, and to answer. Twice daily the tea table was provided with a variety of suitable delicacies. The visitors were welcomed at the entrance, their names known, their outer wraps taken; they were brought to me, each given a seat, — right according to position, status, and temperament, — and served with refreshments.

There was not one lady or gentleman who did not comment upon the unobtrusive, faultless service. After the first day I played a game with myself, betting for and against this comment being spoken. The affirmatives won ten times in ten before the guests' departure.

Every Chinese lady followed this by asking how my serving matron was adapting herself. I replied that Bald-the-third did not complain. Each lady said, "The serving matrons from the House of Exile are wise in the art of settling the bride to contentment."

Every foreign lady and gentleman said, "Your husband's household staff is famed in all the ports of China. Some lucky bachelor will get them. A man's servants never stay on after he marries."

But I had a feeling that the staying qualities of Chang and his clan were equal to mine.

8

During the winter I spent some part of every day with Mai-da, and I wrote in my balcony room. But in the spring Mai-da quickened with child and had to go north to her husband's family homestead for the birth. I had written one story which had been accepted by the *Pictorial Review* and had two others in the post, but I had no more ideas with which to occupy myself.

My hands itched to work with the soil.   My husband noticed this.   He suggested that I do what I liked with the garden. He added that as Liu the Elder had to return to Peking because of his mother's ill health, I could take on a gardener who had been recommended to me.

My neighbor sent the man to me.   Together we dug, raked, and sowed.   He liked the touch of the warm brown earth. So do I.   He spoke a Chinese dialect that I did not then understand, so I never heard in words what lay behind his weather-beaten brow.   But I knew that no toil I planned was too arduous, because he too believed that a seed is a miracle.   We communicated happily by gesture.

But one morning he was gone.   When I failed to find him, Chang informed me that he was from Canton and that all Cantonese men are worthless.   He repeated a verse which is two rhyming couplets in the northern dialect: —

> "Fear not Heaven,
> Fear not Earth,
> But be wise in fear
> Of the Cantonese."

He advised, since I as yet knew so little about such things, that he select the next gardener — in fact, he had a Peking man now drinking tea in the kitchen court.

There was work in progress which had to go forward before the spring rains.   The Peking gardener proved efficient.   His wages were one dollar less than the wages of the Canton man. There was no possible cause for complaint to "the master."

9

The weeks went by.   Then the small matter of a Madeira tablecloth, when I had said the one with the Irish crochet, drove me to ring a bell.

Cook's wife answered it. She told me that Chang had pre-pared the table. He had gone to the market. He had decided that the flowers we had in our garden were not suitable for a dinner party.

The click of a golf ball as my husband practised strokes in the west garden broke on my ears. I decided to tell him about everything and discover who was who in the household.

But the way to my husband lay through a bower of flowers and across a smooth stretch of grass. Dew glistened on the poppies as they raised their silken petals to the evening sun. The larkspurs were spikes of heaven-sent blue. Old-fashioned pinks were gentle and sweet. Late primroses made a band of pure gold. The first rose was opening. My feet would not move quickly. I was drugged by the odor of new-cut grass mingled with the incense of flowers.

Nature had her way with me. The knowledge came that life is too crammed with beauty to hold the pettiness of rankled personal feeling. Roast duck or chicken, clear soup or thick, east rooms or west, Canton or Peking gardener, Madeira or Irish crochet — what does it matter who is who?

Life, so I knew that evening as the sun went down behind my garden wall, is too wonderful for bickering over material details. I remembered that my husband was accustomed to his staff. I comforted myself with the assurance that he would yield to anything I asked and make things right if he knew that anything was wrong. But I resolved not to disturb things. His household knew his shirts, his socks, his taste, his habits. They had served him well before I came.

I ceased to fume and began to rejoice in house and garden. I no longer concerned myself with the routine of domestic duties or with menus. In time I congratulated myself that my superior indifference to mundane matters had brought about a change, as my few suggestions were met exactly, and the down-stairs flower arrangements came to be copies of those I did for my balcony room.

When my era of trouble was so remote as to be a joke, I told my husband all about it and ended with the theme that as soon as I rose above pettiness the household had recognized my virtue. He said, "Yours is a pretty tale. I do not like to spoil it with doubts, but when did the change of household spirit begin?"

"I was really conscious of it on the first day of the month, as that was the day Chang and the Cook paid me the compliment of asking me for a recipe for pickled peaches."

"The day I settled all accounts with him, and told him that thereafter you were the holder of the Privy Purse."

Perhaps it is because I am a lady of superior temperament, perhaps it is because I am Chancellor of the Exchequer; but whatever it is, Chang is a diplomat of rare ability and a very worthy house boy.

I came to the end of the house money with which my husband had entrusted me. I asked him for some more.

"Let me see your accounts, please," he answered.

Thus was staged one of those domestic dramas which must always occur when a man who records his expenditures in little red books entrusts his money to a woman who considers herself extremely economical but never writes down the dollars and the cents, and they attempt to adjust their difference handicapped by his calmness and her temper.

I went to my room. Drew a check on my Philadelphia account for the exact amount of housekeeping money I had handled. Packed my trunk despite Bald-the-third's opposition, and pushed her out with the warning that she make herself ready to go or else be left behind. I had changed to my traveling dress, when Chang tapped at the door. "Pardon, mistress, but perhaps you have need of the housekeeping book."

He handed me a little red volume of English manufacture, in which

| Salt | .03 | Sugar | .20 | Pepper | .10 | Matches | .06 |
| Lemon | .07 | Vinegar | .30 | Flour | .16 | Soap | .12 |

and so forth were noted, day by day from the beginning to the end of my husband's money.

I turned through the twenty-four pages that the total had reached. When I lifted my eyes from the last entry, I saw my husband's face in my dressing-table mirror. It had come unfrozen. His eyes twinkled. I threw the book over my shoulder. Chang picked it up and handed it to "the master."

"It seems all right," said my husband when he had examined it. "If anything the money seems more economically administered than usual."

And just before he closed the door on his discreet, velvet-slippered departure, Chang answered the challenge: —

"A house where there is a sensible wife is always a more economical establishment than the establishment of the most careful bachelor."

CORRESPONDENCE WITH SHUN-KO

1

THE HOUSE OF EXILE, twentieth day of the Budding Moon, 1923. — I direct my love with special thought toward thee, sweet child of my heart. I thank thee for thy letter, delivered by Su-ling, and for the length of Nanking brocade into which thee has had the weavers put the life story of Kuan-Yin, blessed Goddess of Mercy. I consider the brocade too lovely to keep selfishly in my own apartment. The entire household are delighted with it and it has been hung to face south on the wall of the Hall of Family Gathering.

As I have so carefully instructed thee a wife should have no disagreement with her husband which survives the night, I trust that thee was again in harmony long before Su-ling arrived here with thy letter. I should have felt delighted to look upon thy face again, had thee been permitted to come home with Su-ling for the Welcome to Spring Festivities. Yet even though I should have been gladdened by thy presence I am well pleased that thee was restrained from coming.

I do not approve of the dangerous freedom Su-ling is permitted. It makes one feel that her husband is a man of no strength.

Mai-da and Su-ling leave to-morrow morning. They will be escorted as far as Peking by their fathers, and Mai-da's husband is to meet them there. As it seems so much more intimate than dispatch by post, I am sending this letter to thee by Mai-da. In it my chief desire is to admonish and encourage thee to devote thyself to accomplishment in bridge, tennis, golf, and ballroom dancing.

Whether or not a wife finds personal pleasure in the activities which occupy the society surrounding her husband, it must be her pleasure to do them. Writing stories or verse is an avocation to woman. Well enough, if she has time to spare from her vocation, which is marriage. Thee has found thyself inadequately educated in the subjects thee needs now for successful daily life, so thee must apply thyself to mastery in them.

In my visit last month, I saw that thee is at a disadvantage in having approached Western society in China through the byway of a Chinese homestead. Nuan is eager now to go down to visit thee. I have discouraged her for thy good. My summary of thy situation is that it is best for thee not to be seen in close relation with Chinese people just now.

Kuei-tzu, our beloved homestead mother, is writing thee for dispatch also by Mai-da. She is inviting thee to join our annual procession of worship to the sacred mountain, Tai-shan, in Shantung. As thy mother by affection I command thee to refuse this first year of thy marriage. Make thyself secure now in thy husband's esteem. Then in later years thee may do in all things as thee chooses.

All men, regardless of the particular race, are much influenced by society's opinion regarding their wives. Supremacy in the activities which are the daily occupation of the other women around him will give thee an advantage which nothing else can give thee. Doubtless thy husband whispers into thy ear, when it lies on thy pillow, that thy difference makes thee divine. Men do say such. But remember that sensible women take no notice of what is whispered on the pillow. Difference is a serpent that poisons contentment as time passes.

Mai-da came over from her husband's homestead and spent all yesterday with us. She brought her son. He is now two months old. After many trials a nurse whose suckle is satisfactory to his stomach has been found and his cheeks are again rosy. Mai-da has no further excuse to tarry with her firstborn. But she finds it hard to leave him.

She asked us all within the Orchid Door of her birth-home to join with her in fervent recitation of the Goddess of Mercy's rosary and to pray that her next-born be a girl so that she may keep the child with her.

Su-ling is loudly outspoken in advice that Mai-da should take her son back to Nanking. Su-ling has her son with her here. She takes him everywhere, as thee knows. At Canton he lives with her in that tiny flat she rents. She has moved three times since his birth. In less than a year he has had his home-sureties three times shattered. Fortunately Mai-da is wise in the knowledge that it is best to nurture sons inside the homestead wall.

Little Dragon may cry for an hour when his mother departs. But the administrations of his nurses and the loving faces of his grandparents, uncles, aunts, and cousins, will soon blot her from his memory. She is convinced that her place is with her husband, so long as he is exiled from home by government appointment, even though her marriage contract clearly stated that she need not accompany him outside his clan homestead. She is just as firmly of the opinion that Little Dragon should grow quietly in the home-place, that all his early happiness will be there, and his child-mind will be filled naturally with the folklore of his clan tradition. Only thus can a son's roots be fastened so that, no matter where life may take him, he will always return home.

I have been interrupted by Camel-back. He brought me a message from Uncle Shao-chun. Also asked me to write down his kowtow, which is the wish that you dwell in peace.

Uncle Shao-chun's message is that I include his greetings in my letter to you and that I request you to remind the Governor of Kiangsu, if you have opportunity to address his august ear, that your Uncle by affection, Lin Shao-chun, is grievously concerned about the neglect of China's waterways.

The Governor may have been so distracted by other reports that he has not read the report Uncle Shao-chun sent to him before the New Year.

So mention that there are nine places of dangerous weakness in the Grand Canal directly menacing Nanking's province.   If these break, as they will at the next flood-rain, Nanking will be submerged.   He is a cousin-by-marriage to the war lord now governing the Yellow River Valley.   It may do some good to call his attention to remembrance of the historical annals recording the antics of the Yellow River at periods in the past when its grooming was neglected.

Finally, if the opportunity to converse continues this long, remind him that the Yangtze, when ignored, is a dragon that not only takes toll of human life irrespective of class or rank, but devastates the fertile midlands — the rich treasury from which the taxes which support his governorship are collected.

These three waterways are so interrelated that when one breaks the bonds that hold it in its channels, the others almost always do the same.   Their power is such that once they are out of control the most capable engineers can do nothing except run for their own lives.   Nanking is at the place of threefold danger.   The house in which thee dwells is handsome, but I wish that it was on a hill.   I shall be relieved when thy husband is transferred elsewhere.

The House Beside the Big Horse Road, Nanking, March 3, 1923. — The Japanese Consul-General and his wife gave a dinner on Thursday night.   We arrived about half-past eight, to find the large double drawing-rooms already well filled, with Chinese, Japanese, British, American, French, German, Russian, and Scandinavian men and women.   Mostly government officials and their wives.

Three kinds of cocktails and innumerable kinds of small

bits of egg, pickle, fish, sausage, cheese, bacon, olive, onion, and caviare, on tiny rounds of toast, were being offered to guests, as we entered. The refreshments were passed about on silver trays by Chinese menservants, uniformed all exactly alike in long white linen gowns and scarlet sleeveless silk jackets, marshaled by a Japanese butler who wore a dark kimono and large white cotton gloves. The trays were replenished

NANKING

as emptied, from a source behind a Japanese screen embroidered with a picture of Japan's sacred mountain.

Our host and hostess circulated diligently from guest to guest, introducing those not known to each other and making every possible effort to promote geniality. They both speak English, French, German, and Chinese, in addition to their own language. They have recently hired a Russian tutor, who now lives with them, to teach their three children and themselves Russian.

Our hostess wore the Japanese dress — a lovely heliotrope cloth kimono, embroidered with a branch of wistaria and held at the waist with a dove-grey obi. Her husband wore black tails and a white tie, as did all the Western men and the younger Chinese — Mai-da's husband too.

There were only young Chinese wives present. They all wore Chinese dress. The elder Chinese men wore the usual silk skirt and short coat: the civil governor's skirt was made of that aspen-leaf, seventeen dollars a foot, at which thee and I looked covetously in the Lia-Chang Silk Shop when thee was here. The Chinese naval and military officers, young and old, all wore splendid gold-braided uniforms and arrived in their plumed hats. There were also three Japanese army officers in uniform.

The Western women were very décolleté. I do wish thee could have been present. Thee would have been most thrillingly shocked. I wore my blue. The one thee said I should never wear in the presence of Chinese men. Truly I was prudishly dressed beside the other Western women. Some were bare right down to the waist in the back, and one Frenchwoman was nearly as uncovered in front. I grant that this Western fashion is not beautiful. It would be if women had beautiful bodies. But so few have. I saw only one, a Scandinavian, who was beautiful, among the many present.

At nine-thirty the Japanese butler stood stiffly against a wall and said, in English, "Dinner is now served." Then he made a deep bow. The wall behind him was slid back, from a break in the middle, by the two eldest of the Chinese servants. Our host led the way with the British Consul-General's wife. We all followed in a two-by-two procession. Each woman on the arm of a man.

There were name cards. Our host and hostess had distributed the nationalities, but taken care to put guests speaking a common tongue next each other, and yet held to the Western custom of seating men and women alternately. I was between the Chinese Civil and Military Governors. So I had two august ears into which to put Uncle Shao-chun's concern regarding the neglect of China's waterways.

The dinner, a combination of the recipes of all nations, was twenty-three courses long. We were at table until midnight. I had time to discuss the Grand Canal, the Yellow River, and the Yangtze.

But there was a circle of wineglasses around each plate, as there has been at every official and private dinner I have attended at Nanking. Red or clear or amber or emerald wine, bubbling or silent, was served with each dish. Diligent servants kept the glasses refilled as emptied. We had already had an hour of cocktails before dinner.

The Chinese Civil and Military Governors did not sip a little of each wine as they ate, as the Western guests did. As soon as we sat down they fell to playing that game with fingers in which the loser empties his wine cup to the bottom each time. The butler deputized one servant who was entirely occupied in keeping their glasses filled. I did not drink anything. They used my wineglasses too.

I did my best to say all that Uncle Shao-chun wanted said. Neither stopped playing to listen. Between swallows they both promised to attend to the matter. But I did not think anything I said was comprehended.

Then this morning the Civil Governor's Second Green Skirt called. She came to ask me to send Uncle Shao-chun a message from her husband. The Governor regrets that there is no money in the provincial treasury to hire engineers to mend the waterways. All he can do is to lead an official procession to worship the Rain God and petition that there be no flood rain this year.

The procession took place this afternoon. I attended it in a glass-windowed carriage with the Governor's wives. It began at the Municipal Buildings and went to the City Temple. The Civil Governor led. He was dressed in his embroidered ceremony robes. He was attended by all the provincial civil servants, including the Deputy Governor and the servants who open doors and fetch tea. All walked humbly.

A little boy carried a cloak woven of roses. The Governor draped this cloak around the Rain God's shoulders. The God was worshiped with music. Grain and fruit offerings were made. Tapers were lit for each month in the year.

Peng-wen surprised me by being at my house when I returned from the Rain God procession. He thoughtfully stopped off on his way from Canton to the House of Exile, to see how I am and to take anything I wanted to send up to thee. He will carry this letter and he has promised to reassure thee regarding the diligence with which I strive for accomplishment in the activities which thee advises will make me a successful wife.

A paid teacher gives me lessons in the waltz and the fox-trot one hour daily. She says that I have natural aptitude. It is simple really. One has just to memorize a few steps. Then go on the music. Western dance music has a rhythm that carries one along.

Often Bald-the-third manages the victrola and I practise alone. I like doing it alone. My teacher pronounces me nearly finished. She says that I must soon put what I know into practice with men partners. I should not mind just one partner whose rhythm was suitable to mine. But I do dread — fat men, thin stiff men, men gay with wine, men who talk all the time they whirl, blowing hot breath on one's neck. This dancing is the amusement of the majority of the "civilized" world to-day. I hasten to reassure thee, dear little mother by affection, that I heed thy advice that it is a part of my wifely duty. I make my début next Saturday night at the Bachelors' Ball in the Nanking Club.

My husband has had a green wall made for me. A white

line is painted on it at the height of a tennis net. I bounce the ball against it. Quite often it goes over the top. Four little tennis boys, sweet in blue and white uniforms, find and fetch the balls back to me. I have to do this every morning to "get my eye in." Twice weekly after tea, my husband gives me a lesson on the proper court.

Golf I do three times a week. The course is where the old Manchu city stood before the Revolutionists leveled it. Thee will remember the place. On the other side of the Nanking city wall, and nearly under the brow of the Purple Mountain. My ease and joy on a horse, which is really no accomplishment at all, has surprisingly been met here with acclaim. It seems that jumping over a wall quite excuses one for stupidity at cards. Even though it is the horse that jumps and one just sits on.

2

The House of Exile, last day of the Kindly Moon, 1923. — To-day completes twelve moons of thy marriage. Nuan and I have been making sweets most of the day. The weather continues clear, cold, and sunshiny, so the syrups and honey all set well. We have skewered candied fruits on bamboos with fancy handles carved by Camel-back for the delight of the children, and shaped sugar flowers of every variety. This delicate work has tired my hands and the writing brush shakes, but I do not want to let the cycle of thy year close without writing my blessing to thee, thy husband, and thy daughter.

Excepting young Tsai-fu, we are all in good health and spirits. He has moped and coughed ever since it was decided, in assembled Family Council, that he is to go abroad to school. His general health has always been too good for him to get sympathetic excuse by the ruse of hacking his throat, but I am in sympathy with him.

Since my world tour, I doubt the wisdom of sending our sons abroad to finish their education. I think that we Chinese are very foolish in chasing our boys to America, England, Germany, France, Italy, Russia, and Japan, in pursuit of whatever magic it is that gives the Western civilization world supremacy in this era. Hundreds so finished have already come home. To me they seem like unsuccessfully grafted trees: weak both in root and branch.

But it is settled that Tsai-fu is to go. Since he must, he has chosen Tokyo University as the nearest to home. The Elder Uncles are well pleased with this choice.

They have just returned from a tour of Shantung and Manchuria, filled with indignation concerning Japan's aggression. They have influenced a vote through our homestead Family Council donating ten thousand dollars to the Japanese Boycott Society. They are also filled with admiration of the competence with which Japan accomplishes her designs, and convinced that there is advantage to be gained in study at Tokyo.

Life goes on quietly here within our courtyards, but we have heard echoes of the warfare and strife in every province. Our clan has been most unmercifully taxed, to no good purpose, this year. Our decision is to make investment of moneys in America sufficient to assure the future.

My husband has been selected to take Tsai-fu to Japan, by boat from Tientsin. He will then travel from Japan to Shanghai, to join the Elder Uncles and the representatives from the House of Lin, and act as interpreter in the transactions which are to be done with the American Banking Corporation. It is planned to put one third of the money decided upon into U. S. Government bonds, one third into basic commodity shares, such as drugs and food and clothing, and one third into small-house property.

The Elder Uncles will travel to Shanghai by train from Peking. They will need five personal servants for the journey. Camel-back has never seen a train. He has asked for one of the places.

Uncle Keng-lin has trained a bird-of-one-thousand-bells to sing for thy Small Girl. En route to Shanghai Camel-back will bring the bird to thee with instructions how to feed and exercise it. The one-thousand-bells has a lovely plumage and a wonderful répertoire of trills. His red cage is pagoda-shaped. It was made to Uncle's own design in the bird-cage shop on the Street-of-the-Sound-of-Thunder-on-the-Ground.

We hear from Canton that Sun Yat-sen has finally clasped the Russian hand. Even though previously the influences of the West, particularly Great Britain and the United States, have always been evident in all his activities, Sun's act is but the natural sequence of events.

Keep it secret, but Sun Yat-sen is afflicted with a sickness which warns him that he cannot be here in body much longer. He has spent himself for China like a saint. He is distressed because he has not accomplished a Republic.

Our Republican Revolution which overthrew the decadent Manchu dynasty was inspired by the study of Western books. The government planned by the Republicans was based on the American model. Sun Yat-sen's emphasis on a written constitution was American. His legal system was copied from that of England. Although we naïvely expected assistance, neither America nor Great Britain has been willing to help us practically. Our models have shied away from any responsibility for us. Both played into the deceitful hands of Yuan Shih-kai.

Their concern is not our successful establishment of a peaceful Republic, but how activities within China affect their mercantile trade or their Christian missionaries.

Early this year Sun Yat-sen sent a mission to the United States to recruit civilians and World War veterans to help reorganize the Kuomintang and to advise our party how to train a model army. He also sent Eugene Chen to London to ask for the same assistance. Both missions failed. A mission sent to Germany also failed. Then Sun wrote to Mr. Karakhan, the Soviet representative at Peking, asking him to send a man with whom to discuss these matters.

Michael Borodin has arrived at Canton. We hear that he has submitted Moscow's offer to repudiate the old treaty rights and to provide us with civilian and military experts. Sun Yat-sen endorses these proposals. He has asked that Mr. Borodin be appointed High Advisor.

The majority of the Kuomintang, our clan included, have signified support of Sun Yat-sen's proposals. The minority, mostly aged members, find them dangerous. They have sent in their resignations. Their withdrawal weakens the party. Sun Yat-sen believes that a unity of all citizens is possible. His faith embraces the Elders who have resigned and the young secret society students and laborers. To impregnate us all with unified ideals, he has commenced a series of lectures entitled, "Three People's Principles."

Su-ling has already organized a club of young women to spread the People's Principles. They are each pledged to do one hundred courtyard calls. She is very much occupied with hers, as she is resolved to speak with and convert the Lady of First Authority in each homestead she visits. Then to tell the Principles in each Garden of Children.

A copy of the Principles is included in our letter. Also notice that a copy has been sent to Mai-da and to thee. I believe that they will have wide influence. I advise thee to read them.

The Astor House Hotel, Shanghai, en route to Canton, March 29, 1924. — I wired thee of my husband's transfer to Canton. Now I write thee in detailed sequence.

Thou wilt remember that we had a Dutch guest last summer. On leaving, he promised to send us five thousand tulip bulbs. We got three carloads of special earth from Pukow and had beds ready to plant the bulbs a good time ago. So immediately they arrived, by the kind hand of a German merchant who traveled via Siberia, the gardeners and I set to planting them.

The task occupied us several days. We had just finished dividing the last hundred, when Chang came out and said: "It is futile to plant more. We are transferred to Canton."

Chang's superior manner still annoys me at times. Especially when I am tired. I asked him, "How do you know?"

"The master's *t'ingch'ai* gives me a ring on the telephone when the master leaves," he answered. "It is an arrangement I have with him so that I know when to put the teakettle on. He told me of the receipt of the transfer orders."

Just then my husband arrived. He confirmed what Chang had said about transfer. My first emotion was chagrin that I shall not see the tulips bloom. This was soon gone in a glow of satisfaction that I shall see Canton.

The Chinese Helpers did all the practical work of departure. Unknown to me, Chang had added my worldly goods to his inventory of my husband's possessions when I entered the family. A Mr. Wu came from the office with an inventory of the government things. They checked together. Then Chang packed ours. I have never before seen such systematic and perfect packing.

He had boxes for everything. Books were done in packets of four, all neatly tied. The silver was cleaned and covered with polishing powder mixed with pounded camphor, to make certain that it does not turn black. The legs and rungs of tables and chairs were wrapped with cotton wool, then with paper, then tied with string. China and glass were fixed with straw. I asked Chang to be sure to pack my cut-glass fruit bowl so that it would n't break. To illustrate how well he had done it, he threw the straw-wrapped bowl across the room.

He made three lists of the contents of each box. One was tacked on the inside of the lid. One put in his notebook. One laid on my husband's desk.

I had only to get tropical clothes ready for Bald-the-third, daughter, and myself, and to make farewell calls on all the community.   I felt sad about leaving Nanking.   I was happy there.   The place is beautiful.   The people nice.   And the house *was* my first married home.

From the time that it was public news that we were going, so many luncheons and dinners were given for us that we were entertained almost daily.   At the dinner the Civil Governor gave us, he asked what I should take, if a fairy gave me one wish, as my last memory of Nanking.   I said that I would attend the Spring Sacrifices at the Palace for the Worship of Confucius.

This temple stands on the site where the Taipings destroyed the Taoist Palace for the Worship of Heaven.   It covers eighteen acres.   All the courts, gates, ponds, pavilions, walls, steps, altars, terraces, and even the trees, were arranged by the builder as symbols of Confucius's teachings.   A thirty-foot wall screens it from the world.   During the monarchy no one but the Emperor could enter the Big Gate.   Twice a year the seventy-two scholars to receive literary degrees were permitted the honor of entering the Temple by the side gates. Now the Civil Governor conducts the Autumn and Spring Sacrifices within it.

The Civil Governor did not grant my wish then.   But five days later his Third Green Skirt drank tea in the garden with me.   She brought a card on which her husband had written admittance for my husband and myself to the Palace on the night of the Spring Sacrifices.   She said that she would meet us at the gate over which is written "His teachings unite the past and the present," and conduct us to a place behind the vermilion pillars in the Court of Perfection, from which we could watch the rites on the Moon Terrace and yet not distract the attention of the worshipers by being seen.

Spring Sacrifice night, we fox-trotted and one-stepped away the hours from ten until two in the morning, to the syncopation of the Nanking Club Jazz Orchestra. Then I read an affirmative answer in my husband's eyes to the question I sent him over my partner's shoulder. A few seconds later, having donned practical shoes and covered my dress with an all-enveloping coat, I slipped out of the back door to find him sauntering leisurely along the path with the forbearing manner men have of hinting that it takes wives longer to make themselves presentable than it does husbands.

A word from our chauffeur to an armed sentinel, and we turned into the Big Horse Road to glide five miles over smooth asphalt cleared of traffic and guarded at intervals of twenty yards by soldiers with drawn bayonets. Such is the custom at Nanking when the officials go abroad at night. I held the card of admittance tight in my hand.

After the first mile our motor fell into line behind the cars of the Civil and Military Governors and their many attendants. We rode past shuttered shops and closed compounds — without even a stray dog to remind us of the daytime activity of this road — to the Gates of the Temple. The governor's Third Green Skirt kept the tryst at the western gate.

She took us across the entrance court and past a great screen on which "The greatness of Confucius is beyond measure" is cut, through a park of beautiful old trees which has a semi-circular pond, and so brought us to the lovely arched gates called "Golden Sound" and "Silver Lilt." Then, as it was still early, we walked through the place of tablets to "Men honest and faithful to the teachings of the Sage, despite poverty," before going to our place behind the Vermilion Pillars in the Court of Perfection.

Keeping concealed, we watched attendants lay red silk cushions to the east and the west sides of the lowest level of the court. This court is three flagged squares. It has double flights of marble steps leading up from one square to another. The upper terrace is called the Moon Terrace. It is directly before the five massive doors above which is written, "The Holy and Divine Confucius Equal to Heaven."

When the cushions were placed, the attendants opened these doors and lit lamps within the hall. The lamps illuminated a high throne on which stood a tablet holding the name Confucius. At each side of the throne were boards wide as a man's height, each a deep crimson with golden letters, "He was the greatest born of men", and "He was the Holy Son of Heaven." Tables for the sacrifice were placed before the throne.

Myriads of colored lanterns in every imaginable shape and color, mostly made of transparent shells, were hung along the marble balustrades leading up to each square level and massed along the sides of each terrace. At the top of each flight of stairs, two great iron baskets were placed on high standards and heaped with knots of wood.

Musical instruments were massed on the Moon Terrace before the central door of the sacred hall. The Governor's Green Skirt told me that some of these very instruments are mentioned in the Annals of Nanking at the time Confucius walked on earth. They have been collected through the centuries. They have been used to call Heavenly Spirits, to raise the departed, to instruct Emperors in their duty, and to inspire men and women with a love of virtue. Now they are all collected here to use in praising the great Confucius.

There were tiny bells like buttercups. Bells of transparent blue glass. Bells of silver. Bells of rose porcelain. Soft-voiced bells of pewter. And one large bronze bell into the molten metal of which the maker's lovely daughter is chronicled to have thrown herself as a sacrifice to perfect the tone. Six different kinds of wind instruments. Immense lyres, one made of the hollowed trunk of a great tree of some pale amber wood, polished until it reflected the lantern light in color. Miniature lyres, so dainty that their sound was like

the song of fairies.   Cymbals of brass, bronze, wood, and glass.
Many colored sonorous stones, tapped with a gong stick.   Tiny
drums, and a huge drum of dull red on which an entire family could picnic.

Thirty-six musicians in blue robes came and sat among the
instruments.   The rites-conductor, called the "Marshal of
Music," had a baton covered with scarlet satin figured with
gold velvet.   The musicians were closely followed by a procession of thirty-six boy sopranos, dressed in long blue cloaks
and mortar-board hats.   They filled the place on the terrace to
the west of the instruments.   Next came thirty-six Harlequins, or boy dancers, who occupied the eastern side of the
terrace.

A withered old man, Crier of Time, famous for having sung
the liturgy here through the seasonal cycles of six decades,
stood at the top of the highest flight of marble stairs.   The
Civil and Military Governors and their two hundred attendants came quietly into the Court of Perfection and knelt
on their red silk cushions.

A long silence lay like a benediction over the temple grounds.
Then a voice from the lower level chanted the request for
permission to pay homage to the great Confucius.   Clear, rich,
and resonant, the voice of the Crier of Time repeated the request.   The drums broke into a thundering roar that spread
through the bells, the stringed instruments, and the pure
high soprano of the choir boys, who held the last note long
after the other music had ceased.

This was repeated three times.   Then the Crier sang out
the answer bidding the supplicants come.

A match was set to the baskets of wood.   Flame darted
skyward.   The gentle-faced, aged Governor, dressed in the
long embroidered robes of the Sung dynasty, slowly climbed
the three long flights of steps, supported by officials similarly
gowned and preceded by bearers carrying flaming torches of
pitch-dipped bamboo, to perform the first ritual of worship

— the sacrifice of an ox before the altar that held Confucius's name.

During the performance of this sacrifice, the musicians played a hymn of praise to Confucius on the lyres, to which the choir sang six verses exalting the Sage, while the Harlequins danced an intricate sword dance.

Then the Governor returned to his cushion on the lowest level. Again he cried for the privilege of worshiping the Sage. As before, his cry was repeated by the Crier, and echoed through the drums, the bells, stringed instruments, and the choir. After the third time of asking, the Crier sang the permission.

Five times in all this was repeated before the intricate ritual, which has been invented since Confucius's departure from life, was completed. Five times the Governor came up the stairs and performed a sacrifice. During each sacrifice the musicians played different instruments, to which the choir sang and the dancers danced.

The Military Governor, who is of Western education, remained on the lowest level throughout the service. At intervals I found myself wondering what thoughts were under his blue plumed hat.

When the last rite had been done, we stood with bowed heads for several moments of silence. Then silvery music played on the air, the Crier led the boy sopranos in a soft chant, and the dancers danced the most lovely rhythm, called the "Golden Pheasant Feather," using the long feathers "that may not be bought or sold."

One by one the lanterns were extinguished. The servants who had helped in any way to work for the service went forward to receive the white slips of paper that entitled each to a share of the sacrificial meat on presentation to the temple butcher before noon.

The Civil Governor, pale from two hours of worship, came and spoke to us. He took my husband to the room where refreshments of tea and cake were laid. His Green Skirt and I, being only women and thus not served with men, were free to wander about the temple, where dawn was breaking.

She was indignant about the worship. She said that she was certain that Confucius, who was such a simple man, would not approve of either the animal sacrifices or the elaborate ceremony with which his name was coupled here. I was so charmed by the temple seen in the dawn light that I did not listen to her much; so, to make her point, she led me around the courts and read aloud some of his teachings, which are written on tablets of red in gold-inlaid characters: —

Better do a kindness near at home than walk a thousand miles to burn incense.

A man of noble mind seeks to perfect the good in others and not their evil.

The inferior man always embellishes his mistakes.

If on self-examination I find I am not upright, shall I not be in fear even of a beggar? If I examine myself and find that I am upright, I will go forward unafraid against thousands and tens of thousands.

To see the right and not do it is cowardice.

Sincerity is the way of God: study it wisely, inquire into it searchingly, reflect upon it carefully, discriminate about it accurately, and practise it wisely.

When Fan Che asked Confucius, "What is Humanity?" the master answered, "To love men." When he asked, "What is Knowledge?" the answer was, "To know men."

He who desires to know men must first know God.

Why should God speak in words? The four seasons follow in their course and all things come to life.

III

A MATRON

Ch'ih p'i fei pao, ts'un yin shih ching.

("An inch of time on the sundial is of greater worth than twelve inches of jade.")

— CHINESE PROVERB

I

BESIDE THE PEARL RIVER

1

W E came to Canton by river, as the early Westerners came. We left Hongkong just before midnight. The moon rose shortly after we entered the river and gave light until the sun touched the rims of the morning clouds with gold. I found every knot of the way familiar.

Luxuriantly verdant land undulated fertilely away into the distance from both banks of the pearl-smooth river, just as chronicled in a seaman's log written when John Midenhall passed during the reign of Queen Elizabeth. Fishermen's craft were lemon-sailed in the moonlight, and clustered at the bend in the river channel where they are recorded as waiting for the dawn when Captain Weddell went this way in 1635.

It was spring again. Flowering apricots half hid the pagodas, as they did when Mr. Flint hopefully approached the Viceroy's Yamen in 1759. The Bogue Tiger Forts overlooked us peacefully, as they overlooked the good ship *Perseverance*, six months out from Philadelphia, when she put in to Canton with a sprung fore-topmast in 1805.

We steamed over the Anchorage where the eighteenth-century Westerners had to wait on their ships while their foreign cargoes were taken off and their Chinese cargoes put aboard. We saw the Fati flower gardens, to which the early-nineteenth-century Westerners were permitted the refreshment of a walk. At six o'clock on the morning of April 2,

1924, we tied up at the Bund, paved with bricks from the city wall torn down by the twentieth-century Republicans.

Although the hour was early, we were welcomed to "The City of Rams" by several government officials. Sedan-chair bearers, uniformed in the green of my husband's department of government service, awaited us. These bearers were tall, fine, old men of splendid lean physique. When she saw them, Bald-the-third whispered, "Formerly Manchu banner-men!"

CANTON

They addressed us in Mandarin, the tongue of the North whence we had come. I saw that both Chang and Chou, who had been apprehensive about our coming to "treacherous Canton where men speak a jabber only monkeys understand," were relieved. When we had exchanged bows and formal greetings with the officials, we had the same exchange of bows and good-word phrases with our new bearers. Then our "personal helpers" bowed with the officials and with the bearers.

This done, Chang was left with one of the banner-men to attend to our boxes. We got into chairs and were carried along the Bund and over a bridge to the house the government rented and furnished for our residence on Shameen. In our service, there is a "permanent staff" that stays on at each official residence, rising, through the years, to retirement.

At Nanking we left the house cleaners, the gardeners, the gateman, the night watchman, the laundryman, and the chauffeur, as motor cars were not permitted on Shameen; at the entrance gates of the Shameen dwelling, house cleaners, a gardener, gateman, night watchman, and a laundress greeted us with bows and wishes for long life, health, happiness, and the birth of many children while at Canton. These, with our chair bearers, were the permanent staff, who — such is custom — were lower in rank than, and took orders from, my husband's house steward, Chang; or, in his absence, from Chou the Cook.

We had baths and breakfast. My husband went to his office. Bald-the-third and I explored our new home. We found it as large, as modernly equipped, and as handsomely furnished as the house we had left in Nanking. I liked the drawing-room even better than the Nanking drawing-room, as it had the charm of two fireplaces, one at each end of the room.

The house faced the river and was built with a long frontage. Each floor had a wide verandah running the entire length of the house. The grounds were limited. There was a modestly sized kitchen court in the rear, a narrow garden-border at each side of the house, and a small garden in front.

Every possible inch of space was abloom with lovely, delicately scented flowers. The gardener was doing something to what he said would be a poinsettia hedge next Christmastime. He left it to draw our attention to the deep garden boxes, filled with lupines, ferns, and trailing geranium that glorified each window ledge and hung in beauty from each verandah rail. Then he led us around the homestead, to show us the sweet peas on their bamboo trellises which veiled our high brick wall.

The second-floor verandah was above this homestead wall.

From it one had an extensive view both up and down the river and of the country hills on the opposite shore. I was on this verandah, and had just resolved to make it my living room, when Chang came through the French windows and joined me. I told him my resolution, and he immediately began to help plan it, discussing a large aviary for birds, wicker furniture, and copper-wire screening for this and the entire house, to shut out the mosquitoes.

"The house is good," he said. "The plumbing is good. There is a servants' bath. The laundry is the best I have had, but I do not like this Southern fashion of a woman doing the clothes. When we have our boxes unpacked the living rooms will be just like the home we left, as the official furniture is exactly the same, even to the color of the rugs."

Chou, the Cook, came to us with a market basket on his arm. He was eager to go and discover what edible produce this strange province had to offer. He was accompanied by a little lad whom he introduced as his new apprentice, a boy who could translate for him from Mandarin to Kungtungese.

Old Nurse followed Cook on to the verandah. "We are safer here than I dared to hope," she said, waving her hand towards the warships of five Western nations anchored in the reach of river before us, so close that we could observe the activities on their decks. "That is the American flag on the biggest cannon-sender. The British flag is on the two smaller craft. Those ships to the east fly the colors of France, Italy, and Portugal. We Pekingese ought to be safe with these battle vessels to protect us, even if the Cantonese are our enemies and the nasty Japanese live right at the top of this island."

A large gasoline launch, flying our service flag, chugged up to the river steps just below us. It was heaped high with our packing cases. The captain of the launch crew saluted. We returned his salute. Coolies began to swing the boxes off and carry them on bamboo poles into the house, singing "Hi-ya-hi-ya-hi-ya" in time to their unison movements.

Chang the faithful had arranged the master's house now for twenty years, and he said, "Unpacking is both noisy and messy. I find the banner-men trustworthy and I have arranged that they carry you under the shade of the banyan trees for a tour of Shameen while we put the home in order."

I demurred, saying that I had not yet decided how I wanted things arranged. Chang bowed to me. Then politely but firmly he explained that there was nothing to decide. Those furnishings that belonged to an Englishman's drawing-room went into the drawing-room, and so on through all the house. The master's bedroom was always the bedroom with the bath-room that had the best light for shaving. The master's wife would naturally always have the best remaining room. My dress boxes would be put there for my woman to unpack. Adjoining the room I was to have was a room for Small Girl. Her things would be arranged therein by Old Nurse.

The weather in Canton is tropic. The atmosphere is heavy, especially in the spring. I did not find the climate suitable to dispute about such details and I was languid with the growth of the child under my heart. Bald-the-third and I did go through the house with Chang and observe how he planned to use the rooms. I could not better his plan, and Bald whispered to me, "Quarreling for superiority will gradually destroy the affairs of a family."

I went out in the sedan chair. There was a comfortable place for Small Girl on a cushion beside me. We were carried by four bearers. Two in front and two behind us. The bearers acted both as bearers and guides, explaining all we saw.

"The Western traders were not long satisfied just to wait at the Anchorage," the Number One began. "They wanted a place on which they could leave one of their crew to purchase merchandise and prepare another cargo while the ship was away. To secure this privilege they exploded a tremendous lot of gunpowder that we Chinese had invented."

"They did not explode it all in the Pearl River," the Number Four put in. "They ran along the coast, right up north to within a hundred miles of the Emperor's palace, exploding it. The people were alarmed at such profane use of gunpowder, made only for festival use. The Son of Heaven had to do something quick to stop it."

"But the Son of Heaven had no intention of letting the blue-eyed people into China. So he said, 'Yes, I agree to give you a place if you will stop this noise,' " came from one of the bearers behind our chair.

"They stopped, and the Emperor gave Shameen," said Number One. "Shameen was a sandbar, under the river water even at low tide in the driest season. All the Viceroys proclaimed the Son of Heaven a clever Emperor. The people rejoiced in the good fortune of possessing such a wise king. But in those days we in China did not understand blue-eyes as we do now. They accepted Shameen."

"Look to the east, the west, the north, and the south," exclaimed the four bearers together, and turned us the four points of the compass that we might look. "Would you believe now that this lovely paradise is really not an island but just a sandbar?"

I agreed that it was difficult to call it a sandbar now.

They trotted on, the Number One talking.

"In every voyage the Occidentals made after they had accepted Shameen, they brought fertile earth in their ships as ballast. They put earth on the sandbar and built it up higher than the level of the water. The sailors turned masons and put a circle of wall around it. The traders brought banyan trees from India and planted them. The roots of the banyan trees grew amazingly. The roots wove the soil together more firmly than silk is woven on the loom."

"When the island was woven," Number Two continued, "the Westerners brought all sorts of Western materials. With these they built homes and offices of such pattern as had not been seen in China before. They planted flowering shrubs, seeded green lawns. And used some magic force by which they make unboiled water safe to drink and freeze ice here in tropic Canton even on the hottest days — ice such as the people in the north cut from the canals in winter."

"Then, in copy of the Chinese regulations, the Westerners made counter-regulations for their sandbar," Number One explained. "No Chinese person can build or even lease a house or office here. No Chinese can put his foot on Shameen except in dispatch of business or as a servant to a Westerner. A Chinese here in either of these capacities cannot sit down to adjust a shoe fastening on one of the comfortable benches under the tree shade on which Westerners enjoy the river breezes."

Number Two spoke next.

"It was not intended that the Westerners should be comfortable or above water here. But they insolently made this tiny sandbar nicer than any park in the proud ancient city of Canton. So the Chinese people want it returned to them. According to Chinese concept of land, it all belongs to the Chinese Government. No matter how many years one has been permitted to use it, the government can demand it back to use for greater good of all the people. But the Westerners won't give it back."

"All my lifetime," said Number Four, "this has made bitter talk in tea shops on the mainland. On summer evenings when the tide wind blows the sweet perfume of the flowering shrubs on to the mainland, one hears that we Chinese must rise up and take the sandbar, which is rightly ours, back again, so that all may come here to enjoy the flowers."

"My brother-in-law has a pleasure boat," put in Number Two, "and he says that the same talk is spoken angrily by his passengers in all seasons, and that the voices are loudest on winter evenings when the lamps glow cozily in the handsome homes the Westerners have built. The trip around Shameen is the trip most often ordered by his customers. In the pleasure-boat trade jargon it is called 'Grumble-about-the-intruding-blue-eyes-tour.' "

"These Russian advisers, newly come to Canton, are fanning this bitterness among students and laborers. In another twelve moons Shameen will be attacked," predicted Number Three.

"I doubt it," said Number One. "It would take more courage than the Chinese soldier possesses to charge into this island, protected as it is by Western battleships. There has always been fortune for the merchant class of Canton in Western trade. The Westerners are doing no harm living here. All this wasted grumbling energy ought to be used to make another place as good as this. There are plenty of better sites."

Shameen is so small that even at a leisurely walk one cannot occupy more than twenty minutes in encircling it. In addition to the paved Bund, which curves around under the shade of wide-branched banyan trees, there is just one central avenue running the length of the bar.

The dwelling houses are on the Bund. All face toward the water and are set well back. None have much private garden. The space between the houses and the paved part of the Bund is communal lawn. It is kept planted, pruned, and mown by the Shameen Council and is used by all residents. One part has swings, seesaws, merry-go-rounds, sliding-boards, and sand piles for the children. Another, a cricket pitch and football field. Another, a bowling green. Another, eight grass tennis courts.

The French flag flies over the east end; the Japanese over the west; the British over the middle. The American flag flies only over the American Consulate. But American homes and offices are scattered over all the Shameen Concessions.

The sedan chair, carried by barefoot or sandaled men, is the only vehicle permitted on Shameen. Vendors are not allowed: they must sell from their boats at the water steps.

The central avenue is a grass park like the space between the dwelling houses.   A cement walk runs down each side of the avenue.   The Western banks and the shipping offices are built facing on this inner street, back to back with the dwelling houses, which face out to the water.   All the building on Shameen is of good material and of commanding but simple design.

Shameen is connected with Canton now by two bridges. My chair bearers explained that in quarrel-times sometimes the Chinese shut off intercourse first by barring their end of the bridges — and sometimes were insulted because the Westerners were quicker and got their bars up first.

2

Su-ling came in mid-afternoon.   I woke from a nap to find her stroking my hand.

"Not changed in the least," she said as I opened my eyes. "Just as fond of sleep as ever."

She had her hair cut in a new fashion which, she told me, was called a "windblown bob," and wore a dress that had been sent to her by a friend in Paris.   It was orange voile.   A straight sheath, sleeveless, low-necked, in length just to her knee, held around her narrow hips by a white suède belt.   Her legs were stockingless, her sandals white suède.

"The new dress of freedom," she laughed, as she twirled around, laughing at my astonishment.   "As soon as your figure is flat again you must dress like this.   You can have no idea how comfortable it is."

Bald-the-third came in and was shocked.   Su-ling did enjoy Bald's scolding, which closed with the declaration that she would tear to ribbons any dress of that variety that I attempted to wear.

Su-ling said that the House of Lin would be pleased if I bowed my respects there on the very first day of arrival, as a daughter of the House of Exile should. Su-ling had a two-seater motor boat moored at our steps. She and I sat side by side, and Bald sat on the floor behind us. We backed away and turned down river at greater speed than I should dare leave a garage in a motor car, but we slid between greater and lesser boats with no mishap. After a time we left the Pearl channel and branched west and southwest, coming to a halt before a high grey wall in which a scarlet door, flanked by a stone tortoise twice a man's height, is set.

Broad stone steps go up to this door from the river. At each end each step has a peg on which to fasten a boat. Five steps were above water and we tied to the lowest of these. Then we clanged the asking-admittance-bell — three short and one long pull of the clapper, which is the ring of a married daughter of the clan.

An aged gateman, not unlike Camel-back in feature, bade us enter. Su-ling's own serving woman ran to us, clasping my hands, and then Bald-the-third's, in warm welcome. A serving woman behind her said that the Lady of Lin awaited us in the Court of Fragrant Balsam.

East and west in this small river-entrance court stood a stone phœnix screen and a stone unicorn screen, as in the Court of Dignity in the House of Exile. We passed behind the phœnix screen. Serving matrons clad in lavender linen heard our approach and drew aside curtains of opaque shell that closed the Orchid Door. We stepped into the court with green-leafed vines bearing golden fruit carved on the porticoes, of which a replica was built for the "Bride from Canton" in the House of Exile.

The House of Lin at Canton and the House of Exile in Hopei are architecturally the same. The small single-room houses have green-tile roofs that extend well over pillared verandahs. The roofs tilted upward in graceful curves. Faëry legends are painted in bright color under the eaves. These dwellings

are built foursquare around paved courtyards, and the courtyards are connected by gateways cut in fantastic shapes.   The
dwelling courts cluster about the taller Hall of Ancestors
which rises inside a circular grove of bamboo.

"The House of Lin is our parent house," Su-ling said as we
walked to the Court of Balsam.   "In the library archives that
surround this court we shall cross next, there are one hundred
and four generations, previous to the branching off of the
House of Exile, recorded in the genealogy book begun by the
first couple who mated here.   Our family history is long,
but there are none among our clan who do not know its principal events.   It is the custom here, as in the House of Exile,
to have the family genealogy committed to memory by each
child during the first year in the schoolroom; for the Family to
repeat the genealogy aloud in unison in the Hall of Ancestors
at each family anniversary; and for each Family Elder to gather
the homestead women and children about him for the relation
of family incidents, axioms, and life stories in the mornings
and the afternoons of all seasons.   I sometimes think that the
long continuity of our race must be because the Family has
always been the centre of our civilization: Family perpetuates
continuance by prudent use of each experience and so inci-
dentally has perpetuated our race."

Peonies, balsam, and flowering plums were in blossom in
the Court of Balsam.   The Lady in First Authority in the
House of Lin sat on a bamboo divan under the cool shade of a
papaya tree.   She was a woman beautiful in age.   In women
who have filled their years well, in every race, I find age has
greater charm, grace, and beauty than is ever an attribute
of youth.   I knelt to her as I had been taught to kneel to the
home-mother in the House of Exile.

She signaled me to rise and sit beside her.   Su-ling sat on
her other side.   The servants brought tea with lichi and
placed them on a table in front of us.   I had to tell of my
farewell visit to Hopei and of my journey from Nanking.

Su-ling told us of her two-month-old twins. The Lady of Lin called us both "my daughters from Exile." I began to speak of the house to which I had come on Shameen.

My hostess toyed with her fan and I was silent. We sat, a long uncomfortable pause. Then she put her finger tips under my chin and raised my face so that she could look down into my eyes, and said: —

"It is unfortunate that you are to live on Shameen. One foot can't stand on two boats. But all through life one must make compromise. You have to live on Shameen because it is your duty to dwell where your husband dwells. There is no social intercourse between Shameen and Canton. Yet it has been decided in Lin Family Council that you are to be treated here as any other married daughter of the House of Exile. The Elder of Exile made formal request for this and we agreed to it."

"That means," Su-ling interrupted, "that no Lin, except incorrigible me, will ever enter your dwelling place; but that you will be welcomed here whenever you knock."

"We will want you at all festivals and celebrations," the Lady of Lin continued. "You can join the circle around the Family Elder when you will, and there will always be place for you in our carriage or boat wherever we go. You will find that no Chinese call on you at Shameen as they did at Nanking, but I think it will be well if I give a garden party 'to meet you,' inviting those who would call if they could, on the birthday of the Goddess of Flowers."

I thanked her, and the garden party was agreed upon. That settled, she said, "Come, I must now introduce you in the Garden of Children, the Springtime Bower, and the courts of Wives and Green Skirts."

Just as we finished these calls, the gateman came running with a telegram. "The Elder of Lin," he gasped, "asked me to give it to his lady before the daughters of Exile went out of the homestead."

The telegram was from Mai-da.   It told that her husband was transferred to Canton.

"The gods seem bent on sending me all the daughters of Exile," the Lady of Lin laughed.   "Her coming so soon saves expense.   You can both be introduced at the Flowers garden party."

3

Through April, May, and until the end of June, life went pleasantly.   There was neither fuss nor confusion connected with the unpacking and the arrangement of our household goods.   Our home was soon as at Nanking.   Windows, doors, and verandahs were screened.   Craftsmen wove furniture of reeds for the verandah in replica of pictures I cut from the *House Beautiful*.   Old Nurse, Bald-the-third, and the laundress helped to sew the cushions of gay English cretonne from Hongkong.

When she learned that we had no conservatory, the Lady of Lin sent a florist from the Fati Flower Gardens to bargain with Chang.   He provided us with an abundance of fresh-cut blossoms and seasonal flowering trees in pots for five dollars a month.   Small Girl's bird-of-one-thousand-bells, when given the freedom of the verandah, recovered from the malady of which he had sickened in travel and trilled his songs merrily in and out of his cage.

The river life fascinated me.   I never tired of watching the boats, and soon the river dialect began to be understandable, so I could exchange conversation with the river people.   They are a distinct tribe at Canton.   Exiled from the land for some misdemeanor against the Emperor centuries ago, they are born, reared, married, give birth, and die on their boats.

More than half the pages of the journals of my Canton years are filled with the festivals, marriage celebrations, worship of water gods, homely axioms, mating songs in the nuptial season, and such incidents in the lives of my verandah neighbors — the river people.

Shameen is small. Society is formal. All the community walk on the Bund to take the air every evening before dinner. I walked there each evening with my husband. Yet no person smiled or spoke until we had met properly. The Shameen ladies waited until they had given me time to settle into my house. Then, hatted and white-kid-gloved, they left cards in the little box that was on our gate when we arrived.

I demurred at doing it, but I had to go around in my best hat and white kid gloves and poke my cards and my husband's cards in correct number in the boxes on their gates. Then we were invited to dinners at which we were carefully seated according to "rank," the highest places belonging to government officials in precedence of the dates of the establishment of their service, and the next places to merchants according to the date of the establishment of their firm's China trade. Afterwards, those people to whom we had been introduced at the dinners bowed when we walked on the Bund. I did not meet any Chinese people in the homes in which we were entertained.

I could not have any Chinese people at my return dinners, because the family in the House of Lin were the only Chinese people I knew and they would not come. The wives of the Chinese officials did not call.

Mai-da arrived. She found, as I had, that here only her own race took notice of her. At Nanking all the Western officials' wives had entertained her, but at Canton no Westerner tried to know her.

We decided that South China was a series of cliques, each living as if on a different planet. I did not meet any missionaries in the homes of the Shameen community. The House of Lin is not Christian. They not only have nothing to do with the Shameen community but they also have no association with Christian missionaries.

And the river people proudly spoke a dialect of their own, distinct from the "land people": the land and the river people both regarded each other as uncivilized rascals.

Mai-da and Su-ling were in and out of my house daily via the river steps. They were the only Chinese, except for "helpers," who ever crossed my Shameen threshold; even though the House of Lin gave the party "to meet our Exile daughters" on the nineteenth of the Peony Moon, and thereafter I was accepted as included in all invitations extended to the House of Lin by the circle of Chinese families in which they visited.

My husband was almost entirely occupied by the delicate political situation. I seldom saw him outside the brief hour he always kept for me just before dinner. Then we usually walked on the Bund so that he could get exercise and air as well as conversation with me.

I had much leisure. I had no Western friends. I spent my time mostly on my verandah, visiting with the river people, or in the House of Lin.

Within the Lin homestead wall I found industry and prudence, kindliness and affection. "There is no ladle that never strikes the cooking pot, and neither is there ever a family in which there is never a difference of opinion," the Lady First in Authority often said, "but harmony should always be the policy of the family and diligence the habit of the individual."

In the House of Lin the axiom "Although you become First Lady in a wealthy homestead, remember that the only way to keep a family in existence through the generations is to mend the clothes and be economical in the kitchen" is practised. The wives attended to all household details in rotation. The girls learned to sew, to cook, and to spend prudently. I used often to join in the homestead tasks and let my daughter play with the other children in the Garden of Children.

The work is well planned and soon done. Afterwards on most days we sat around the Elder in the cool deep shade in the library courtyard. Sometimes we sang folk songs. Other days we listened to the lute. Best of all I liked those times when the Lady of Lin read poetry aloud in her musical voice. Next best I liked the occasions when the Elder of Lin told us dramatic incidents in clan history. Often the children repeated legends they had heard from their nurses. Occasionally maidens of the Springtime Bower enacted historical pageants, dressed in costumes from the old family chests.

Life in the House of Lin is more urban and less pastoral than life in the House of Exile. The House of Lin holds government leases to over seven hundred acres of farm land, but it is all let out to tenant rice-farmers. The Family do not cultivate a home farm, and stable no beasts inside the homestead wall. They buy their food in the market place and have small concern about the weather.

The principal part of the family income is derived from trade. Much of it from medicine shops that make a world chain on which the sun never sets. But one of the younger uncles has responsibility for the revenue from the rice-rents. Mai-da and I rode out with him one May day when he went to survey the crops.

We traveled much of the way by canal boat, on which we carried our sedan chairs and bearers, using them when we had to go up inland paths to view rice paddies in sections away from the canal. We picnicked at noon in a fruit grove beside a bubbling spring. We served just such a lunch as we like to serve Uncle Shao-chun when we inspect the Exile farms with him. It was a peaceful, happy day. Neither Mai-da nor I had ever seen such abundantly fertile land before: here it seemed that men had but to drop seed to reap a rich harvest. We rode home into the sunset.

The walls of the House of Lin are stout and high. No one other than folk of family connection enter here. If the Lins have need to entertain others, they hire a city restaurant or use their guildhall. The home is occupied with clan activities, clan incidents, and clan celebrations. National events are important there only if they personally affect any member of the Family. The House of Lin makes liberal donation to each government as it comes into power and the Family Elder counsels against other participation in politics in this generation, "because the affairs of the Family may be ruined." "The House of Lin must go on despite civic irregularities" is the policy of this clan, which traces descent back through seventeen dynasties.

But Su-ling was independent. She had secured a handsome allowance from her husband's family at Ningpo and lived with him alone in a modern flat. She was deep in Republican activities and continuously assumed more than she could accomplish. Then she would scold Mai-da and me for lazy indifference to world events.

Neither Mai-da nor I ever assumed any regular tasks. But sometimes we assisted Su-ling by pouring tea and passing cake. She was "at home" four afternoons each week. Few of the older Republicans came to her drawing-rooms, but they were filled with young Chinese men and women of means who had been educated in Western universities.

These were bright, attractive, energetic young people at loose ends. They were all from the provinces. They had gathered at Canton because, on return from Western schools, they could not fit themselves into their homesteads and because Canton was the headquarters of the republican movement. They spoke in English because they had no common Chinese dialect.

The men dressed either in Western clothes or in soldier uniform, even though not attached to any regiment. The young women wore Western fashions or Chinese dress according to what they thought most becoming. Each one with whom I conversed had a scheme for the unification of the country. All could tell me exactly why all the previous revolutionary activities in China had failed. They danced to victrola records, played tennis, raced speed boats, flirted, and theorized continuously about what they would do with their learning as soon as they got the opportunity. They were restless and dissatisfied.

One afternoon, Sun Yat-sen came. He stood by Su-ling's tea table and asked her for tea. As he was recognized, talk ceased, cups and plates were put down. For forty years, longer than the lifetime of any of this group, he had devoted his life to an attempt to elevate China to a state of unity, freedom, and independence. He had accomplished the overthrow of the decadent Manchu dynasty; but again and again, within touch of the establishment of a national Republic, he had failed.

Yet there was no smirch on his reputation. His life was an open book. These young people held him in the deepest veneration. With his hand resting on the back of Su-ling's exotic cubist painted chair, he asked for three minutes of silence, for self-examination, for consideration of the doctrine of republicanism, and for self-determination. The silence was emotional, yet peaceful and profound. At the end of it, he made the finest call to leadership of the masses that it has ever been my privilege to hear.

One felt his spirit steady, true, and undaunted. His eyes were bright, his cheeks flushed, his countenance illuminated, his body straight and vigorous. I found it impossible to believe longer the rumor that he was afflicted with a fatal organic malady. His appearance in Su-ling's drawing-room effectively refuted this gossip in the minds of all her friends.

His speech was conversational. Yet it rang a louder call to unselfish service than any dramatic oratory could have done. When he had finished he introduced his companion, Michael Borodin, as a genius of organization who understood why feudalism had become entrenched during the Republican period and had generously come from Russia to help establish a true Republic.

Mr. Borodin bowed. He did not make the mistake of speaking.

In the days that followed I heard much from Su-ling about the formation of auxiliary societies to make the Kuomintang an effective agent of revolution. These societies had such names as "League for the Freedom of the Race"; "Youth Movement"; "Republican Wives"; "Revolutionary Scouts"; "Federation of Farmers and Laborers and Students." They touched every walk of life.

Sun Yat-sen was unquestionably the leader of the Kuomintang Party, with power to give membership to what other groups he chose. As each new organization was formed it was given membership in the national party. Organizations were formed almost as soon as anyone in Su-ling's crowd suggested a name. Her crowd were no longer restless and dissatisfied. They were active and happy.

Mr. Borodin dropped in continually at Su-ling's afternoons. He advised the placement of young Western-educated people of private income, who would ask no salary, in the secretariats of all the new organizations. Sun Yat-sen approved. Thus, through these secretariat positions, these young men and women eager for national service came into pivotal positions in the Kuomintang Party.

The news spread north that a returned student had but to appear in Su-ling's drawing-room to find his or her life work. The Western-educated students flocked to Canton. The Russian advisers, experts in each type of organization, came from Moscow and trained this new leadership for specific, usually propagandistic, enterprises.

It is so easy to become interested in one group and think that they are the only people about. When I had poured tea at Su-ling's I was quite certain that the Kuomintang was the only active party in Canton. Then one morning I went with my cook to market.

He had just purchased two live ducks and instructed his

apprentice to carry one under each arm, when a Yunnanese soldier entered the market and demanded the contents of the shopkeeper's till. The man was slow in unlocking it. To quicken him, the soldier pulled the trigger of his gun.

Cook's apprentice was frightened to forgetfulness of the ducks. They flew squawking out of the shop. Cook sat down flat, upsetting his basket of vegetables. I found myself under the counter. Blood from the merchant's forearm dripped on my head, but I waited there until the soldier had emptied the cash box, Cook's purse, and mine.

On the way home, Cook told me that these Yunnanese soldiers were hired henchmen that Sun Yat-sen had brought to Canton to police the city some years ago, and that what I had witnessed was a frequent occurrence. He said that the merchants were arming themselves against both these Yunnanese and the new youthful activities of the Kuomintang.

Four days later, Cook borrowed my chair bearers. He wanted them to help him carry home a week's supply of food. He explained that it was necessary because the markets were closing. Fighting between the Merchant Guilds and the Koumintang would start that night. The merchants had sandbags, bricks, and solid iron gates ready to barricade all the business section of the city. This could easily be done at Canton because the business section is a complete unit. At sunset the merchants would declare an embargo on trade until such time as the Yunnanese soldiers should depart to their own province and the young organizers stop their restless activities of which the merchants disapproved.

The rumble of guns began just before daybreak. Battles by night and sniping by day continued most of the week. Stray bullets fell on Shameen, but the only damage done on our sandbar was a bullet hole in the fire engine.

The river people gave me news of the progress of the war and told me how the merchants were routed. The barbers belong to no recognized guild. They were forgotten in the merchants' alliance, so were not loyal, and yet were not suspected of treachery. They were inside the barricades. A bribe was passed in to them. They punctured the water mains; then set fire to a dozen shops.

The merchants surrendered their weapons. The Kuomintang helped to put out the fire and clear away the barricades. We had peace again.

Mai-da, my small daughter, and I spent the Festival of the Summer Solstice with the House of Lin.

I helped serve at the Door of Compassion, where tea and food are given to the poor in the Hour of the Dragon on Summer Day. We had a long queue of hungry people still hopefully approaching the altar when the Time Stick had burned out the hour. The Lady of Lin gave orders that they must all be served. So we were kept busy until nearly noon. Fifteen catties of tea and one hundred and ninety-seven catties of rice cake were used.

New Year's Eve, Summer Day, and Mid-Autumn are the three settlement days of the year according to custom. All accounts must be paid up on these days. If a family does not pay they are shamed in public by tradesmen following them closely with lighted lanterns to show that the day has not yet dawned for them. Mai-da helped the wives who checked the tradesmen's books and made just settlement.

These tasks done, we gathered in the Court of Women's Gathering, where the maids of the Springtime Bower had arranged refreshment tables, and refreshed ourselves with Ch'u Yuan cakes. These are triangular cakes made of rice flour, yeast, and candied fruit. They are eaten on Summer Day in honor of a statesman and poet named Ch'u Yuan. He was an honest and upright man who dwelt in the State of Ch'u during an unprincipled and dishonest age about four centuries before Christ.

When we had rested and re-tidied our dress, we went out through the river To and From the World Gate and distributed ourselves on the five family junks, painted red and purple, awaiting us there.

Posters at street corners and on the notice-boards at the Yamen that year reminded the populace that the "Gregorian calendar of the West is the calendar of the Republic and that celebration of the Summer Solstice Festival — a heathen festival — is forbidden."

But the Lin junks were all decorated with dragon banners, lotus lanterns, and the flowers and ribbons used always on Summer Day. Every member of the Family had a dragon somewhere in his or her dress, either as a silver pin or embroidered on the stuff. All the other craft we saw, even those on which Republican officials enjoyed the fine weather, were dragon-decorated. Folk laughed and joked about it with each other, calling from deck to deck, "Shame, you heathen god-worshiper!"

First we went to the reach of river where the guilds had their rival displays. The jade merchants' procession got first prize. It was forty boats long. The first boat held the god Pan K'u, who made heaven and earth. The next, the goddess Nuan, who modeled fish and fowl, beast and man, of clay, and blew life into them. The third, Yu Ch'ao, the builder of houses, and Sui Jen, the producer of fire. The fourth was filled with the five legendary tribal chieftains, who led the Chinese from savagery.

Then boat by boat down through history to the last boat that carried a banner, "June, 1924, Gregorian Calendar." The helmsman in this was a Kuomintang official, according to the label on his sleeve. He wore a stiff straw hat, a black-and-white-check suit, horn-rimmed spectacles, and brown leather shoes. The oarsmen were dressed as a Russian and a Japanese. The passengers were ragged coolies and supercilious returned-from-abroad-scholars.

Our boatmen knew where to find the forbidden dragon races. We went to them next, and found that thousands of other people knew as well. Sampans, slipper boats, launches, craft propelled by coolies in a treadwheel, motor boats, and junks painted in every bright color, were parked so closely along the course that we had difficulty in finding a place.

Reed sheds had been erected along the shore for the comfort of people who possessed no water vehicle. They were strung with gay colored balloons in dragon shape, which hovered above their roofs. The sheds, as the boat decks, were filled with a merry holiday crowd, all dressed in brilliant gala costume.

Before the races began, a golden-dragon junk drifted along the race course. It held an orchestra of little maids dressed in the legendary costumes of the dragon-king's daughters. They played serpent-bellied *san hsien*, and sang the love songs of Summer Day. The clear pointed notes of the instruments and the soft contralto voices of the maids were charming in combination as they floated to us over the water.

Too soon, the race-starter cried "Hao! Hao! Hao!" and the orchestra cleared away. Then, amid wild applause from us all, the contestant dragon boats came out so that we could admire their beauty and choose one on which to bet. Clans, schools, shops, clubs — any group or individual who wishes — may race a dragon.

Boats in a dragon race must be over ninety feet long and resemble dragons. The rowers may be any number the contesters choose, but they must be seated in pairs side by side. Builders make the boats as slim and light as possible. The prows are high, and shaped as a dragon's head with snarling or laughing mouth and long fangs, and are moved by ropes held by the front steersman. The sterns are also high, and made in image of a dragon's tail: they have long steering paddles in the likeness of fins that rise well above the gunwales. The body of the slim craft is painted with scales. Gold and silver touches give brilliance.

Each dragon boat has a coxswain with a drum. He times the oarsmen's movements by beating "Tum-tum-tum-tum-tum." Some dragons are raced with as few as thirty paddles and others have as many as a hundred. All have men in gay dress with bells, gongs, and cymbals standing at intervals between the rowers to excite them to mighty effort.

The dragon boats went slowly up and down the course before us. They were a gorgeous, never-to-be-forgotten pageant of extravagant splendor. Those that had won in previous seasons had their victories in gold lettering on scarlet ribbons hung about their dragons' necks. I bet on a sea-green dragon entered by the Rainbow Silk Shop. My daughter favored a blue dragon flecked with white, — entered by the House of Sui, — which had a particularly agile tail.

Men wearing coats of cloth made to resemble dragon's skin went about in slipper boats collecting the bets. When we had given ours, we found that we of Lin had money on all the contestants.

The dragon king's daughters, their gold junk moored now at the top of the course, clanged cymbals. The dragon boats lined up abreast of each other. The starter threw a line of lighted firecrackers into the air. The boats were off.

They passed us in close formation, the sun glistening on the bare backs of the oarsmen, and disappeared in a flash of color far down the river. We waved excitedly and shouted our partisanship into the deafening crowd roar.

A black dragon and a rose dragon crashed and were out of it before the boats passed us again. A yellow dragon, rather too shallow, capsized. The third time in passing five boats were more than two lengths ahead of the fleet. Their supporters ran along the shore or leapt from junk deck to junk deck, shouting their encouragement as the dragons shot like knives through the water, leaving white foam on the waves behind them.

In the fourth round, three boats were snout and snout to

the front. Excitement reached a peak when it was seen that one of these was the scarlet dragon, oared by the Blacksmiths' Guild, which had been at the very rear in the second round. Cheers rose and the beat of the coxswains' drums throbbed as the heartbeat of the populace.

In the fifth turn down river, the Blacksmiths' scarlet dragon and the sea-green dragon of my bet were alone at the head of the race.

A ribbon was stretched between our junk and a junk that moved out opposite us. The dragon that touched this ribbon first would have it and be proclaimed the winner!

The dragons came forward. The beaters of gongs and cymbals were quiet. The oarsmen were pulling a swift speed, but appeared to be nearly spent. The coxswains beat fast but careful time. In silence tense with excitement, we of the crowd strained forward to watch.

Length by length the dragons came on together, neither seeming able to gain on the other. Then, within a yard of the ribbon, one of the Blacksmith oarsmen lost the rhythm and the scarlet dragon shipped water. She recovered without flooding. But the sea-green dragon won by half a jaw.

There were more races still to occur before the regatta finished, but the hour approached at which my husband expected me to be at home. Su-ling had come in her motor boat. She ran me to my steps.

After nightfall the dragon boats came down river and idled about within sight from my verandah. They had been rubbed with phosphorescence and hung with lotus lanterns from prow to stern. The oars gleamed with light at each stroke and at the prows waves of fire seemed to fall away, brightening as they ran in the darkness, then suddenly dying like blown candle flame.

Among the dragon boats drifted the golden junk carrying the soft-voiced daughters of the dragon king.

4

June passed like a fair dream.   I spent it in happy anticipation of the hour when I should look upon the face of my second child, now moving actively.   My sister arrived from America. Everyone did innumerable kindnesses to make me comfortable. Shun-ko sent me an air-mattress.   My household helpers, my husband and sister, the Lins, and the boat people watched over me to see that I did not tire myself in any way.   All the Chinese I encountered in any way greeted me with best wishes for the "babe soon to see the beautiful light of day."

Among the Chinese fertility is normal.   A woman who approaches childbirth with fear of the birth-pains is considered a coward not worthy of life.   Birth is woman's career.   Creation is the purpose of marriage.   Frequent fruitfulness is considered healthy.   Barrenness is unhealthy.   People do not speak shamefully of a woman *enceinte*.   Neither are they awkwardly silent concerning her condition, as in America.

Strangers, seeing that a woman carries a child, congratulate her.   At such times the most honorable place at every table is at her right.   By common law she is exempt from trial or punishment for any crime, until after the birth of her child.

The weather was very warm and damp.   I felt extremely languid, but otherwise all right.   I no longer even lifted my daughter up when she pressed against my knees asking for the ever-entrancing story of the child coming soon to stay with her.

On the evening of the twenty-eighth, I suddenly lost consciousness while Bald-the-third was solicitously tidying my hair in readiness for dinner.   When I knew the world again, I saw my husband's face first.   He knelt by my bed.   It was a strange bed.   I glimpsed a nurse's white skirt.   I asked to see my child.

Before my husband could reply, I heard the authoritative voice of the doctor say that I must not be talked to just now.

I tried to attend to what they were saying to each other, but I lost them again. Next I saw my sister. Her hand was cool on my forehead. I asked her for my baby.

A nurse slipped a thermometer into my mouth, but by concentration of will I stayed with them this time, and as soon as it was removed I asked again. The nurse muttered something about the doctor coming to me soon. I persisted about my baby, sitting up suddenly, and doctor and nurse were both at my pillow. They made me lie down, telling me to keep still or I should tear the stitches in my wound. But I resisted and sat up again, strong with fever. I heard my sister's clear young voice say that it was best to tell me, as all my life I had always persisted until I knew anything I wanted to know.

Then, my husband holding my hands, they told me.

I was in a Christian Mission hospital. The Shameen doctor, in consultation with the American missionary doctor called to help him, had decided to operate. They could not do it so safely in my own room. So I had been brought here. I was unconscious. There had been no opportunity to consult me. My child was dead. He had been sacrificed to save my life.

July passed and August began, but I had no count of the days as I grasped and then lost hold on happenings. My sister lived at the hospital with me — supposedly to share duty with the English nurse, but if I stirred I found her hand reassuringly on mine. I did not suffer pain, but my fever came and went, complicated by malaria and dysentery and eight stitches in an abdominal cut which would not heal. My bed was on an open verandah. One day I saw bearers carry a stretcher across the hospital court and knew that the little shape beneath the sheet was my daughter.

I insisted that I must have her in my room. She had fever. The doctors available at Canton — the missionary doctors were now away for the summer holidays — could not decide what fever. When my husband came I said that I must take her to Hongkong. He was wan and thin. He confessed that he had wanted to take me to Hongkong but had been told that to move me would be fatal. Yet the populace of Canton were in an angry mood and war might start at any moment. We went to Hongkong.

Sir Edward Stuart-Taylor met us with an ambulance and took us to the hospital on the Peak. Under his care my daughter was running merrily about in one week. That week, August 25, fighting began at Canton, between a group who called themselves the "citizens" and the government.

The "citizens" feared that the Kuomintang had become Communistic and so decided to drive them from government office. But the returned-from-abroad students, tutored by the Russian advisers, incited the laborers to strike. No work was done in Canton. Servants' brooms did not sweep. Men did not load cargoes. Clerks did not sell their employers' goods. Life was paralyzed, and the government blamed the "citizens." Martial law was declared against the "citizens." It was announced that if the merchants did not get the strike called off, the government would not hold themselves responsible for law and order. The strike continued. There was considerable exchange of gunfire. The "citizens" had finally to ask the students to call off the strike. As a result, by early autumn there was a split in the Kuomintang. The anti-Russian-adviser element, headed by Sun Yat-sen's own son, resigned and came to Hongkong.

5

In September we all went up to Canton. When I weighed eighty pounds and could walk alone, my elder sister left us to accept a professorship at the Government University at Nanking. My youngest sister was on her way from America. In the first mail given me after I returned to Shameen was a letter from the editor of the *Atlantic Monthly*, accepting an article entitled "Justice While You Wait," and asking me to send more.

Only one born and bred, as I was, to the traditions of the *Atlantic* can comprehend what that letter meant to me. I had work published, without receipt of a rejection slip, in every other magazine to which I had submitted manuscripts. But for seven years, in a ratio of one manuscript every two months, I had sent articles, poetry, and short stories to the *Atlantic* for consideration. And they had all been returned.

In failure to give the child entrusted to me life, I was crushed by an overwhelming consciousness of my worthlessness. This letter from the *Atlantic* was the tonic I needed to make me well.

6

I seldom left my verandah during the winter of 1925, but Su-ling and Mai-da came often. They told me of the continued quarrel between the radical and conservative elements in the Kuomintang, and the valiant effort Sun Yat-sen made to unite the party. Finally, despairing of unity in the group at Canton, he went north to rally Shanghai and Peking to consciousness of the need to end feudalism and establish a strong national party. He held conferences and interviewed the Elders of the principal clans until, worn out, he finally had to go into the Rockefeller Hospital at Peking.

Trouble brewed in Canton over the succession to party leadership just as soon as the report of his illness came. While he was still alive, the question of relationship with the Christian schools arose. Sun Yat-sen was a Christian, educated in Christian schools. He repudiated his family-arranged marriage and wedded the second daughter of the House of Soong at Shanghai. The House of Soong is the strongest Christian family in China. The parents are active, professing Christians, and the children are educated in Christian schools. So long as Sun Yat-sen was well and active, he protected the Christians. But the radicals in the Kuomintang thought the missionary school curriculum contrary to the principles of free citizenship.

When Sun Yat-sen was on his deathbed, the Russian advisers pushed the young Kuomintang members to demand an investigation of Christianity. Following on this, all Christians were expelled from the party. Next the Kuomintang programme extended to the expulsion of all Christians, of whatever nationality, from Nationalist territory.

Sun Yat-sen died on March 12. It seemed at first as if his death was to result only in war. Kuomintang Party members in all the provinces fell to quarreling over party leadership. There is a Chinese proverb which I often hear: "When the heron and the mussel quarreled, the fisherman got the benefit." In the fable referred to the mussel nipped the heron's beak as the bird was endeavoring to extract him from his shell, and as neither would give way, both were caught by the fisherman. While the Chinese quarreled over party control, the Russian advisers, paid from Moscow, seized control, evolving a party organization which made Michael Borodin party dictator.

But in death Sun Yat-sen's power in China, among the great mass of the populace, suddenly became greater than in life. While the Kuomintang quarreled, I began to hear his name spoken with veneration on the river, in the streets, in the markets, and in courtyards where he had not previously been mentioned. My household helpers, shopkeepers, vendors, and minstrels coupled him with Confucius. His will, after publication in the vernacular press, became almost a religious testament. I found Bald-the-third committing it to memory, word by word. When I questioned her, she said that she did it because it was good.

On the first day that I was strong enough to go to the House of Lin, I saw that Sun Yat-sen's portrait had been hung in the library. The Elder asked us to consider the purposeful, unselfish life of this great republican. Then he read the will: —

"I devoted my life to my country in a futile attempt to raise our nation again to a state of good internal government and a place of independence among world nations. My experience has absolutely convinced me that to attain this goal we must enlist the support of the great mass of the people at home and abroad to work in coöperation with those nations that treat us on a basis of equality.

"The revolutionary movement has not succeeded. It therefore is imperative that all my fellow workers should do their utmost in order to realize my 'Reconstruction Plan,' my 'Outlines of Reconstructive Policies,' and my 'Three Principles of the People.' Fight on, my fellow workers, with renewed vigor, to bring about a People's Convention for the solution of our national problems and to abolish the unequal treaties with foreign nations. These things must be done in the shortest time."

This family reading of the Sun Yat-sen will astonished me. I had read in the daily press that it was thought a forgery framed by the Russian advisers, and spoke of this to Mai-da, as we walked home. She told me coolly that the Chinese people did not think it a forgery but a direct message from the greatest spirit of modern times.

Three days after Sun Yat-sen's death, his former secretary, young Chiang Kai-shek, who was in residence at Canton, led a movement to clear out the Communists and prevent Michael Borodin from returning. Warrants were issued for the arrest of all Communist leaders. Communist pickets were disarmed, and the Russian advisers at Canton sent off on the Russian ships. He accomplished this much before the attention of the Radicals was turned upon him.

But Mr. Borodin returned. He seized control of the Central Executive Committee, and accomplished the expulsion of one hundred and twenty-four conservatives. Holding the Central Committee in his hand, he forced a resolution through the Kuomintang which gave greater freedom to the army being created by the Russian advisers. This done, he made peace with Chiang Kai-shek, astutely convincing that young man, so Su-ling explained, that Russia was friend, not foe.

Then, on May 23, the Central Executive Committee of the Kuomintang passed a resolution stating that it could no longer work with the existing government at Peking and that the only government in the world to-day with which it could work was Soviet Russia.

On the morning of May 31, while I was dressing, Bald-the-third read aloud an account of the Shanghai Municipal Police firing on a Chinese mob, from the vernacular press. In the afternoon I had a letter from Shun-ko.

Shun-ko wrote that the sons from the House of Exile, who had been at boarding school in Shanghai, had been brought home. It had been decided that it was unwise to allow them to stay there longer.

All spring a man named Li Lieh-san, trained in Moscow, had been spurring on boys in the school to agitate against Japan. The House of Exile sons had taken part in the destruction of one of the Nagai Wata Kaisha's Mills, and as Uncle Shao-chun had learned in Peking that the Soviet Ambassador was pushing the circulation of ideas that would soon lead to some serious incident between the Chinese and the Municipal Police they were glad to get the boys home before they were hurt.

On June first, I went to afternoon tea at Su-ling's flat. Mr. Borodin was there, and made a speech. He seized the details of the Shanghai incident to stir the young crowd to an expression of antiforeignism. He urged them to concentrate on Great Britain first, as "she is the most powerful of all the nations, and if she falls, the entire structure of foreign rights and privileges in China will fall. We must focus hatred on England. . . ."

II

THE RISE OF THE CHINESE NATIONALISTS

1

ETURNING from the Swimming Baths, in the torrid forenoon of June 6, my little daughter and I found hundreds of Chinese people pouring over the British Concession bridge from Canton city to Shameen. We counted sixteen bedridden old mothers carried on the backs of strong young daughters-in-law. Scores of rheumatic old men leaned on sons and grandsons. Hastily dressed ladies from luxurious homes hobbled along on "lily" feet, supported by natural-footed women servants. Babies were strapped to the frail shoulders of brothers and sisters of five and six years.

The more able-bodied folk had been left free to transport household goods — charcoal stoves, saucepans, crockery, bundles of chopsticks, foodstuffs, rolls of bedding, bunches of cloth shoes, silver water-pipes, tobacco, crackers for saluting the heavens, lanterns, and kitchen gods snatched from the slumbering peace of kitchen nooks.

"Whither goest thou, Respected Grandfather?" my child asked an old man.

"We flee before the God of War, Small Girl," was his reply.

The refugees were not stopped, and with childlike simplicity the populace took for granted the protection of the French and British flags. All that day and the following they continued to flock to Shameen. They camped in comparative comfort in the cool shade under the wide arms of the banyan trees to wait for accommodation by river boat to the still more certain protection of Hongkong. The island soon became as crowded as a native bazaar. Beds were spread, cook stoves set going, and tea made. Market boats pressed along the Bund, offering foodstuffs and even bedding and clothing at exorbitant prices. The riverside echoed with shrill bargaining.

But among the refugees there were many poor folk. It was a time of broken barriers. Those who had plenty shared of their abundance with those who had nothing. We regular residents on Shameen sent out rice and loaned the use of our water taps. My Pekingese servants donated five catties of charcoal.

Mai-da and Su-ling came to spend the afternoon of the seventh with me. I knew that their trunks were packed and that they were due to go that evening by boat to Shanghai and then overland, to the "House of Exile" to visit their parents. Bald-the-third had been homesick ever since we came south, so we had arranged that she should accompany them north, acting as Mai-da's maid, while Faithful Duck, who dreads travel, should take her place with me.

When Bald saw Su-ling and Mai-da aproaching, she hurried away in excitement to complete her dress for travel. But they had come to tell me that their husbands had requested them to delay their departure. At this time it would appear too much like flight. Their example was needed to help quiet the people.

They said that serious trouble was brewing, and that although they heard little, they knew that there was danger of its spreading in any number of directions. They told me that the Lin clan would remain at Canton; but that patent locks, which did not show from the outside, had been put on the homestead To and From the World Gate and the Gate of Compassion. When she had gone, I found that Mai-da had left patent locks for each of my two gates in my sewing basket.

The refugees on Shameen crowded right up over the lawn to the stone wall which shut them off from my house. From my upper verandah I could hear their conversations without leaving my chair. They sat in groups on the ground, their legs folded under them, and talked of the rising strength of a new party kindled from the embers of the late Dr. Sun Yat-sen's ideals.

They murmured rumors of a fierce conflict with guns soon to take place. They said that the mercenary army had been "even without the grace of lambs — who suck kneeling." They spoke of Dr. Sun Yat-sen suffering silently and dying with "tears flowing into his own stomach" because his hired henchmen had broken the yoke of control to bleed the city privately.

They told tales of the collection of unauthorized taxes at the points of guns, of the emptying of shopkeepers' tills by force, of raids by night to secure the savings of many years from homestead Elders. But they said it was better that things should continue as they were, even with the Yunnanese making such trouble, than that there should be civil war again, with the future uncertain.

"This new party echoes winged words of freedom — how are we, the people, to know the future? Since 1911, by the Republican calendar, we have heard many golden words. Change is not good. It is best always for life to continue in the ways of the past, and then when disaster occurs it is disaster to which we are accustomed."

As fast as opportunity permitted, the refugees moved on to Hongkong, to wait there until the future should be revealed to them.

In the brilliant moonlight, about ten o'clock on Sunday evening, the Nationalists opened fire. On Monday defenses were organized on Shameen as a precaution against a rush of refugees, from whichever side might lose, and against the danger of enemy pursuit.

Tuesday and Wednesday occasional bullets whizzed over the island, — one of them cutting a hole in our neighbor's chimney, — but with no decisive victory on either side. On

Wednesday afternoon three Soviet Russian women, wives of men said to be in charge of the Nationalists' army, came to stay at the Victoria Hotel on Shameen.

So far the Chinese gunboats had manœuvred aimlessly up and down the river, taking no part in the conflict. On Thursday morning my gardener told me that the "navy" had been bought at a good price, paid in silver coin, by the Nationalists. Walking along the Bund just before lunch, I saw a Russian man in civilian clothes summon a sampan to the French Concession steps and go out to a Chinese gunboat in midstream. The boat got up steam and entered into the firing against the "Conservatives."

On Friday, June 12, I was awakened from my afternoon nap by Old Nurse shaking the foot of my bed violently. I sat up and stared at her face, which was overspread with a greenish pallor.

"Kuan Yin, have mercy on my ten parentless children in Peking," she wailed. "The Nationalists have control of the City of Rams. We Chinese know that the Cantonese mass will now rise up and butcher all the Chinese of other provinces found here. The anger of the populace has seethed for many moons against the strangers within their gates — they will not distinguish between the Yunnanese and other folk from other provinces. Murder and death! Ai-yah, ai-yah . . . !"

Unable to stop her wails, I rose and began to dress. I opened the door of my wardrobe and found fat little Chou Chung-hung, son of my cook, wrapped up in the flimsy mass of my favorite chiffon dress. In the bathroom I discovered that Bald-the-third had failed to prepare my bath. I opened the wicker laundry basket to throw in my pyjamas, and saw dirty clothes level with the top. Surprised to find it so full, I plunged my arm in to pull them out and see what it contained — and found Bald hidden there.

As I went through the house I discovered other Chinese members of my household crouched in fear in dark corners.

Chou, the Cook, had pasted thick brown paper over the glass door and the windows of the kitchen. Chang had laid tea in the stuffy, tightly closed dining-room and refused to move it to the usual cool corner of the verandah.

"The Cantonese loves only himself" was the refrain. There was no interest in the theory which I presented in the kitchen — that perhaps it was natural for the Cantonese to dislike the Yunnanese, who had bled their city.

I pushed open a shutter and went out on the verandah. A hundred yards away in the Pearl River floated a badly mutilated body. The kindly old man, Number One of my husband's official chair bearers, had followed me out and begged me to come inside quickly. I asked him why he was at home, and he said that "the master" had refused to take the chair at two o'clock but commanded all the bearers to stay at home. The others were hiding in the coal cellar, but he had come up because he was anxious about the master's lateness.

Just then we heard my husband enter the front door and speak to Chang in his usual quiet voice, asking him to tell the servants that they were all quite safe so long as they did not leave the place. I saw Lee, the gardener, come around and fasten the high iron garden gates with double bolts. My husband said nothing about conditions as we had our tea, but I knew by the slight twitching of his thin face that he must have walked through hell on his way from his office in the centre of Canton city.

From three o'clock that afternoon until Monday morning the Cantonese massacred the "strangers within their gates" with the cruelty of mob insanity. The Yunnanese surrendered their arms when the Nationalists defeated them in battle. They cast aside their uniforms at once to hide their identity, but in the arena of the masses this did not save them from death. All "strangers" alike were the prey of the maddened crowd. Only those who could speak the Cantonese dialect were passed over.

A victim beseeching mercy was cornered, and while he kowtowed the persecutors pierced holes in his head with nails on the end of long sticks. They shrieked with crazy delight at the welts which rose on bambooed flesh. Women and children screamed wild approval when a can of oil was poured over a man and a match set to his trousers. The mob secured flat-bottomed boats and carried on their massacre while drifting before my verandah. They flung dying men into the Back Creek, allowed them to strike out for the Shameen shore, then gently pushed their heads under water with broad boards.

We Westerners sought to intercede in the unequal conflict, and one business man brought three wounded Yunnanese on to the island; but the consuls, knowing the grave danger of Western interference in native affairs, forbade participation in the trouble. On Shameen, nerves were taut as violin strings. Unable to succor the afflicted, we threw ourselves into artificial activities as a means of escape from thought. There was a nervous whirl of dancing, bridge, and high stake poker. Cocktails fomented laughter. Men dreading to be alone filled the Club bar.

Chang, our faithful house steward, who had served my husband loyally since 1904 and twice saved his life, went raving mad and attempted to assassinate all three of us. Frothing at the mouth, he attacked my little daughter with a pair of long scissors, cut me through one cheek, and struggled desperately, slashing right and left, before my husband could control him. He had to be sent away to an insane hospital at Hongkong, babbling that the Cantonese were after us in ten motor cars, and it was many weeks before he recovered.

On Monday morning, June 15, a proclamation was issued from the Government Buildings, announcing that a new government had been formed and that peace and order were now restored for the good of the people.

The massacre stopped. Crowds dissolved. The city waited with empty streets for the first move of the new government.

2

The new government numbered some prominent names among its members. Hu Han-min, a returned student from Japan, later replaced by Eugene Chen, was Minister for Foreign Affairs. Liao Chung-kai, born in San Francisco and well known as a leader of the Canton Labor Party, and, later, Soong Tze-ven, educated in the United States and a brother-in-law to the late Sun Yat-sen, were in charge of Finances. Young and able Chiang Kai-shek was soon to be Commander-in-Chief of the Army. Hsu Him, a teacher at Canton Christian College, headed the Supreme Court. Sun Fo, son of Sun Yat-sen and American schooled, was announced as head of the Department of Reconstruction.

The city was quiet. The seventeenth was the birthday of the wife of the Elder of Lin. I took her a present and stayed for the meal in the Hour of the Snake. Mai-da and Su-ling were there also. After I had said good-bye, my hostess said that she wanted to show me the patchwork pattern of the bed-quilt she had received from the House of Exile. We went to her room. She showed me the quilt — then took my hands tight in hers. She spoke in a low agitated voice.

"Please do not ask any questions, but take the advice of an old woman who loves you — take your child and go home to Pennsylvania."

I thought her old and nervous, but I kissed her and explained that I could not leave my husband any more than Su-ling and Mai-da could advertise the troubled times by leaving theirs.

Mai-da was waiting for me at the gate. "I'll go back with you and help you pack," she said.

In astonishment I stared at her, and said, "You know I am not going away."

"It is these Russian advisers. Rebuffed by the Western countries on whom we counted for assistance in establishing the Republic, our party have made a mistake in accepting the proffered hand of Soviet Russia . . ."

Sometimes my tongue is quicker than my brain. I retorted: "You Chinese do not know what you want. I have met the Russian adviser, Mr. Borodin. I've talked often with him. I think that if the ideals he voices were put to work in every country the world would be a much saner place."

Mai-da's lip curled. "My husband and his confederates are fooled just as you are. Western education must blind folk. We who have been brought up inside courtyard walls, with no broadening advantages, have sharper eyesight. We recognize a flight of stairs leading to calamity."

So we parted at the corner of the Road of Seven Springs and the Street of a Thousand Blessings.

All remained quiet in the city. On the morning of the eighteenth I spent two or three hours roaming about the streets, as is my custom when I have nothing else to do. I stopped to listen to an ardent youth of about fifteen years, wearing foreign clothes, who stood on an overturned fish tub making a speech. His remarks were a stirring appeal to the citizens of China to unite against the "Imperialistic Foreign Devil."

At six o'clock on Sunday morning a small Cantonese boy came into my kitchen court with a red paper, ordering my servants to cease work and march off the island at nine o'clock, and stating that a general strike had been ordered by the Labor Department, as, now that the Yunnanese and other alien Chinese within the province had been punished, the British, French, Americans, and other Westerners were to be disciplined by having their domestic help withdrawn. As my cook, Chou, was now senior of my staff, since Chang's removal to the hospital at Hongkong, he received the order. Fearing the treachery of the Cantonese, he brought it to me.

That morning a general strike of employees working for Westerners went into effect. In long rows the strikers paraded off Shameen, crossed the French Concession bridge, and disappeared into the city. They mostly went in fear, marshaled by the strike masters. My "helpers" were all Pekingese. They dared not trust themselves to the Cantonese. So they hid in a dark storeroom and refused to come out even for food. I carried boiled rice and tea to them twice a day.

After two days of this, my cook, realizing that I was cooking for a household of twelve with the heat at ninety in the shade, volunteered to come from the storeroom and cook as usual if I would move the oil range and necessary utensils into an inner hallway. We enjoyed a delicious meal that day. Old Nurse insisted upon changing the plates to prove her devotion equal to that of her husband. Bald-the-third came out as well and they refused my offered help with the dishes.

At lunch there was much laughing banter about a Chinese anti-Western procession rumored to pass along the Shaki Road about two o'clock. My sister's fiancé lunched with us. He was of the Volunteer Corps assigned to afternoon duty. He went to his post on the Back Creek with unloaded rifle, according to orders. I settled down to read a new novel which had arrived from the States the day before.

I had quite forgotten China and her civil wars when I found a British marine shaking my arm. He ordered me to get my household together and join the women and children, who were to be carried by naval launch out to the American gunboat *Ashville*. Then I became conscious of the sound of battle — the rapid snap-snap of rifle fire, and the rumble of machine guns. My servants pushed in through the door of my bedroom. "The Cantonese are on Shameen!" they wailed hysterically.

My little daughter sat up wide awake, and pulled Old Nurse down on the bed, admonishing her to be quiet. My sister awoke and smacked little fat Chung-hung, who was so astonished that his howl broke in mid-air. I gathered up my child on one hip, thrust the bag which had stood packed and ready into Nurse's left hand, grasped her right one, and sped down to the waiting launch at the foot of our steps. My sister ran beside me with the Chinese baby Chung-hung on her hip, and dragging "lily-foot" Bald-the-third by one hand.

The launch was already well filled with Shameen people. One, an Indian woman, had been struck by a bullet and was bleeding so that her dress was a bright red over the right breast. While bullets splashed in the river around us we sped across to the *Ashville*. Not until we were on board, and my neighbor, Ruth Bender, called my attention to the fact, did my sister or I notice that Chou, my cook, held the scanty rear of my short skirt tight in both fists — and thus was safely quartered with the women and children.

On the *Ashville* we waited for real news of what had happened. Anchored next to us were two Japanese gunboats, and we watched their marines equipped in readiness should they be called. Down river we could see that the marines on the French, Italian, and British gunboats were dressed for action. The American marines fretted to leave the *Ashville* and go to the aid of Shameen civilians. But although bullets continued to splash in the river, the gunboat commanders and the consuls, who were ashore, sent the marines no command.

Finally a ship's officer came aboard with a report. The Chinese procession had passed peacefully at first, headed by school children and representatives of the various guilds, armed with banners declaring their unity with their fellow citizens against the Westerner. Then came a group of very young soldiers, who presented arms quite harmlessly. Then suddenly, from behind them, the first shots were fired toward Shameen — and the trouble was started.

We learned that three bullets had struck the wall beside the chair of an American woman, as she sat on the verandah of the Victoria Hotel, but that she had escaped uninjured. That Mr. Edwardes, Commissioner of Customs, who had lunched with us, had been shot through the leg below the knee. That an elderly Frenchman, much beloved, had been instantly killed while walking near the Catholic church. And that, while the firing continued, it was being carried on from behind, and over women and children, which made the consuls quite certain that the men at the Chinese guns were not of the calibre necessary to charge across the open Back Creek, without cover, as they must do if they fulfilled the declaration of their procession banners and seized Shameen. The doyen of the consuls, Sir James Jamieson, a Britisher born in China, who had spent all his life except his school years among the Chinese, and had won honor among them for scholarship in their language, was of the opinion that the Chinese, even Russian-officered, were certainly of divided mind as to whether they wanted to seize Shameen.

After a while word came that it was over. The procession had run away. No naval help was needed.

About seven o'clock we women were told to go on shore in the naval launches provided, and pack small bags to take with us to Hongkong. We were not asked whether or not we wanted to go to Hongkong; we were simply told that we should be conveyed there by naval escort.

The island was in complete darkness. I groped my way to my house and got out candles. Then I busied myself putting out supplies of matches, food, and towels. At last my husband came in. He told me that I should have to obey the order and go to Hongkong, as Shameen was to be completely evacuated of women and children, and he urged me to return to my home in the States until trouble was over.

Hongkong was full to overflowing with Western refugees from all over South China. Women from Swatow repeated tales of atrocities and of starvation by boycott. People from the interior towns told of mob cruelty and long treks across country to river boats; of red pamphlets inciting the natives to drive out the "Imperialistic Devil" which came in advance of every instance of hostility.

Our friend, Mrs. Hayley Bell, had taken us into her home.

My child was happy with her two children and the English nurse in their nursery. My sister had volunteered for the Mothers' Help Corps of Hongkong and was busy all day, as native nurses had been forced to walk out at the same date as the Shameen strike began. My servants were fitted into Mrs. Bell's household and given work. I spent idle hours doing nothing but roaming about from one person to another, listening to wild talk. Soviet Russia was blamed for the situation. Days passed; the Governments took no action.

People began to say that we were forgotten. Inconvenienced by the servants' strike, the shipping boycott, the fear of financial ruin, the crowded discomfort of the city, they found it hard to understand that local action might only start a more serious war.

Telegraph wires to Canton were cut; mail interrupted. Only an occasional naval boat ran up river carrying food supplies. I knew that in Canton my husband, an official under the Chinese Government, of which the only diplomatically recognized head was the party at Peking, would be going into the city every day, maintaining an attitude of absolute neutrality; demanding of the thousands of Chinese under him in the same service, the same integrity. Carrying on as always, in the midst of civil war as though there were no war. Flying above the Government Buildings the flag of the last internationally recognized Chinese Government, until such time as he received a dispatch stating that another group were now the recognized Chinese Government.

Unable to leave for the United States in contentment, and still more unable to stand the idle uncertainty in Hongkong, I loitered by the wharf one afternoon and watched the preparations on a native boat about to sail. From the dock I asked a Chinese woman passenger where the boat was going. She answered, "Canton."

I have never known fear. Through the years of my life in China I have seen soldiers mistreat their unarmed country-

folk, and I have seen the masses in their passion commit fright-
ful cruelties, but I personally have always been treated gently.
So I handed the woman my purse.

A young girl beside her grasped my wrists and helped me
aboard, as the gangplank had already been drawn in.   The
vessel was packed with Cantonese men, women, and children.
I recognized many faces I had seen among the refugees who
had run away before the Nationalist capture of Canton.
Thus, without premeditated decision, I was among them.

"Thou returnest home, Honored One?" I said to the woman
who held my purse, and who now made room for me to sit
beside her.

"We return — and thou?" she responded.

"I also return to my home," I replied.

The afternoon passed in idle talk in which we women compared ages, told the number of our children, and sympathized
with each other over babies we had lost.   We ate salted watermelon seeds, nibbled chocolate, and quenched our thirst with
fresh lichi fruit.   They smoked their water-pipes and laughed
at my clumsy efforts to keep one alight.   At the Tiger Forts
we discussed the signs of new fortifications — earth had been
thrown up and rough shelters of bamboo placed at intervals
over the hills.   They explained to me that in "old" China the
forts had no guns; only pictures of fierce tigers pasted over the
windows.   My new friends said that these had served as a
device to remind people of the power of the law and had been
better than modern methods.

All about us was the drone of men's voices discussing political events — the discomforts to be borne if there should be a
boycott against all Western imports, and at the same time the
necessity of teaching the Western merchants certain truths
regarding the supremacy of the Celestial People.

Night came.   The boat dropped anchor.   The last breeze
died down.   Mosquitoes came in millions to torment us as we
lay in the sultry heat, crowded so close that our bodies touched.

My nostrils rebelled at the mingled odors of putrid water, sour salt perspiration from my unbathed fellow passengers, and the nasty offal of our cargo of live pigs. From nightfall to dawn the hours dragged to the slow torture of the squeal of

A YOUNG CHINESE MOTHER

thirsty pigs and the raucous voice of a political agitator haranguing the assembled multitude, who were attempting to sleep, on their cowardly submission to the indignity of Western interference in China. My new friend and I moved restlessly in vain attempts to find comfort on the hard boards of the deck. I longed for a drink of water.

With the dawn my eyes rested upon the muddy waters from

which had risen the rancid odor of the night. Lifted high on strong clean stocks above glossy wide leaves, lotus buds were open to the light. They covered all the space to the shore — pure white just touched with shell pink. Dainty beauty rising out of foul slime — each blossom as fragile as a floating wisp of cloud.

When we were within sight of Canton, two launches flying red flags came out and escorted us to a position opposite the Customs wharf. Delegates came aboard from the launches, wearing sleeve bands announcing that they came from the Strikers' Headquarters and the Seamen's Union. They made speeches of greeting, welcoming the returned refugees to their homes and assuring them that all former discomfort had been the fault of the interfering Westerners; that the back of the Western influence in China had been broken by the new Nationalist Party; that all Christian missionaries were to go; and that all teaching of the young was to be done under government control. One of the speakers asked me in English if I was a missionary. I answered "No." He said that it was a good thing, because the new régime would not tolerate Christian teaching.

Another delegate questioned me about my business. I said I was just a housekeeper. A crowd gathered. Someone suggested that I might be a spy. They shook their heads and agreed that there was something wrong about a white woman speaking both Mandarin and the local dialect. The woman who had befriended me said that she thought I was quite harmless, but a little queer in the head. I sat down on a box and waited for the business of disembarking to draw their attention away from me.

The wealthier of my fellow travelers, suspicious of free rides to shore offered by the launches, gave polite evasive answers to the invitation and hired sampans. The launches finally went away with the shabbier of our company. Two slipper-boat women vied with each other for the opportunity to row the last passenger ashore.   The one who lost cried "You take the bread out of my mouth" after her successful rival.

I leaned over the rail and offered her a good sum to convey me to shore.

"I have no leisure," was her calm reply, as she rocked on idle oars.

3

The red flag with the Rising Sun, symbol of the Nationalist government, fastened by the Labor delegates to the mast of our boat, drooped in the breathless heat.   My friendly companions of the voyage had melted away the instant suspicion was pointed to me by the red-necktied committee.   Even the woman who had vouchsafed that I was harmless had gone without farewell.

Red flags hung like strings from buildings on the Canton Bund, and from every junk, steam vessel, flower boat, and sampan in sight.   The boatwoman who had declined to accept me as a passenger lay down in the bottom of her craft.   I saw a bright twist of red cotton cloth plaited in her long black hair.   Then I noticed a similar red in the braids of all the boatwomen.

On the faces of the cook's coolie, the boat's guard, and all the children on near-by craft lay a blank mask of unconcern — which I recognized as intense interest in the drama of a woman stranded in mid-harbor on an empty vessel.   The Chinese are a race of infinite patience — they waited for the next act in the play.   Life among them has taught me the art of patient waiting also.   I stretched out on the top of a long packing box and closed my eyes as though in sleep.

After a weary, apprehensive hour, I saw a trim government launch, flying a new flag — the Nationalist red and white. I signaled it audaciously on the chance that there were no officials on board at six in the morning, and that the men in charge, accustomed to obeying orders and rattled by the rapid changes in authority of recent days, would obey me without question as to my right to give commands.

The launch turned and came up. I rated the boatswain soundly in Mandarin for his slackness in keeping me waiting. He murmured polite apologies. I was bowed aboard. The folk on near-by craft waved me a cheery farewell — the people always like a drama to end with pomp. The launch landed me without question at the steps of the British Concession.

The British sentinel — a young civilian volunteer — stared at me in amazement as I came off the "enemy" launch. Then he recovered his senses sufficiently to repeat the order that no women were allowed to return to Shameen. He had been a guest many times in my house — he could n't very well push me backward into the river. I suggested that he walk to the other end of his beat so that he could not see me come up the steps. He did.

The imported shrubs and flowers which had made Shameen a beautiful garden were dead for lack of watering. The native grass had in one short week grown to a tangled mass. Only the banyan trees, native to the tropics, were in full green. Hastily thrown-up trenches, barbed wire, and walls of sand-bags added to the desolation. The Punjabi troops had been quartered next to our house. They had flung out white tents and tethered black goats on the grass. Bright-turbaned cooks were preparing food over open charcoal burners. A circle of men in khaki shirts, the tails of which were worn outside their breeches, played cards under our flame-of-the-forest trees. Two bearded men were smoking a hookah between them. Several others were enjoying a morning dip from the stone em-bankment in front of our gate: they rubbed their copper bodies with oil from a green bottle until they glistened in the morning sun, then one by one they dived slowly and gracefully into the muddy river. Each swimmer exhibited a different dive.

The flowers of my garden were withered corpses. In the

dusty, littered breakfast room, my husband explained to me the enormity of the offense I had committed in returning to my home when I had been sent away by the British and American Consuls. But a man in our house lay seriously ill. I busied myself with the tasks which a woman can do better than men, and kept quietly out of everyone's way. So they let me stay.

Despite the intense heat — for three months the thermometer hung around ninety — the Western men, shut up on the tiny island, kept up a wonderful spirit. The heads of big businesses, who faced bankruptcy because of the stoppage of trade, whistled as they trundled home their daily supply of food from the distributing station and prepared it in stifling kitchens. They kept up their morale, their clothes washed, their faces shaved; they took pride in inventing edible dishes out of available ingredients, and they accepted without grumbling the heavy community duties assigned them by the Emergency Council.

Once we did not have bread or flour for eight days. Fruit, fowl, and green vegetables were a far-between luxury sent up from Hongkong when possible, but there was a scarcity there also because of the antiforeign boycott. Down the river past us floated flat-bottomed craft piled high with the rich produce of Kwangtung Province: plump young chickens and ducks, high pyramids of juicy oranges, pale yellow, much-needed lemons, baskets of papayas, spinach, lettuce, new potatoes, and snowy cauliflowers — all those foods that the palate, fed too long on salt and storage meats and canned stuffs, craves.

Once, just at twilight, I sat alone on the steps of the deserted boathouse. A boat loaded with golden papayas floated slowly downstream, poled by a kind-faced old man. Scarce above a whisper I bartered with him. His boat drew close. A coin passed from my hand to his. When he had gone two ripe melons lay under the fold of my skirt.

Many months later I learned that the poor old man paid with his life for that transgression of the boycott against

Westerners.   Convicted in the Hall of Justice, he was wrapped
with thin wire and laid out in the sun to die of slow strangulation.   A sampan woman whom neither of us noticed made the
charge against him.

Long, monotonous days passed.   The Chinese Nationalist
officials, still uncertain of their own saddle, refused to treat
with the Western world.   Internal disruption claimed their
attention, and with canny wisdom they knew that only by
distracting the attention of the multitude with the decoy of a
common Western enemy could they mould a national unity.

On July 29 Michael Borodin, the Russian from Moscow,
was announced openly as the chief adviser to the Government.
Mr. Norman, an American and formerly adviser to Sun Yat-
sen, sailed for home.   On the morning of August 1, five hundred thousand dollars consigned from Russia were brought by
ship to Whampao, to aid the Nationalist Party.   A day later,
ships laden with much-needed oil arrived from the Black Sea.

On August 4 an order was issued by the newly formed Central Bank of China that henceforth only notes issued by that
bank would be legal tender in South China.   The Telegraphs,
Customs, Railways, and Post Offices were directed to accept
only such notes after the fifteenth.   The order had no authority
from Peking, but such was the strength of the rising Nationalist Party that it was put into effect.   The Bank redeemed its
notes daily with the Posts and Customs, giving them the
face value in silver.   By making the paper the only acceptable tender in such places of public service the government believed they would win the populace to a trust in the
Nationalist notes.

New import duties were declared, in addition to the regular
Customs tariff.   No boat was allowed to move cargo until these
duties were paid.   Contrary to the regulation that all Customs
revenue be sent to Peking, the local party declared its right to
put them into their coffers.   Thus the long battle between the
Customs authorities and the Nationalists was inaugurated.

Unsigned letters began to reach Shameen showing great ap-prehension on the part of certain Chinese Conservatives, and calling upon the Foreign Powers to use their "magnificent" battleships to "break the back of the bloodsucking, upstart" Nationalist Party.

Letters came also from servants who had left their jobs at the instigation of the general strike of June 21. They told of the horrors of road building, under Russian overseers, into which they had been conscripted; they complained that they were paid no wages and given only one small bowl of rice a day. They begged their "masters" to find a way to smuggle them back to the island.

On August 18, with the heat at ninety-nine degrees, the workers in the native waterworks, which supplies the entire city, walked out in protest against an order of the Nationalist government. We on Shameen had our own waterworks, manned by Westerners. But the Chinese people were reduced to carrying water from the river, which is the emptying place for sewage. An epidemic of typhoid broke out. People died by the hundreds.

On August 21, Liao Chung-kai, the "strong man" of the Nationalist government, was shot as he left a public meeting. News travels on wings in China. There was a difference in attitude at once on the part of the boat people in front of our house. For the first time since my return to Shameen they passed the time of day with me as I watered the flowers in my garden. They commented upon my clean starched frock, and asked me if I had laundered it myself. They explained as carefully as though I knew nothing of the Farmer's Calendar that *Chu Shu* or the "end of the great heat" was due in two days.

On the afternoon of *Chu Shu* I ventured to suggest that it would give me great pleasure if one of them had "leisure" to row me across the river to the White Heron's Nest, so that I might have a change of air and take tea with some friends there.   Several of the sampan women exchanged glances, but all shook their heads.   An hour later, however, the tap-tap-tap of oars on the stone steps below my verandah called me to conference with one of them.

She said that she had occasion to cross the river, and as I was of no weight at all I might just as well sit out of sight under the hood of her boat.

I went to Su-ling's house.   Su-ling gave me tea.   I heard that a group within the Nationalist Party, including Chiang Kai-shek, were somewhat afraid that the Russian Soviet advisers were not sincere concerning the Chinese purpose.   There was suspicion that the Russians were cleverly working to use the Chinese people as tools of the World Revolution.   The wives of the Russian advisers were known to have packed their personal belongings in readiness for flight if necessary, and were keeping out of sight.

Su-ling told me that both C. C. Wu and Mai-da's husband had pleaded within the party all the forenoon before the Shaki procession and the planned firing against Shameen.   And that the following day Mai-da's husband had told her to pack to go home, as the health of his mother called them north.   So they had gone.

A week after my visit to Su-ling, I received a check from the *Atlantic Monthly* for my second contribution.   It was for the exact amount for which Fong, the dealer in "beauty," had promised me an old Chinese painting which I coveted.   Elated by my secret journey abroad the previous week, I cashed my check at the National City Bank and journeyed under the hood of the friendly sampan to the Street of a Thousand Blessings.

Canton presented much the same appearance as ten weeks previously, except that the streets were cleaner, the police in new uniforms with new revolvers, and the river front picketed by men in blue costume with red arm bands — the new examiners of entering and departing goods.

Seemingly no one took any notice of me. In the Street of the Water Lily Well I met a German woman of my acquaintance, accompanied by her husband. They said that they had lived unmolested through the trouble, in their home in the heart of the city; but that all Germans had been given arm bands to wear so that the common people would know that they belonged to a Western country whose foreign privileges in China had been abolished.

They told me that there were possibly two hundred and fifty young foreign-educated Chinese men and women gathered in Canton city — all arrivals within the last two months, drawn there by the new social freedom as much as by political feeling. These young people held all sorts of offices. Most of them came of good families and gave their services as volunteers. They worked by day and enjoyed themselves when off duty in dancing and in parties, much the same as in Western countries.

Just after I left these Germans I came upon a crowd gathered about a street orator. The speaker was a pretty young girl in Chinese dress. She spoke to the people in cultured Mandarin about the beauty and the natural wealth of their country. A murmur stirred the crowd. A man pushed his way to the front. He explained to her that the people were so badly educated that they could only understand the local dialect. She explained that she knew not one word of Cantonese and could lecture only in the northern dialect. He offered himself as interpreter. She accepted his offer. The lecture proceeded.

She called to the people to rally around the Nationalist standard and throw off the shackles of the military governors and their imperialistic Western allies. She assured the crowd of the purity of the Nationalist's purpose. The crowd began to drift away.

Then the interpreter ceased to interpret truthfully — he threw in human interest to draw the crowd back to attention. He said that what was wanted was for the people to punish

Wong, the cigarette vendor at the near-by corner, for having wares with "British-made" stamped on them.   Interest picked up at once.   The first stone was thrown at Wong.   His goods were trampled underfoot.   He was surrounded and mauled about.   The new police stood at ease, offering no interference. I went quickly on to the shelter of Fong's shop.

When I went to live at Nanking, I took with me a letter of introduction from Fong, the Cantonese ivory dealer at Peking, to Fong, the Cantonese dealer in ivory and "other treasures of charm" at Nanking.   When my husband was transferred south, I carried a letter from Fong at Nanking to Fong the clansman at Canton.

Fong at Canton had been paternally kind, so that I had felt that he was not just a merchant from whom I occasionally bought goods.   He had invited me to his New Year celebration in honor of the God of Wealth.   His wife had presented my daughter with a pair of embroidered shoes on her birthday.

He had always served me personally when I went into his shop.   But this day his lowest clerk asked my desire.   I could see Fong drinking tea alone in his office.   I asked the clerk to carry my name to him.   I knew that Fong saw me through the door as the clerk passed in.   The clerk came back with word that the master had nothing worthy of my notice.

On the wall in front of me hung the painting I had been promised.

I knew Chinese etiquette well enough to feel this treatment like a slap in the face.

I left the shop with tears smarting in my eyes.   At the Flowing Flowers Bridge, I saw the young Chinese poetess whose name in English is Little White Jade.   I hastened to overtake her to tell her how much I had enjoyed her verses in the last number of the *Hsiao Bo*.   She returned my greeting with an icy stare and went quickly down a byway.

At the water front I was allowed to depart in peace after my pockets and my handbag had been carefully searched by the blue-clad pickets. They counted my money and returned it to my purse. They turned around in every possible direction a piece of paper found in my pocket. One of them put on a pair of horn-rimmed spectacles and peered at it upside down. In the end he said that he would have to retain it. It was a list of my menus for the week.

I did not get into the city again until November. Someone had reported to my husband that I had left the island on two occasions. And I was forbidden to venture abroad again under threat of being sent immediately to Philadelphia if I did. So although my husband went into the city each day, I stayed inside the high barbed-wire barriers on Shameen, except for a trip by launch to Hongkong on which he took me along.

4

The British boycott continued. But the Chinese desired Western products, to which they had become accustomed by some centuries of trade. The Nationalist Party found it impossible to decree the use of only native goods. So finally any vessel was allowed to do business so long as it paid the duties and had not put in at any British port on the way to China. The harbor was soon busy with the coming and the going of Norwegian, American, French, Portuguese, Italian, and Russian ships.

The Nationalists chose to use the rallying cry against the British, but they permitted British firms to do business — even encouraged them, so long as they acted under Chinese names.

At last the barriers to the gates of the French and the British Concessions were opened. American, French, and British women returned to their homes. Missionaries came back and took up the difficult task of carrying on their work in the face of government interference and supervision. Things took on the face of normal life — with the exception that the order forbidding servants to work for Westerners was enforced. Later this order was slackened in cases where a heavy contribution was made monthly to the Labor division of the Nationalist Party.

My husband was told that as a Chinese Government official he need not do without servants, but, as earlier, he answered that we did not need them until our countrymen had them also. As it happened we did very well with a French maid.

Pickets continued to search everyone who went into the city. I foolishly purchased some roses to decorate my house for Christmas. The picket took them gently away from me and threw them into the Back Creek. He told me, almost sadly, that "the wives of barbarian devils must not barter with the inhabitants of the Celestial land."

An Englishman caught attempting to smuggle an old servant back to his house, in answer to a piteous letter, was led through the streets with a chain halter on his face and head, and tied up in a cage. The populace were invited to come and jeer at him. But he had to stay in the cage only one night. He was released unhurt the following day at Sir James Jamieson's request. The offending servant was hung up by the thumbs and beaten to death, by order of the Laborers' Court of Justice.

On January 1, 1926, the Nationalist government circulated a printed report showing a credit balance in their finances and a statement that all employees of the government — including teachers, clerks, and soldiers — had been paid regularly since the party came into power. They truthfully stated that they were the only party since the Revolution in 1911 who had accomplished such a feat. They showed that a definite sum was regularly applied to the education of the people concerning the Nationalists' movement, and that propagandists trained in publicity were sent out systematically in advance of the army, to convince the people of the high purpose of the cause and to enlist support without bloodshed.

On the twenty-seventh, Mai-da and her daughter and servants returned to Canton, following her husband, who had been invited to return to his former post. She brought messages and gifts from the House of Exile for both Su-ling and myself.

In February I heard from an authoritative source within the Nationalist Party that a split between the left and right wings of the party had been averted by the timely arrival of Mrs. Sun Yat-sen from Shanghai. On election day she mounted a platform in the room where the party were assembled and made a passionate appeal to both sides to hold fast to the ideals of their departed leader, Sun Yat-sen, and forget slight personal differences. She was supported by her stepson, Sun Fo.

Near the end of the month I was invited to a party at the home of one of the Nationalist officials. It proved to be an afternoon tea dance. The house was filled with young officers and officials, both Russian and Chinese, some in long colorful silk gowns and some in smart uniforms — all dancing Western dances with self-possessed young Chinese women, both maids and matrons. The young women had shingled heads, Eton crops, straight pagelike bobs; heads with long braids wound in smooth coronets; heads with firmly set marcel waves; and heads smartly chic, yet dressed in Chinese fashion with flowers caught in shining ebony nape coils. Their dancing feet were clad in dainty high-heeled shoes.

The note of the party was youth, self-confident; a little hard; very practical beneath a dash of devil-may-care. They had set up a government and run it for several months. Life was good. They had a flaming ideal for which to live. Before them lay the whole of China — a wondrous unconquered adventure.

Keeping pace with their banter were half-spoken dreams of the future when the Nationalist flag should wave over all China and they would dance in the ancient city of the Mings,

Nanking, proclaiming it again the "Golden City" and making it their capital.

Two weeks later I accepted an invitation to lunch with an elderly Syrian Jew who has dwelt for many years in Canton city. I knew him to be a merchant much respected by the Chinese people. With his halo of abundant white hair, he is well known in the streets and his pithy speech is often quoted by tea-shop minstrels. I had heard in Western circles on Shameen, and in Hongkong, that the native merchants were suffering great loss in trade — in fact were facing bankruptcy — because of the hostilities against the Westerners and the absence of tourists. He had promised to take me on a tour which would disprove this.

We went first to the Pearl Market, which had been closed during the previous two years. The shops were open. Elaborately clad women sat at velvet-covered tables making their selections. We were shown pearls of a milky beauty which took on the warm color of flesh when held in the palm. We saw necklaces worth thousands of dollars, matched in marvelous perfection.

"There is law and order under the new régime — we no longer need to hide our treasures," one merchant stated.

We went to the Street of Jade. Jade is the most sought-after of all ornaments by the Chinese. Here again was the same pageant — men and women making their selections.

"Chinese customers are buying again because they no longer fear to possess beautiful things. Formerly they feared looting and wholesale robbery. We have brought up rare jade from the underground cellars where it has lain buried for years," a shopkeeper said.

We went through Blackwood Street. The wares usually displayed to catch the eye of tourists were gone. In their place were rare pieces fashioned to conform to Chinese use. I ran my hand over the satiny surface of a long table. The figures on it were carved three inches deep.

"There is no work like this done now," the blackwood dealer said. "This new age has no artistic patience."

"But this is the altar table from the Temple of Five Hundred Buddhas!" I exclaimed.

"You have recognized it," he replied. "The temple is to be abolished — the new régime does not believe in religion. The furnishings have nearly all been disposed of. The money goes into the coffers of the Nationalists."

"But what has happened to the kindly abbot and his priests?"

"Abbots, like blind minstrels and fortune tellers, must now earn their livelihood by practical trades, according to the decree of the Nationalist government. I, too, remember that this abbot was a sweet spirit. I have not heard what happened to him — but he has gone."

After lunch my Syrian friend took me out to what was formerly the golf course of our Western Club. It had been taken as a drilling ground for the Nationalist army. Officered by Russians, and clad in well-tailored uniforms and smartly trained, the soldiers were an impressive sight.

"It is a small army to conquer all China," I said to the Chinese man who accompanied us.

He laughed. "This is only a part of Chiang Kai-shek's army — yet you have spoken the truth. The Nationalist army is a small force with which to conquer all China. It is not by military force but by propaganda that the Nationalists plan to conquer our land province by province. The army will come up behind to give form to the advance. It is wise at this time to have it small. China has been bled too long by unruly troops. While the army is small it can be well controlled, well clad, and well paid. Then the trail of our conquests need not be dirtied by looting or by mutiny and desertion."

During this winter we heard much concerning the movement of money. The remittances to Canton homesteads by

Chinese abroad, from the States, Australia, the Straits Settlements, and England, kept the usual level, which averages about ninety million dollars a year in postal money orders and bank drafts. These are often as low as one dollar, and rarely larger than one hundred. They are the regular contributions towards homestead fortunes from members of families in business abroad.

There were generous donations to the Nationalist Party from Russia. And there was a new movement of money to the Western world, money dispatched in large drafts — the prudent action of young Western-educated Nationalist officials, who thus in their finance programme prepared a solid defense against future civic upheaval by the salting away of millions of dollars in securities in France, the United States, Canada, and England. This has proved a long-sighted wisdom which has provided the means for the furtherance of party aims through all the civil turbulence since and has given a sounder financial base to these officials than any others in China have yet possessed.

Shopping at Canton, amid anti-Westernism, continued so difficult that on March 19 I took my rapidly growing daughter to Shanghai to get her some needed clothes. My husband accompanied me as far as Hongkong. We went out to the boat the night before, to save the trouble of coming aboard in the early morning. About six o'clock next morning I heard a lot of noise outside and peeped through my cabin window. I saw a group of people coming on board from a launch flying the red flag.

Mrs. Sun Yat-sen came first. Then Sun Fo, her stepson. Next came Mr. Cohen, a Russian Jew, formerly in Sun Yat-sen's personal bodyguard, who is reputed to be able to throw two coins in the air, draw two pistols from concealed pockets inside his coat, and shoot a hole through each of the coins before they touch the ground. And after him Mrs. Sun Yet-sen's brother, T. V. Soong, the Minister of Finance, followed by two

young women whom I did not know.   Coolies from the launch
lifted two heavy boxes after them.

I woke my husband to tell him what I had seen.   He did
not show any particular interest.

"But they preach a British boycott," I protested.   "They
signed the order forbidding any vessel that touched at a British port to drop anchor in Canton harbor.   This boat moves

HONGKONG

only under British naval protection.   It carries armed British
guards.   And it is going to Hongkong."

"British hostility is only a political ruse to create support
for the Nationalist Party.   They have to have an 'enemy' for
their cause, or they cannot collect the attention of the populace.
That does not mean that the Nationalists have any personal
feeling which prevents them from traveling to Hongkong as
guests under the British flag, or proceeding on to Shanghai, as
I expect these people intend to do, on a British ship.   It is the
safest and most comfortable way to travel."

"Won't the captain put them off?"

"Put them off?   What in thunder would the captain put
them off for?"

"Because of the anti-British boycott, because of those vulgar
posters at street corners, because of those handbooks stating
that the purposes of both the British merchants and missionaries are vile!"

My husband smiled at me.

"But how can they feel safe here?" I ventured as I rang for tea.

"Safe?" He was puzzled. "Of course they feel safe. The Chinese are a people of long memory. They know that we are not chameleons. Although they are making us the goat just now, they know that they can trust themselves to our care, because they know that we never act until we have convinced ourselves that the blow is for justice, and we never strike, even then, until we have given our foe ample warning of our intent. We have not taken up the challenge and accepted the Nationalist Party as our foe. I do not think England will need to do that; the Chinese are intelligent. They will understand Russia before long."

They journeyed with us. Playing bridge, eating British food, and chatting genially — with their publicly declared political enemies.

They transhipped at Hongkong on to the *Empress of Asia*. As I did. So we traveled up to Shanghai together, and I could write back and tell my husband that his prophecy was correct.

5

The Lin medicine shops are all managed by Lins, exiled from home for that purpose. All the buying of the products used in the compounding of the medicine is done by Lins who travel to the far borders of China to secure what is needed. So the men of the family are scattered over all the provinces. They write frequent letters home.

The Elder of Lin believes that all things of concern to the exile are of concern to each member of the House. Business reports are not kept secret. Here, in the House of Exile, and among my own servants, I always find the feeling that women are more prudent in money matters than men and quicker to see the way to monetary advantage. From one who lives quietly inside the home wall may come wisdom which will help the man in the outside world who is too close to a problem to be able to judge it sagely.

So the letters "from the world" are read aloud in the library court. Their contents are discussed. During my years at Canton, so many paragraphs in these letters related incidents in civil war between military overlords that I felt all China to be convulsed by battle. The policy of the House of Lin was to maintain the business at as comfortable a compromise as possible, and to pay such tribute as they must to whoever won in each conflict. They put these items down on the cost side of the business ledger and charged accordingly for their medicines.

Peking was the Capital of China according to the acknowledgement of the Western Powers. But the President changed with surprising frequence and according to the Lin letters was never other than just the appointee of the particular war lord holding that district at the moment.

In the provinces, whatever man had sufficient private army to seize the "seal of office" was governor. The Lin in Szechuan wrote, in April 1926, that there were six governors dividing that province between them, and told how the House of Chen, dealers in silks, had found it expedient to marry a daughter to each of these war lords so as to keep their inter-provincial taxes sufficiently low to be able to continue business.

The various battles, as explained in the letters from different places, were not serious warfare as war is fought in the Western world. Few of the combatants were killed. Usually as soon as the soldiers under one flag saw that their general was losing, they threw down his colors and went over to the other side.

There was compromise and companionable tea-drinking between the officers. Frequently there was no battle at all. The man holding the "seal of office" often accepted a price to hand it to the general marching against him. It was customary for the winning general to leave a "peace gate" open through which the losing general could depart. This, so the Elder of Lin explained when I was puzzled about it, has been the polite custom in China for centuries. A man who disregards it is a man of no breeding or education.

The Lin men often wrote that the departed governor and the new governor were of equal merit. It was not important which ruled. But in each locality where there was a Western concession, they advised that the Lin shop be maintained in the concession, since the taxes were exceedingly moderate and so regular that they could always be planned for in advance.

The shackle on trade in Chinese territory was caused by the uncertain amount of the taxes and the fact that they were often collected at the point of the bayonet. A governor sure of continuance in office was careful not to paralyze business entirely. But a governor with fear that he had but a short time in office took all that he could grasp from the banks, the merchants, the families, and the guilds, as he had no concern for their future.

The Lins repeatedly complained that it was difficult in this era to secure cheap labor in the way of boy apprentices. War lords recruited their armies by seizing boys between the ages of twelve and sixteen. Families were reluctant to put their sons out to apprenticeship, even though the apprenticeship offered a good future, as they were afraid to have them outside the protection of the homestead wall, lest they be taken to be soldiers before their characters were formed.

China was named Republic. But although I heard details of life in many districts in all the twenty-one provinces, I never heard mention of a franchise. When I had been six years in China I began to wonder why I never heard anything about any elections or knew of anyone voting. I wrote home to the House of Exile about it, and I asked about it in the library court one afternoon when we were gathered about the Elder.

Shun-ko and the Elder of Lin answered me similarly. They both said that in China the word "Republic" merely means not having a monarch on the throne. It does not mean a popular franchise or even a vote to each family or to each guild.　It has no kinship with the word as defined in a Western dictionary.

With the rise of the Nationalist Party there was no change in interpretation of the word "Republic."　Citizens in Nationalist territory were not given the vote.　While flying the new flag, homestead families kept their To and From the World Doors close-barred.　Merchants and bankers were wary of the Russian-advised Kuomintang.　Michael Borodin won the enthusiastic support of the young Western-educated men and women and was able to use them in an organization which also utilized ruffians from the lowest city alleys.　He was a genius of organization and gave the party coherence and forward force such as no Chinese party had yet possessed.　But the Family Elders and the middle-aged business men held aloof, judging him Russia's tool, not China's friend.

From the beginning of Mr. Borodin's dictatorship, indignities were inflicted on Westerners in all territory as it came under Nationalistic control.　At Swatow, as at Canton, not only were Westerners forbidden to buy food or other products, but any Chinese family known to aid a Westerner was punished by having the first of its members to go into the street arrested by ruffians, tried in the National Hall of Justice, and condemned to some torturous death.　The Masonic Hall was looted.　The Anglo-Chinese College was seized and used for soldiers' barracks and horse stables.　The British Consul was attacked and beaten with bamboos when removing Communist posters from the wall of the Consulate.

At Wuchow, the Memorial Hospital, an American Missionary institution, was attacked, the Christians escaping from the town only because of the arrival of an American gunboat. At Nanning the churches were forbidden to hold services and all Christians persecuted.　At Pakhoi the Western cemetery was desecrated.

These incidents, especially the impious desecration of graves, so the Lady of Lin informed me, were viewed with serious concern by all prudent clans. A party that perpetrated such outrages could be of no good to China.

But Borodin and his colleagues were clever men. He explained the need to drive the Westerners out of China so well that the young people were convinced of his wisdom. He was shrewd and careful. He kept his workers occupied in work suitable to the temperament of each. Sensitive young folk were not sent where they saw outrage. In Su-ling's drawing-room he pooh-poohed the vernacular press reports that such things occurred; or that, if they did, they were in any way connected with the Kuomintang. He used to say that such incidents, if true, were the acts of the populace and a sign of popular uprising against the oppressive imperialism of the Western nations.

6

In the autumn I had to go to England. I expected to be away from China a short time; but I was taken ill in London, and it was after New Year 1927 before I could plan to return. In the meantime, my husband was transferred to Tientsin.

Just before I sailed, I received a letter from Ching-mei, — one of the twins, — who, since her marriage, lived at Tientsin. She wrote: —

The Nationalists are moving steadily northward. They have kept their planned formation — orators and publicists to the fore, assisted by young volunteers, both boys and girls, who distribute handbooks to Village Elders and stick posters on courtyard walls.

Then the army, coming in the rear to establish material government in the territory, made a spiritual conquest as well. Thus there are few battles, and funds are not wasted in purchasing ammunition. So the government is able to clothe and feed the soldiers. And the people are delighted when they discover that in the Nationalist Army "pay day" is not permission for the soldiers to loot the countryside for twenty-four hours, as has formerly been the custom in China, but government money spent in local shops to the enrichment of the countryside.

We hope that within twelve moons the Nationalists will control Tientsin. Many of their propagandists have already arrived. The district is well honeycombed for the military advance.

I have joined the Nationalist Party — but I cannot expect you, who must look at the world always through Western spectacles, to understand. There will probably be some travail before the Nationalist flag waves over all the provinces and the government is solidly established. But, according to the sage proverb, "There must be high wind in spring if there is to be good gentle rain in summer to nourish an abundant harvest to fill the granaries for winter."

We have seen your husband twice at public receptions since he was transferred here, but have not talked with him. He looks well, and I read in the vernacular press that he had beaten a Japanese Davis Cup player in a tennis competition — which is a good thing, as the Japanese are wearing hats too tall for them. I think this propaganda against Great Britain a mistake. It should be against Japan.

III

WIND IN SPRING

1

M Y husband sent me a cable in care of the British steamship on which I had passage. He announced that he had just received my letter declaring my intention to embark for China. He advised me that all Western women and children were being sent to their home countries as rapidly as passage could be secured for them. He forbade me to return until he advised me that China was a safe place in which to reside.

I waited in Italy to collect my mind.

The orange trees were in bloom on the hills above Rapallo. The sea came in over the warm yellow sand in blue waves. But the Italian press reported the clever transfer of authority in the Nationalist Party from the Kuomintang to the Communists, with the result that the Russians were masters of the Chinese situation and had instigated a reign of Red terror. Every edition reported outrages against Westerners and unmerciful persecution of the Chinese bourgeoisie; detailed incidents of brutal attacks on Chinese ladies caught outside their homestead walls, and food boycotts by which too haughty families were starved into submission; told of merchants and bankers made to give over their fortunes by the "checkerboard," — a punishment in which a cubic inch of flesh is cut from the victim daily until he either does as requested or dies, — and punishments inflicted on the "bright young people who have been made Borodin's tool" — these I concluded to be Su-ling's crowd — when they dared to question a command.

I had learned to love the folk in the House of Lin at Canton. They were now bourgeoisie in the Nationalist territory. Suling, impudent under authority, was somewhere in the Nationalist movement — if not already chained in some damp cellar. The House of Exile, residence of my mother by affection, was in the direct march to Peking, the Nationalist objective.

My husband followed his harsh cable with a gentle cable. He suggested that I visit Florence, Venice, and Rome. The idea was kind. But I had no heart for those places. My days were a feverish travel from news-seller to news-seller in search of the latest reports from China in every language I could read. My nights were sleepless.

Letters arrived. I was afraid to open them. When I had read them, even though assured that at the hour of writing my correspondent was safe, my reason reminded me that weeks had passed and anything might have happened since then. I cabled Mai-da. First to one place and then to others. When I had tried five possible addresses and got no reply, I cabled Shun-ko. I could get no answer from Shun-ko. I was frantic.

Then my young sister, Anne, who had gone home from Canton to attend Swarthmore College, suddenly arrived in Italy. Her fiancé was at Canton, and she was en route to Canton. Anne believes, and practises, that one should know what one wants and then do it. Before she had taken off her hat, she had convinced me that I was a doddering fool to loiter in Italy when I wanted to be close to people in China.

We had a hasty lunch and went up to Genoa. We sailed that same evening, March 2, on the S.S. *Saarbrücken* of the Norddeutscher Lloyd line. We chose a German vessel because Germany's treaty rights in China were abolished during the European War, and so we concluded that a German vessel would possibly be admitted, even if by the time we arrived all "imperialistic" vessels were forbidden anchorage in Chinese harbors.

The last letter I had received from Mai-da was dated December 29.

We are now here at the ancient city of Nanchang, the capital of a province which is only important because it serves as a corridor between the Yangtze and Canton. We came from Hankow rather hastily. At least we departed without luggage, although my brother Peng-wen now tells me that our departure had been pending for some time. My husband returned from an interview with Mr. Borodin, — to whom he went to protest against the policy at Hankow, which he does not consider a credit to the Nationalist Party, — and asked me to put on my cloak and walk with him. I was beating honey to make sweets for the Kitchen God's festival, but he spoke so seriously that I put the bowl down and came.

My brother Peng-wen was waiting at our To and From the World Door when we came out. Neither man explained. Peng-wen just greeted me, and we all walked down to the river and got into a boat. We traveled until we arrived here, where we joined Chiang Kai-shek and others of the Kuomintang who have resigned from the "Hankow Group." While the men discuss politics, I am occupied doing what I can to replace our abandoned wardrobes.

In the January number of a new magazine published at Shanghai, I had read: —

No one can be blind to Mr. Borodin's capacity and brilliance. His capable reorganization of the Party, his construction of a workable commissary system, and his skillful application of Western revolutionary tactics in China are not to be ignored in judgment of him.

But he is a foreigner. Opposition to foreign domination is too deep-rooted in us for us to tolerate Russian domination. Sun Yat-sen trusted Michael Borodin. But when Michael Borodin was with Sun Yat-sen he was a quiet personality. In Canton, at the beginning of the rise of the Nationalist Party, Mr. Borodin was careful. Now, as the Nationalist movement has conquered province after province, he has changed. He makes frequent public addresses. He uses his voice as if it were the voice of the Chinese people. He dictates policies.

Mr. Borodin misjudges us. We are not a peasant race. We have no class groaning under centuries of oppression, as in Russia. We Chinese people are an intellectual people. Brain with us is not limited to any particular group. Our aristocracy has never, in the many centuries of our recorded history, been other than an intellectual aristocracy. Right to position has never been an inherited right, but a right won in each generation by scholarship — the competition open to all sons, regardless of the father's occupation. The son of a coolie has been born with the brain to win the governorship of a province, and the son of a premier has earned his livelihood in the shafts of a rickshaw. According to our custom, the highest offices in our land have belonged to the most intelligent people. So what need have we of an "adviser" schooled in Russian revolutionary methods? Is it not time that Michael Borodin's luggage was packed?

We are, in this era, confounded by the necessity to adjust our country to world conditions, but no foreigner can help us. No foreigner can understand us, because no outsider can know our history or our system of homestead government, which is the government of the longest world history and the base of all Chinese government. Our Family Government is a system of compromise. Action occurs only when the clan are *agreed* to be unanimous in action. If there is a protesting voice in the Hall of Gathering, the matter proposed is dropped.

Even under a Son of Heaven, in every dynasty, we each had the right to memorialize the throne regarding an edict. To outsiders we appear docile under government, because we are a people who like to abide peacefully by rules so long as they do not confound our reason. But a House or a Guild is soon broken up by an attempted dictatorship against which there can be no question. The members do not make a fuss. They assume an austere reserve and leave the Homestead or the Guild.

In recent weeks, Kuomintang members have been leaving Hankow, the Nationalist Party capital. To-day there is scarcely an important or well-known name there. Many have gone to their homesteads. Others have come into the International Settlement at Shanghai. A goodly number are reported to be gathering round young Chiang Kai-shek, who is resting at Nanchang.

In the London *Morning Post,* I had read a speech delivered by the British Secretary of State for Foreign Affairs, in the House of Commons: —

On the morning of January 3 a mob, after listening to inflammatory speeches made by a Chinese member of the National Government and by Borodin, tried to enter the British Concession. During the afternoon the available naval ratings were landed and employed, with thirty-five Marines who had already gone ashore, to protect the Concession. During the whole afternoon they were subjected to a fusillade of bricks and stones. They never fired a single shot. Some of them were knocked down and injured. There had to be a bayonet charge to rescue them, and in the course of the bayonet charge two Chinese were wounded, but not one Chinese was killed. By evening, these small naval forces were withdrawn to their ships or headquarters on shore, where they were held in readiness during the night. The Volunteer Force of the Concession and Indian Concession Police had been employed all day in maintaining order inside the Concession.

On the next morning, January 4, the Rear Admiral arranged with the Chinese Authorities that Chinese troops should guard the boundary of the Concession, on the understanding that the British Naval forces should be withdrawn. The Chinese did not properly carry out their part of this arrangement, for, on the 4th and 5th, a violent mob entered the Concession and the assistance of Chinese and the military police had again to be called in. The fact of the matter was that it was a mob which you could not control without firing, but our officers refrained from giving the order to fire, in order not to create just that kind of incident for which the mob had been incited and provoked. . . . I perhaps ought to say that something very similar to that mob violence and loot has taken place at Kiukiang, and Kiukiang has been evacuated by us in order not to have to fire upon the Chinese.

Soon after we boarded the *Saarbrücken,* we saw a Chinese girl and boy reading our luggage labels. The two were so like as to be unmistakably sister and brother. We went and spoke to them. They were a son and daughter of the House of Chan, at Kiukiang, and had been at school in Berlin. They expressed pleasure that we were returning to China.

"We read in the Berlin newspaper," the girl said, "that all British and American people are being evacuated from our country by their home governments. We are so glad that the report is not true."

"It may be true," we told her.

The radio news of the following morning announced that

all Westerners had been evacuated from the Upper Yangtze. Great Britain had unconditionally given over the administration of the concession areas at Hankow and at Kiukiang to the Nationalist Government.

We were in the Indian Ocean, March 21, when the news of the fall of Shanghai reached us: —

Shanghai, metropolis of the Yangtze Valley, went over to the Nationalists at noon to-day. The Northern troops have gone. But the Nationalist army has not yet been able to take over the city. Having no means except their feet to bring them here, the victors cannot possibly arrive before to-morrow night.

A reign of terror has disturbed the city during the entire day and is continuing. One foreigner has been killed and thirteen wounded. The leading Chinese newspaper to-night estimates the Chinese casualties at over four hundred men and women killed and innumerable wounded and raped. The trouble began at dawn when an armed group, Russian-officered, who call themselves the "Civilian Corps" set up a Commune in the deserted Government Buildings, from which headquarters they issued arms and ammunition and are conducting systematized looting. Chinese shops and homesteads are closed. But the desperadoes, when refused admittance, set fire to shop shutters and homestead doors. We have not recently had rain, and the fire is spreading rapidly. . . .

The 1,500 American marines and an equal number of Japanese marines are on duty to-night, assisting the French soldiers and the Shanghai Defense Force, sent out from England in February for this emergency. So all is well within the International Settlement. But nothing can be done for the defenseless Chinese populace outside who are petitioning piteously for admittance.

At the first breakfast table beyond Colombo, the ship's "Wireless News" reported: —

Nanking was evacuated by the Northern forces on March 23 and occupied on the following day by Nationalist troops under General Chen Chien. The Nationalist forces immediately made for and attacked the Foreign Consulates, as well as foreign firms and residences and missionary institutions. In the course of the day Dr. J. E. Williams (Vice-President of the University of Nanking), an American, Mr. Huber, the Harbor Master, an Englishman, Dr. L. S.

Smith, a British medical practitioner, and a French and an Italian priest were murdered. A British bluejacket, on *H.M.S. Emerald*, also succumbed to a sniper's bullet. Mr. Bertram Giles (British Consul General), Captain Spear (British Intelligence Officer), Major Nemoto (Japanese), Police Superintendent Mori (Japanese), and Miss Anna Moffat (American), of the Presbyterian Mission, were wounded. Several foreign women were stripped and subjected to the grossest indignities, as was the Japanese Consul also.

Looting and attacks upon foreigners, and all Chinese who attempted to shield foreigners, continued throughout the day. Nanking lies well back from the river and is enclosed within a very high wall. It was not until a party of Americans, under the guidance of the American Consul General, J. K. Davis, had reached Socony Hill, the summit of which is in sight from the river, and signaled for assistance, that action was taken. On reading these distress signals, flagged with a white flag made from the petticoat of one of the children of the party, *H.M.S. Emerald* and the American destroyers *Nao* and *Preston* opened fire, placing a barrage of shrapnel around the hill. Molestation of foreigners in all parts of Nanking immediately ceased. The women and children on Socony Hill were lowered down over the wall on to the marshy plain below, across which they ran, under the protecting fire, to the boats; but it was not possible to secure the release of other foreigners inside Nanking until forty-eight hours later, when the Foreign Naval Authorities sent an ultimatum that unless their nationals were given safe escort outside the city wall by six o'clock on the evening of the 25th, Nanking would be seriously bombarded. Then all foreigners were brought safely outside, and those in need of medical attention rushed to hospitals in Shanghai. Looting continues at Nanking.

At Manila, the hotels and the restaurants were so crowded that we had great difficulty in securing a table for lunch anywhere. The crowd was mostly American, but included other Western nationals and Chinese in flight from Nationalist territory. We talked with some, who said they were Christian missionaries.

They told us that from the very beginning of the Nationalist movement the missionaries of all denominations had sympathized with the party. Missionaries had assisted in Nationalist publicity abroad by lecturing and writing. Within China they had preached the Nationalist programme from their pulpits. Nevertheless, as the Nationalists had secured control of a district, the village mobs were excited to torment and stone all Christian missionaries and their converts, persecuting them by such insults and outrages that the Home Boards had had to issue orders for the complete evacuation of all Nationalist territory.

As we left the restaurant we met Mai-da's brother, Peng-wen. Our excitement at finding each other here was mutual.   Greetings done, he assured me that although they had had a perilous journey down from Nanchang, he had left his sister domiciled at the Astor House Hotel in the International Settlement in Shanghai, with Faithful Duck, four days previously.   She desired to go home, but she could not travel north until it was discovered what attitude Chang Tso-lin, the Manchurian war lord now governing the home province, would adopt towards persons who had been so closely associated with the Hankow group.

Peng-wen was at Manila as Chiang Kai-shek's agent, to try to secure American military and civilian advisers to help purify the Nationalist Party.   Herculean efforts had been made until now to prevent the breaking up of the Kuomintang, but it had been impossible to secure a majority in the Central Executive Council to expel Mr. Borodin, although Chiang Kai-shek, and many older and more sagacious Chinese, realized now that the Russians were intent on hampering China.   The development of the mob had been very skillfully done, so that on the surface it might appear as an expression of popular feeling. Until the Russians were forced to go home, and the mob spirit quieted by sensible information, the Nationalist Party, whose armies were loyal to Chiang Kai-shek, would conquer no more territory.

Peng-wen told me that the Nationalist army had marched to the Yangtze almost without battle, often being one or two days' march behind the departure of the "enemy" troops.   The homestead elders in each town believed the young boy and girl propagandists of good family who traveled before the army assuring the people that the Kuomintang would give them a sensible government. So the Elders usually were able to persuade the persons then governing to leave their offices before there was need for war.

"Governors in China, even feudalistic war lords," Peng-wen declared, when I questioned this statement, "never remain once they are convinced that the people of the place are of one desire for their departure. But the Nationalist army is small. They just come up and pass on. The establishment of a government was left to civilians. The policy of the Russian 'advisers' was to undermine law and order by sending on paid agitators to excite the unreliable, unstable persons of the district (of whom there are some even in every good family) to silly mob violence. Thus Mr. Borodin's intent is to break homestead government, turn the inexperienced young against their Elders, and set the lazy and shiftless against the industrious and thrifty, while discrediting us Chinese abroad by outrages against foreigners resident among us. As time has passed, paid agitators have even been sent into the Nationalist army to stir up trouble in the ranks.

"Incensed by this policy, the elder party members have been slipping away from the Kuomintang in large numbers. This Chinese characteristic of leaving a situation when one disapproves of it has helped the Russians until now. It has made control of the Central Executive Committee easy. We young men have tried to remain in the party and purify it from within. The situation has been acute since last October. In December, Chiang Kai-shek left the army, and went to Hankow. This was a brave thing to do, because he knew that he was not wanted there, and that Mr. Borodin would be pleased to find a way to bring his life to an end. Chiang Kai-shek's purpose was to force a resolution through the Central Executive Council, dismissing Mr. Borodin from his advisership and dispatching him home. He failed. Instead, Mr. Borodin forced a resolution dismissing Chiang Kai-shek from his appointment as Commander-in-Chief and instigated a Council to control military affairs.

"So Chiang Kai-shek went to Nanchang to rest. Shortly after this, Mai-da's husband and I protested against mob violences at Hankow, and we also had to leave. We went to Nanchang. After some weeks there was quite a large party of us, of one political mind, at Nanchang. While forming a policy for ourselves, we took the precaution to discover just what part of the National army was loyal to its dismissed Commander-in-Chief. We decided to go down river to Nanking, the ancient Ming capital, and establish a new Kuomintang headquarters, to which members who had left the Hankow group might come if they wished. We passed this intention on to Ho Ying-chin and Pai Chung-hsi, two generals in the Nationalist army whose loyalty could be trusted. They were to march into Nanking, as close on the heels of the departing Northerners as possible, and we would greet them there.

"But this message was intercepted. From Hankow, Mr. Borodin wirelessed to Chen Chien, a Hunanese soldier in Russian pay. Chen Chien was ordered to rush his army into Nanking before Ho Ying-chin and Pai Chung-hsi could arrive, and so disrupt the city that Chiang Kai-shek 'would not have a place in it in which to lay his head.' This was done under systematic and strict military discipline, as if by direct command of the deposed Commander-in-Chief, with particular care to be drastic with Americans and Japanese, because it was suspected that Chiang Kai-shek intended to ask either America or Japan for support of his new Kuomintang headquarters.

"We started down river from Nanchang in boats. When we approached Nanking, the outrage occurred. We at that time intercepted a message and learned that a similar incident was to occur at Shanghai. The date was set for Sunday, March 27, by which time it was expected we should arrive there.

These intercepted orders said that, as large contingents of foreign troops around the International Settlement at Shanghai made an antiforeign uprising impossible, the Communists would concentrate on creating a reign of terror against the Shanghai bourgeoisie, equal to the 'commendable achievement at Nanking,' and make it appear that it was done by Chiang Kai-shek's orders.

"We rushed down river. We arrived at Shanghai on Saturday, March 26," Peng-wen continued. "We were thoroughly tired and discouraged. I was one who believed that an attempt to quell the Communist uprising would be futile. I joined in trying to persuade Chiang Kai-shek not to land. But he would not listen to advice. He gave the order to land, and we landed. He led us boldly to the Lunghua garrison and entered in the manner of a Commander-in-Chief who expects the salute of his officers and men. From there he sent out a call for all persons who chose to support him to come and review the Shanghai situation.

"None of the material elements were in Chiang's favor at Shanghai that day. But he was determined to purify the Nationalist party of Russian influence and to stop the planned Communist uprising at Shanghai.

"It did not seem at all probable that evening that he would be able to stem the Communist tide. A General Labor Union, supported by Hankow with Russian money, appeared to control organized workers in all the Shanghai factories, and even the domestic servants. A Commune, well supplied with arms and ammunition, had been established by armed Communists, Russian-officered. The Nationalist army, who had marched up to Shanghai two days after the departure of the Northerners, only numbered three thousand men. We knew that agitators had been busy among them.

"Hankow authorities had published in Shanghai an offer of half a million dollars for Chiang Kai-shek's head, but when supporters failed to come to him at the garrison, he went into the

streets to seek friends.   First he visited the Red and the Green
Secret Societies and convinced them of the need for action.
Then he went to the Ningpo Guild.   He is a native of a village near Ningpo.   Ningpo provides Shanghai with the bulk
of her proletarian population.   He secured a hearing, which
collected the folk from his home district solidly behind him.
This done, he walked boldly into one after another of the labor
headquarters and addressed whomsoever he found present.
Then at twilight he reviewed the troops.   He had them stand
at attention to listen to a brief address in which he recalled
them to memory of their sainted leader Sun Yat-sen.

"The meetings planned for Sunday morning were held at the
exact place and hour ordered.   But instead of being signals
for a reign of terror, each was a demonstration of gratitude to
Chiang Kai-shek — a leader come to save the people of China
from Russian Communism.   Chiang did not attend any of
these demonstrations.   We attended them for him, to tell
the demonstrators that Chiang Kai-shek does not desire personal acclaim but just to help the people to do right."

2

We came to Hongkong two days later.   I found the wives of
missionaries, merchants, and consuls of all the nations, and their
children.   They all had glassy eyes, as though still too close to
fear, and an eagerness to talk to one who would listen.   They
told of the peaceful departure of troops, and the peaceful
entry and passage of Nationalist troops welcomed by a populace; then of strikes, stones thrown, the growl of mobs; and
escape, sometimes hidden under loads of farmers' hay by kindly
folk, sometimes in the bottoms of boats with fruit piled con-
cealingly over them, and sometimes on gunboats sent to rescue
them.

I also found Chinese men, women, and children refugees
everywhere.   In the tea-dance room of the Hongkong hotel,

I was turned away because there was no place for me.   As I
went, I saw a table of people gesturing, but did not suspect that
they meant to beckon me, until one of the children ran to my
side.   They had nine tables.   They were the House of Ping,
from Samshui — relatives by marriage of the House of Lin, and
folk loud in declaration against British ownership of Hongkong
during my residence at Canton.

Greetings over, I asked about the House of Lin, and learned
that they were all at Canton when last heard from.   Then I
twitted the Pings with seeking refuge in Hongkong.

"Canton is safe — if one has a house as powerful as the Lin
clan, of whom all governors are afraid; but the reign of terror
is such at Samshui that we just had to come away.   To stay
would have been folly.   We moved everything valuable down
here, and paid room rent in advance for one year, last Pepper
Moon," one of the young wives said, blushing.   "It is true
that we, and many other families, favored the return of all concessions, but in this spring a foreign settlement, governed by
foreign law, is our only place of safety."

"We talked idly in the courtyards," put in the Lady First
in Ping Authority, "but we never really meant that China is
ready yet to take on the administration of the concessions.
We never had the matter up even for discussion in the Hall of
Gathering."

"By just such careless talk," said one of the men, "we have
got the concession at Hankow returned, and now the families
in the Upper Yangtze have no place of refuge."

"The Hunanese are people who always leap before they look.
This will teach them prudence," said the Family Elder, biting
into a cream puff.

"We ought to get a stable national government established."
One of the daughters educated in Japan spoke.   "The House
of Lin, so I have heard, are supporting Chiang Kai-shek.   I
think we ought to support him."

"We will wait and see how he gets on before we decide to

support him," jested one of the children, with a twinkle in his dark eyes.

I sailed that night for Shanghai, where the *Saarbrücken* loaded cargo four days before going on to Tientsin. Peng-wen had wired Mai-da, and she was on the jetty.

Her husband had gone away on some unknown political errand the day after Peng-wen left. She was lonely in Shanghai, and longed for home. I was relieved to find her well and looking just as usual — which is pretty in a plump, dimpled way. We cried, in the foolish manner of women, even suddenly beginning again, after carefully drying our faces; then, more composed, we went for a tour of the International Settlement in the limousine that Mai-da's husband had hired for her.

She was charmed by the British Tommies and the American marines, and insisted on taking me all around the defenses they guarded so that I might appreciate them also. Mai-da knows that I do not approve of soldiers of any nationality. But she is always trying to convert me to a different opinion, as she believes that soldiers are necessary to prevent war. The British and the Americans appeared jolly men. Many of them had their laundry out to dry on the barbed wire. They were all on genial terms with the Chinese on the inside and the outside of the barricades.

One fat American marine cook was ladling his beans, from a pot set in a wagon-canteen, into the cupped palms of a group of Chinese boys. Further along a young British sentinel was attempting to extract a splinter, with a penknife, from the bare foot of an old Chinese farmer who had thrust his injury in under the wire.

"Do you remember," Mai-da said, "the Elder of Exile reading to us, from the Book of Mencius, in that part where a governor named Yen oppressed the people and a king named Hsuan of Ch'i went and smote him? 'Hoping to be delivered from fire and water, the people met Hsuan's armies with trays of food and pots of broth.' It is like that here to-day.

"People are flocking to Chiang Kai-shek's standard, hoping that he will prove a bulwark against the rising tide of Communism, which has thoroughly frightened them. The three intellectual leaders of China, Tsai Yuan-pei, Wu Tse-hui, and Li Shih-tsen, whose pupils and associates constitute our intelligentsia, have declared themselves for him. Following on this, poets, artists, and students have written and wired from all over the country announcing themselves anti-Communistic. K. P. Chen, Manager of the Shanghai Commercial and Savings Bank, who previously has always remained aloof from politics, has promised Chiang full support, and agreed to be chairman of a Financial Commission. Other bankers and merchants have followed his lead and three million dollars have been arranged for immediate use. T. V. Soong has arrived from Hankow. C. C. Wu, Wang Ching-wei, and C. T. Wang have telegraphed that they are in sympathy and want to help. It has been agreed to abandon the Hankow Government, even though Mrs. Sun Yat-sen continues to support it, and to ignore its decisions. A Plenary Session of the Central Executive Committee, open to every person who desires to attend, will be called at Nanking on April 15, for the purpose of purifying the party. I do hope Peng-wen will get back in time to attend it."

"I expect he will," I said. "Are you going?"

"I? Whatever for?" Mai-da exclaimed.

"Lots of Chinese women will attend."

"They will. But I am not interested in politics," she answered. "I wish that I had married a man who was content to be a farmer, and that my only brother was content to be a farmer also."

I did some visiting among Western people at Shanghai, and I did not find much confidence among them in Chiang Kai-shek or any Nationalist. A fear psychology possessed them. They were nervous, tense, irritable. The weather was getting hot and the Settlement was overcrowded. There were over eight hundred missionary women and children refugees, perhaps half that number again of other women and children refugees, and innumerable men who had been ordered in out of Nationalist territory by their consuls. People were having to live and sleep four and five in a room. Everyone with whom I talked had either suffered or had those they loved suffer stoning, insult, or nasty handling. They had been looted and robbed before departure from their upcountry homes. In the hospitals and the nursing homes were victims of Chinese violence, among them raped women whom the doctors were trying to protect both from venereal disease and from childbirth. Among these were many Chinese as well as Western girls and women.

Like the refugees at Hongkong, the eyes of the Western refugees at Shanghai were too bright. Pressing in upon them, whenever they walked in the Settlement streets, were thousands of Chinese refugees. These had suffered just as greatly from mob violence, but there was a surge of anti-Chinese feeling which made it difficult even for Christian missionaries to say just then that all men are brothers. There was resentment that the Chinese were in the concession when they had all China to keep themselves in. Also anxiety lest their presence cause epidemics of cholera, typhoid, or typhus. The antiforeign demonstrations in Nationalist territory had left the Chinese, especially Chinese of the Nationalist Party, with very little reputation among foreigners. Even my intimacy with Mai-da was criticized at one house where I dined.

During the first three days of my stop at Shanghai, the Western press were skeptical of Chiang Kai-shek and his associates. The vernacular press were solidly for him. They approved heartily of the establishment of a Nationalist headquarters in defiance of Hankow, and of the reconstruction of the Nationalist Party. They agreed that the new headquarters could not be at Shanghai under the protection of thirty thousand foreign troops and foreign gunboats. They applauded the dispatch of all available troops to Nanking to disarm and disband Chen Chien's Hankow army and then prepare Nanking as the new capital.

But on the day I left Shanghai, establishment of the Nanking government was assisted from an unexpected quarter. Mrs. Borodin had been arrested on the Soviet steamer *Pamiat Lenina*, at the end of February, and had been sent to prison at Tsinan. From Tsinan, in the slow way of Chinese justice, she had been sent on up to another prison at Peking to wait until the judges were ready to try her. Except that the Russian Embassy kept demanding her release periodically, she had been practically forgotten by the Chinese people.

But Chang Tso-lin, governing Peking, had found the papers taken from her interesting, and had them translated. Their content caused him to prepare a search warrant and get it countersigned by the Dean of the Diplomatic Body; then to dispatch police and troops to search the offices of the Russian Commercial Agencies and the Chinese Eastern Railway. And when they saw the offices of the Soviet Military Attaché burning, the searchers put out the fire and searched them. On the last day of my stay in Shanghai, Chang Tso-lin sent out a circular telegram announcing that he had found documents establishing Chiang Kai-shek's assertion that Russia had seized a directing control of the Nationalist Party and that the Internationale was working through Hankow.

3

The coast trip was smooth and uneventful. We put in at no ports and took up the pilot outside Tangku about five o'clock on the afternoon of the fourteenth. He told me that a launch had had steam up since the previous morning in readiness to bring my husband out to meet me. So when he had brought the *Saarbrücken* up as close as possible to the sandbar in the mouth of the Hai-ho River, I said that I would wait.

I waited until ten o'clock next morning. Then, as my husband had not arrived, I started up river in an open flatboat. The weather was pleasant, the boatmen genial. I like river travel, and, as it was spring, the scenery was pretty. Troops, wearing Chang Tso-lin's colors and equipped with umbrellas and teapots as well as muskets, were numerous on both banks. They were playing cards, sleeping, or eating. Twice we got hot water for tea from them, and one especially friendly group gave us bowls of spaghetti, which we anchored to eat. We sighted Tientsin after about six hours. When we had gone a short way into the city, I noticed that soldiers on both river banks were manning their guns.

A light-draught Japanese passenger steamer came out from the wharf. Bullets splashed in the river around it.

"The war with Japan has begun!" my boatman exclaimed, and expertly changed our course.

We backed and waited at the side of the river channel. The soldiers did not fire at anyone. They just put their bullets into the river in front of the Japanese vessel. A crowd gathered on the bank and clambered into our boat and boats around us to have a good view of the happenings. Suddenly the Japanese boat made another attempt to dash downstream. She was struck. After some delay she put back to her original wharf. Soldiers boarded her and took a Chinese man off.

Just then I saw my husband on the Bund. As our relationship began with his disapproval of my habits, there was really very little left by now that he could say regarding my conduct, except to repeat his often repeated injunction that I ought to stay out of China. When he had begun that, after I came ashore, we both laughed so that he could not soberly finish it.

He had not been able to get down to the *Saarbrücken* because of trouble in Tientsin, but he had hoped that I would stay there until he could. The man just taken off the Japanese steamer was the Chinese mayor of Tientsin, who had been accused of being in Russian pay and had tried to escape. We walked along to my husband's house, leaving Bald-the-third to wait with my luggage until Chang could come down to arrange for its transport.

My husband's house was filled as for a house party. When I expressed delight at finding guests there, they answered me soberly. They were not party guests, but refugees from Peking and other inland places. Mrs. Molland, the elder among them, had lived half a century in China. With her husband and four little children she had been trapped in the Boxer rising in 1900. She and her youngest daughter had been badly treated by Chinese soldiers in the Second Revolution, in 1913. Her lovely house on the hill at Nanking, from which luckily all the family had been absent, had been one of those looted of everything, even the floor boarding. Her other house at Kuiliang was now occupied by Chinese soldiers.

Another of the party had escaped the January violence at Hankow only by a miracle, having escaped before the mob with her two small boys, but having to leave all her possessions to their tender mercy. Each person present had had some terrible experience.

They told me that people were clearing out of inland stations and resting at Tientsin, within the circle of foreign troops, until they could collect their thoughts for the future. The guests in my husband's house, and every Westerner I met elsewhere in Tientsin, scolded me solemnly for returning to add to my husband's already intricate problem by my presence.

He would not say that he was glad that I had come. Neither would he say that he was sorry. I think he believes — as, I suspect, not only English husbands but other husbands, as well, do — that it is his duty to keep his wife and child in some comfortable country, yet enjoys having us with him. He did not in any way hamper my friendships with all sorts and kinds of Chinese people, even when I climbed over trenches and crawled through tangled barbed wire to visit them in that period when foreigners were wary of the Chinese.

All throughout 1927 and 1928 Western fear of China con-

tinued.   At Tientsin we were crowded together within a circle
of marines and soldiers — waiting for what might happen.

I have felt akin to the Chinese from the first hour of my
arrival in China.   I have never suffered fear of them and
never been hurt by them.   I sympathize with fear of the
Chinese, just as I sympathize with that equally terrible fear of
foreigners from which I know many Chinese suffer.   I know
that the Chinese have done cruel deeds, nasty wrong things, and
committed sinful atrocities.   I know truthful men and women
to whom they have been done, and I have also seen them done
with my own eyes.

But sin is a universal attribute.   We all sin.   I have never
been able to believe that it is characteristic of any particular
race, or group, or special individual.   I was in my teens and
early twenties, perhaps my most susceptible age, with friends
on both sides, when tides of human feeling were roused to
make four years of what our history books now call The Great
War.   I have not yet got far enough away from that experience, even in middle age, to believe that any one of us might
not be caught up in participation in mob violence — even
Chinese antiforeign violence, if we happened to be born Chinese
instead of American.

4

Meeting the ex-Empress colored with pleasure the spring of
my arrival at my husband's Tientsin residence.

Colonel Buchanan, of the British Army, was with the foreign
forces at Tientsin then.   Sir Reginald Johnston, who lived
within the Forbidden City at Peking with the Manchu Imperial
Family for many years, had given him his place in a bridge four-
some in which the ex-Emperor was fond of playing.   Colonel
Buchanan, when he had decided about me, in his quiet, cautious
way, announced that he had a friend to whom I ought to be
congenial — and took me to the ex-Empress.

A beautiful girl or woman has half won my heart before she speaks. If she has wit, I am her unconditional slave. I have never seen any woman, of any race, equal to the loveliness of the Manchu ex-Empress in 1927. It is said that beauty was sought in all the eligible households to mate with the last scion of the Ch'ing dynasty, but had the seekers looked through all the world and had equal right to take what girl they chose, I doubt if her equal could have been found.

Beauty is elusive to description. To write that she is tall, slim, has ebony hair, rose-petal skin, slender arched feet, perfect hands with perfect half-moons at the base of each nail, and brown eyes, is but words.

She is of such repose that she appears calm at all times; but one glances away having decided that her eyes are like the sepals of a hazel-bur, and looks again to find that they are black pearls; her face is sad, so sad that it twists one's heart — while one stares, it brightens until it holds all impish delight. Her manner has all dignity, yet is so simple that one cannot decide wherein lies her imperial manner.

I was drawn not by her beauty only. I had pleasure in her which would have drawn me if she had been ugly to the eye. Whenever she asked me I went to her, and she asked me often. We both enjoy food, and we exchanged recipes; we both like pretty underwear, and we exchanged patterns. She gave me two coats that I admired; I gave her two garments of mine that she admired.

Through her I met many of her relatives. Among them, the prince to whom Mai-da was attracted on the day of my first journey down the canal to the House of Exile, with whom she corresponded secretly before her marriage, and for whom I suspected she still had a passion. The ex-Empress told me that her cousin had a locket he wore, holding a likeness of a Chinese girl because of whom he had never married.

The ex-Empress lived then in the Japanese Concession at Tientsin. As women do when they sit and embroider together, she told me her life and I told her mine. She had a happy childhood and girlhood, brought up like any Manchu girl of royal blood — strictly and simply. She was surprised and thrilled when she was told that she had been chosen to marry the Emperor.

"My wedding in 1922," she said, "was perhaps the last Manchu pageant. Everything was done with care to fulfill the rites which have been elaborated through the centuries to make the Son of Heaven's wedding the most marvelous of spectacles. Flowers perfumed the courts. All the Banners came, bringing their wives and children. Everyone was dressed in robes jeweled and encrusted with gold according to rank. There was music — "

"And you in it," I interposed.

"Yes — I was the bride in it, and I enjoyed it all. It was a fairy tale, such as my nurse used to tell me, come true," she laughed. "I did my part in it so that when it was over my mother, who had been exceedingly anxious lest I be clumsy, said that I did it all right."

She put a new thread in her needle and stitched a primrose petal. Then she went on about herself.

"We lived peacefully in Peking for two years. We had one part of the Forbidden City. There is a lovely lake there — pink with lotus in early summer. We skated on it when it was frozen, and drifted on it in a purple boat on warm spring evenings. We wrote and gave plays in the blue-domed theatre. There was ample space there for us and for the Manchu families who had been connected with the old court. We lived a secluded life. We did not find it confining, but natural. The Son of Heaven and his bride, according to Manchu custom, usually lived a secluded life. The Chinese did not molest us, although when my husband was in his teens some Chinese tried to make him Emperor of all China again. He had not liked that experience and we did not concern ourselves with Chinese politics.

"In 1912, when my husband, then the six-year-old Emperor, signed the agreement of voluntary abdication prepared for him, the contract promised that he should keep this quarter of the Forbidden City forever as his private property. It never occurred to us that this promise would ever be broken. But one October morning in 1924, when we were at breakfast, my old nurse ran in, screaming that Chinese soldiers were pushing in through the gates to take us. I thought that she had gone silly, and told her to be quiet.

"I was eating an especially delicious baked apple, and I went on eating it. But she was right. The court below our balcony — we were in the Winter Palace — filled with Chinese soldiers. We had to run. We ran through passages and across courts to the streets, arriving breathless in the Foreign Legation Quarter. We knocked at the British Legation, and asked for shelter. It was refused. I wanted to try the American; but my husband said it would be useless, as they would send us away. We had to run again as we heard the Chinese soldiers in close pursuit.

"We reached the gates of the Japanese Legation, exhausted. I tripped on my torn skirt, and would have fallen in the road, but the Japanese guard ran to my assistance. The Japanese soldiers helped us inside and shut their gates in the faces of the angry, shouting Chinese soldiers. My clothes were spoiled. The Japanese Ambassador's wife kindly gave me clothes of hers. We never got anything from our home. The soldiers belonged to the Christian General Feng Yu-hsiang. He captured Peking that day and not only tried to take us but took and imprisoned the Chinese President of the Republic, Tsao Kun.

"He held Peking for only a few weeks. Then he was driven out by some other Chinese warrior. But he announced that my husband's Abdication Treaty was canceled, and all China has treated it as canceled ever since then. Our private residence, according to the contract, is now a museum — people pay a fee at the gate to look at our things. I heard that the baked apple I was eating was one of the popular items until it rotted. The Japanese could not keep us in their Legation, so they gave us residence here."

5

One morning, when the white lilacs were in flower, Ching-mei came into my walled garden. She came to tell me that Shao-yi had been arrested at Peking. His twin, a student at the same school, had just telephoned down to her. Police had searched the school for evidences of Communism and taken Shao-yi, his girl-wife's brother, and five of their classmates, because of quotations — quotations found in their notebooks from a book Su-ling had given Shao-yi at New Year.

Shao-yi is the boy who so often read aloud to his sister and his cousins in the Garden of Children at the House of Exile, during my first winter in China. He had grown to be a thoughtful, kind lad, who seemed principally interested in flowers and poetry. He had never shown any interest in politics at home.

"It is best," Ching-mei said, "to go down and tell the Family Elder at once. Ours is a powerful clan. He will be released by the day after to-morrow, if we start now. The Elder has only to give us a note to Chang Tso-lin."

We hastened to the House of Exile, urging speed in every stage of the journey. We were welcomed and, with care to keep the news from Shao-yi's wife, who carried a child, we told what had happened.

Shock and sorrow showed in every face. But we were confounded when we realized that the Family would take no action. Ching-mei was as astonished as I was. We had to return, knowing that the clan of Lin, as represented by the House of Exile, would do nothing. It was not merely the Elder. He did not speak to influence anyone.

Back again in Tientsin, we telegraphed to the Lady of Lin.

Her evasive message of sympathy convinced us that the Canton relatives would not move.

Su-ling arrived. She saw Chang Tso-lin, and told him that the book the boys had copied was hers. She offered herself for punishment.

"I could not release my own son or daughter, or even save myself," he told her sadly, "if thrown into prison to-day on suspicion of Communism."

There was no trial. No clan took any action to save any of the boys, although three of them were of powerful families. They were used as a warning to scholars. Theirs was not an isolated case of injustice, and not just the stubborn action of a stern governor. They were only an incident in the Spartan stamping out of Communism which followed on the finding, translation, and the wide publication of the Russian documents taken at Peking and elsewhere.

When knowledge that this foreign poison had been injected into their country dawned upon the Chinese people, they sacrificed all else to cleanse it out. It was not a purification directed from above. The tide against Communism was a tide of national feeling in every locality, in which homestead, guild, trade, farmer, and laborer were of one mind. The secret societies were active in it, dragging men even from the foreign concessions. Folk who were possibly Communists, and many who were not, were put to death — some even by their own kin. I did not hear of any clan that asked for release of a member arrested on suspicion of Communism; or of any Family Elder called before a magistrate for destroying a son or a daughter.

I talked with Shao-yi on the afternoon before his death. He was philosophical. He calmly accepted the fact that Communism must go, and that he must be used to help it go. On April 28, with eighteen others, he was put to death by slow strangulation. They went to their deaths courageously. Shao-yi's last words were to beg Su-ling not to cry.

The translated and widely circulated Soviet papers showed that Feng Yu-hsiang, the Christian General, had received large sums of money and vast stores of ammunition from Russia. He did not try to deny this. Instead he sent out a circular telegram explaining that he had cleverly fooled the Soviets so as to get the things. He distributed new flags to his regiments, announced that he was leading his armies forward to fight for Chiang Kai-shek, crossed Shensi, and began to attack northern Honan. But the Japanese sent two thousand troops into Shantung and stopped his advance. They explained their action as necessary to prevent an incident similar to the Nanking incident, at Tsinan, the capital of Shantung, where hundreds of Japanese live.

This roused a surge of anti-Japanese feeling in Chinese courtyards, which was echoed in the vernacular press, by minstrels, and by vendors, but did not divert the Chinese minds from the job of ridding themselves of Sovietism. By the end of June, I heard it said that Communism had been stamped out in all the twenty-one provinces, excepting Kiangsi, Hupeh, and Hunan, where the Hankow government, with Mr. Borodin as Dictator, still had power. On July 27, the vernacular press announced that Mr. Borodin and all the other foreign Communists had run home, escaping across country by the back door through territory controlled by Feng Yu-hsiang. Reading this news, I jumped to the conclusion that China would soon be a Republic united under one flag.

Shun-ko and Nuan came down from the House of Exile to visit me in August. We were playing mah-jongg in my summerhouse when Chang came to say that Peng-wen had arrived. We had him join us. He was on his way up from the Capital to help with the home-farm work. He had left his post at Nanking. In fact, all the Nanking offices were now vacant, awaiting whosoever cared to try to make a government for China. The Nationalist army was also waiting until someone volunteered for the job of Commander-in-Chief. Chiang Kai-shek had gone home. He had been the first to retire to his homestead farm. He had made a speech in a committee meeting, and as it had not been supported he had walked out, got on the train, and gone home. I was bewildered and astonished.

"Mencius," so Peng-wen informed me, "taught that if a gentleman makes suggestions and they are not taken, he should go home."

I concluded that now the Northern war lords would simply re-occupy the territory that they had abandoned to the advancing Nationalists. Northern war lords had been menacing Nanking by sending their bombing planes over it. But I concluded wrongly. The Nanking government had gone home, so, as there was nobody to fight, the "enemy" stopped bombing. The nation waited, while the Kuomintang collected itself again.

Conferences, in this private house and that, occupied some members of the Kuomintang during the remainder of August, September, October, and November. Not everyone gave importance to these by attending. Many members kept their attention on the tillage and the harvesting of their homestead crops. The vernacular press reported that when the House of Chiang had threshed their grain, young Kai-shek might go abroad, as he had never seen America.

6

In China, where mating is controlled by family prudence, it is a paradox that nothing so pleases people as the happy ending to a romance. At festivals, fairs, tea-houses, and homestead parties, I have learned that it is the minstrel who sings love stories based on truth that is the most popular.

Nothing is secret here. We live behind high walls, but the most intimate details of private life spread in some mysterious way from tongue to tongue all over the land — if they happen to be found interesting. At a street corner in Canton, I heard a minstrel sing, in twenty-seven verses, the drama of how the American Consul's wife at Chungking got her husband to buy her a rose-red dress for the Bachelors' Ball. If one stops to listen one does not always hear tales from the distant past. In widely separated places, I heard minstrels lament in sad minor strains the story of the love of Mai-ling, youngest daughter of the House of Soong at Shanghai, and Chiang Kai-shek of Fenghua near Ningpo. Rumor had said, through five years, that Madame Soong would never give her consent to this marriage and that her daughter would not marry without it.

But Madame Soong issued invitations to the wedding of her daughter Mai-ling and Chiang Kai-shek on December 1, 1927. I was told, while shopping, by a policeman, a hot-bath vendor, Liu, the ivory dealer at Tientsin, a rickshaw runner, a copper-smith, a scholarly-looking gentleman with a book, and a pretty girl who was buying pins in the shop where I stopped to get thread. And on my return home I found my invitation. Each person who told me seemed as delighted as if the wedding was that of their own daughter or son. I could not go to the wedding, but I heard a full account of the magnificent festival. The songs were given by the blind singer at Noonday Rest, whose lyric began, "All China rejoiced. . . ."

The Kuomintang were startled into hasty action by a coup d'état at Canton, where in December a Russian named Kovlok led a Communist uprising in which the city was sacked and thousands of bourgeoisie killed.

Chiang Kai-shek was asked to end his honeymoon and return to Nanking as Commander-in-Chief of the Nationalist Armies, Chairman of the Central Executive Committee, and Chairman of so many other things that, when Bald-the-third was reading it aloud from the vernacular press, she just grouped it as "Chairman of all Responsibility." The Kuomintang issued wide publicity, announcing Chiang Kai-shek's appointment, and canceling all previous alliances with Soviet authorities and the Communist Party.

Chiang Kai-shek and Soong Mai-ling, accompanied by her

brother T. V. Soong as Minister of Finance, went to Nanking to reëstablish government. According to Kuomintang regulation, nineteen members constitute a working quorum of the Central Executive Committee. Even though bankers, merchants, and homestead elders, student groups, guilds, trades, and secret societies publish their approval of a government, it is not easy here to secure nineteen proper persons to accept the government portfolios.

All through January Chiang Kai-shek traveled to and from Nanking, in his effort to enlist the men and women he needed for authority. Many gave the excuse "No leisure." Mrs. Sun Yat-sen, now his sister-in-law, whose influence in the Kuomintang is considerable, hampered proceedings by cabling from Moscow to denounce the government under formation at Nanking. But finally, on February 1, a quorum had been secured, when it was possible to take up such business as the demands for restitution of the foreign Powers for the Nanking and other outrages in Nationalist territory, and the formation of a Northern Expedition to bring all China under one flag.

The events of this period touched us intimately. Mai-da's husband, on an errand to secure peace with Hankow, was sent home dead from a dinner party. Two weeks later a private messenger brought me a packet. It contained a letter from Mai-da's late husband. In it he asked me to say nothing, but in case of his death to keep the enclosed packet until after the Three Years' Mourning. I put the packet in a linen wrapper, sealed it, marked it "Not to be opened until January 1931," and deposited it in the bank.

The Northern Expedition began on April 10. Chiang Kai-shek commanded in the name of the united Nationalists. Again there was great anxiety among the Westerners in North China, who were gathered, by consular order, within a circle of trenches and barbed wire, at Tientsin, and guarded by the usual four regiments maintained here, augmented by American marines under the command of General Smedley Butler.

Chiang Kai-shek directed the Nationalist army northward into Shantung. And so came into conflict with Chang Tsung-chang, who had governed Shantung for some years. The Chinese people are peculiar in that, although they will suffer devastating taxation uncomplainingly, they are incensed by a governor whose private life is not fitted to Chinese ideas of morality. Chang Tsung-chang was arrogant in noisy publicity about his harem of fifteen beautiful Russian girls, replenished by purchase in Harbin as they faded. He amused himself by insulting Shantung families. Also, an old woman told Shun-ko and me, when we were in Shantung on a pilgrimage to the sacred Tai Mountain, "The nasty creature has flipped his tail in our faces by regilding the temple of Confucius's wife." When the Nationalists entered Shantung, therefore, they were welcomed. Chang Tsung-chang had to flee to Japan for his life.

As the Nationalists came north, Chang Tso-lin commanded his troops to withdraw peaceably through the Wall to Manchuria. All the other Northern war lords reflagged their soldiers with the Nationalist flag. So they announced themselves Nationalist and there was no excuse to fight them.

In the last week in May, I received an offer from a firm of Swedish publishers to go to Mongolia and write an autobiography of Larson, Duke of Mongolia, for his signature and their publication. The American Consul General, a kind, fatherly man, attempted to protect me by withholding my passport, but I did not need it, as Chang Tso-lin gave me permission to ride north with his deputies when they went to Hwailai to give the order to his troops to return to Manchuria.

I waited at Hwailai to watch the three-mile procession of splendid chestnut horses pull the polished cannon away. I saw them followed by thousands of good-natured, well-clad, pleased-to-go-home infantry. When they had gone, I walked four days across deserted country to Kalgan, which city leans against the Great Wall where it borders Mongolia. I found that there were no rebellious people to conquer in this corner of China. By the end of June the Nationalist flag waved over all the provinces within the Great Wall.

But there were two serious incidents in the campaign. On May 3, the Nationalist troops and the Japanese came into armed conflict at Tsinan. A nasty diplomatic situation developed. Chiang Kai-shek handled it by going at once to talk with the Japanese Commander, General Fukada, and by persuading his

THE GREAT WALL

own commanders not to fight but to trust the Foreign Ministry to make settlement. And secondly, on June 4, the train in which Chang Tso-lin rode in the rear of his withdrawing troops was dynamited outside the Great Wall, in Manchuria, just as it was approaching Mukden, and he was killed. This was less easily handled.

Chang Tso-lin, the self-appointed dictator of Manchuria, who frequently named the President at Peking and often ruled North China, was ruthless in punishment of anyone who disobeyed his regulations, and had a heavy hand when collecting taxes. But he was a popular character. Ever since I came to China I have heard stories, both humorous and serious, about him. His life is the stuff of which historical legends are made. When he was born, his clan were poverty-stricken outlaws, because of a misdemeanor against the then existing government, and he made his House rich and powerful, setting his uncles, brothers, cousins, and sons to rule where the Changs had been outcast. While he lived, his strength, his common sense, his courage, and his gentleness were already the theme of nursery folklore.

Children listen now, and will listen with round eyes a century hence, to incidents illustrating how his wife ruled wisely, often overmatching her lord in some situation where woman's way is best, from the days of poverty up through prosperity; or to the story of how Mrs. Chang chose the pretty Fifth Green Skirt, whom her lord fancied for her beauty, only because she was skilled in arithmetic, and so kept her entirely occupied with the homestead accounts and moulding the tribute gold into bars that were laid in the walls and the floors of the Mukden homestead for safekeeping.

Because it was known that knowledge of his death would disturb the people, every effort was made to keep it secret until the diplomatic committee appointed to investigate the mystery could prepare a just report.

This was impossible. The vernacular press, in all the provinces, printed stories based on the rumors of what had happened, and all declared that such dastardly killing of good old Chang Tso-lin could have been done only by orders from Tokyo. The new Nationalist Government, of one mind in fear of foreign complications, quickly throttled the press. But every Chinese of my acquaintance stopped his ears to Nationalist dictation, and made prompt contribution to the Anti-Japanese Society. In courtyard, street, and bazaar, ill-feeling against Japan was fanned by a rumor that the Japanese were saying that the dynamiting had been done by Chang Tso-lin's eldest son, who inherited his dictatorship.

This summer, for the first time in his life, Chiang Kai-shek visited Northern China. He came as the head of the Nationalist government, but he astonished the people of the North because he came on an ordinary train, accompanied by his wife, and did not bring an army. Although Mr. and Mrs. Chiang arrived at Peking on July 3 and did not return to Nanking until July 29, they did not find it easy to meet the Northern generals, who had declared themselves Nationalists. Finally they announced that they would attend a memorial service to the leader of the revolution, Sun Yat-sen, whose body was in the Western Hills, and hoped that they would find all the Nationalist generals there. Yen Hsi-shan and Pai Chung-hsi attended. When the worshipers were standing with bowed heads for the three minutes' silent self-examination which is a part of the Sun Yat-sen service, Feng Yu-hsiang entered. He wore a sombrero and a leather belt holding two pistols in open-top holsters. He was accompanied by a guard of armed troops.

After the service, Chiang Kai-shek succeeded in winning the generals to consent to a conversation at Peking.

Following these parleys they joined with him in signing a circular telegram. This telegram was proclaimed an official order. It was addressed to the nation. It forbade all further recruiting in all parts of China. It also announced a Special Military Rehabilitation Conference to be held at Nanking, with the purpose of reorganizing the existing troops into a small national army under the direct control of the central government, and to arrange for the industrialization of all other soldiers.

Chiang Kai-shek returned to the Capital and labored through the remainder of the year to prepare for this conference on disarmament. But it was difficult even to keep a quorum of efficient party members, who could and would work together, at Nanking.

The Nationalist flag was unfurled over all China. But the Lady of Lin wrote to me that according to their reports there was more forced recruiting than at any other period since 1911, and every time I went into the country I saw boys taken to be soldiers. The commanders, however, published their personal disbandment plans in the newspapers.   And the majority of my Kuomintang acquaintance seemed content to assume that the nation was now a nation, and disarmament being carried out by army owners — so why bother?

Chiang Kai-shek kept his wife and his friends busy on errands to coax the veteran Republicans back in the government, but politics were no longer fashionable.   All the "bright young people" who had been enthusiastic at the beginning of the Nationalist movement had grown older.   The men had become merchants, or bankers, and their wives were occupied with their families.   The younger generation, who had heard the experiences of their brothers and sisters, were not attracted.   The elders of the party were broken into "left wing," "right wing," and other sectional groups.   Chiang Kai-shek made innumerable trips in the rôle of peacemaker, but without much success.

In November, Chiang Kai-shek acted on the advice of an American newspaper correspondent with whom he had become friendly, and hired a Colonel Bauer, with sixty Austrian and German officers, to help him reorganize his small army as a model, industrializing part of the men and drilling others to police work.   In December, despite the fact that the Japanese Consul and the Japanese Commander at Mukden both advised him not to involve Manchuria in affairs within the Wall, Chang Hsueh-liang hoisted the Nationalist flag over the three provinces north of the Wall, thus declaring friendship for Chiang Kai-shek, who had won him over in one interview.

Chiang Kai-shek now challenged all the military men of the country to come to their capital and confer on disbandment.   The convocation of this assembly appeared impossible. But in January Bald-the-third read aloud from the vernacular press that for the first time in the history of the Republic all the military leaders in China had come together under one roof.

I could not have been more excited, had I been Chinese.   It seemed that the sincerity, unselfishness, and greatness of spirit which are in every Chinese of my acquaintance had triumphed over all other Chinese characteristics.

But the conference failed. Feng Yu-hsiang was the first to leave. After his departure the other generals slipped away one by one. None found it possible to let his army be considered as other than private property. While each was willing to help reorganize another's army, none was willing to let others interfere with his organization.

Each militarist went home and acted as independently as ever, although still flying the national flag. Civil wars, as usual, disturbed the country. Chiang Kai-shek remained at Nanking, harassed by battles around the Capital and by dissension within the party, struggling to make China a nation. T. V. Soong continued to try to keep the Nationalist budget balanced, and C. T. Wang worked hard as Foreign Minister.

By the autumn of 1930 it was considered almost as much a slur on one's family to be in politics as it is in America; and there were frequent complaints in the press that Chinese families were investing their surplus wealth in foreign government bonds and foreign securities, instead of in Chinese industrial and commercial enterprises.

IV

RAIN IN SUMMER

1

SKATING west from Pa Li Tai Bridge on the morning of January 17, 1931, my daughter and I accepted a kind invitation to rest and take a cup of tea in the Hour of the Snake with some people named Wu — a family of emigrants on the way to Tientsin to board the train for Manchuria. Their canal boat, fitted with runners, like the boat on which we travel to the House of Exile, had been pushed off the double-track iceway into the wayside bay below the Village of the Fragrant Forest. There were thirty-seven in the family, counting the youngest girl, who had been born on the boat the previous afternoon. They were all of the same surname, descendants of the two eldest, a man and a woman who had celebrated six decades of marriage.

These Wus had come from "two moons down the Canal." They are farmers, descended from "folk who have tilled the earth for generations beyond count." One of them was born with a club foot and apprenticed to a smith. He has forged farm tools in his home hamlet for thirty years and is now teaching his trade to a nine-year-old nephew who was shot in the hip last year by marauding soldiers. Another, who was stung blind by bees, was apprenticed to the Minstrel of the City of the Third Dyke. He can play the moon guitar and sing songs from the "forty-six centuries of Chinese history, to enlighten the family in times of darkness, because by examining

the past we can understand the present and know the future."
From external appearances and the acquaintance of an hour,
I found the family self-respecting, decent people — good citizens such as China needs now. Yet they were leaving the
homestead where they had dwelt for two centuries and going
out beyond the Wall.

They were dressed in clean, neat, warmly wadded cotton
garments and homemade shoes. Before eating, they washed
their faces and hands, calloused and thickened by honest toil,
in basins of steaming water. In addition to good tea they
had whole-grain flour noodles, grown and prepared at home
before the journey, seasoned with fresh green onion tops bought
from a passing farm boat. After the meal they scrubbed
their strong white teeth with salt, washed their food bowls,
chopsticks, and the cooking pot, then put out the charcoal
fire in the cookstove, saving the bits of once-used fuel. Two
of the women cracked walnuts for the mother of the newborn
child, saying, "She has two to feed, so she must have something
extra." The great-great-great-grandmother told me that,
rolled inside their bedding, they each had a complete outfit of
summer clothes, sewn before leaving their old homestead;
when spring came they expected to be entirely occupied planting crops in new fields.

My daughter asked the Elder why he was leaving the fertile
midlands, where the climate is kind, to farm northern fields
where the cruel winter shortens the growing season to a scant
portion of the year. In reply he said: —

"Thatch your roof before the rains; dig your well before
you are thirsty. We flee from the wrath of the Three of the
Midlands — the Yangtze, the Yellow River, and the Canal.
Shamefully neglected for more than two decades, the Three
are angry. They are not satisfied with a few bright toys flung
into their waters to a mythical dragon at festival times. The
historical annals record more practical appeasement. In the
past, engineers have coaxed the Three into good humor, re-

turning to them part of the riches received from midland harvest: they dredged canals, built and repaired dykes, and helped the Three control the summer rains.   It is now twice ten years since the engineers went away, and we flee from the wrath to come."

"The ice level in the canal is a finger-length higher than ever before in my father's lifetime," said the man who sat next to the Elder as he handed him the pipe he had lighted.   "It is a warning to the House of Wu to move elsewhere, even though we have enjoyed two centuries of satisfaction in that place. Twenty years ago, in the first year of the Republic, we sent petitions to Peking concerning three weak places in the dykes above our fields, that had been neglected by the previous government.   Our cry was not heard.   Four years ago we welcomed the Nationalists as saviors.   We have reported the danger nine times to Nanking.   Our nine cries are not heard. The places of weakness now number twenty.   We have sent foot scouts to other farmers of the rich midlands.   They have reported that it is common knowledge in the village market place that at the next season of heavy rain the Three will sweep out, causing such devastation as has not previously been recorded in Chinese history.   The midlands are the treasure chest of the National Government.   Nanking, their capital, the Queen of the Three Valleys, sits at the place of threefold danger.   Can we judge these new rulers wise men when they are now entirely occupied arguing among themselves about party discipline?"

We skated home with the sun on our backs.

When we reached home we found that Mai-da had arrived in answer to a letter I had written her, in fulfillment of the promise I had made her late husband, informing her of the envelope he had given me to be opened at the close of the customary three-year period of widow's mourning.   We got the envelope from the deposit box in the Western bank where I had put it.   We carried it home and opened it in my upstairs sitting room. It contained a letter, dated on the very afternoon on which he went to that fatal dinner.

MY DEAREST DEAR, —

The moon is not round for long; the sunset-tinged clouds are soon scattered. Before I lifted thy veil and we knew each other, gossip told me that thy heart had been given to another. I approached our union, arranged in accordance with custom, with reluctance; but through six years thou hast made me more comfortable than the gods and given me such pleasure as mortal man knows is seldom given south of heaven. Happiness makes one more intelligent. Continued happiness, long life, and health are the common desire of all men. I have had the first and the third. I know that I am not to have the second. I have erred in political judgment and one day soon, any day now, I shall leave thy arms to ride, to walk, or to dine, and my body, emptied of its spirit, will be sent back to thee. Earth has no feasts that do not break up. Do not continue to grieve now that thee has completed the mourning. Do not probe into the details concerning my departure. I have often instructed thee not to meddle in politics, and I trust thee to obey me in this. Probing would not fetch me back to life, but it would involve thee dangerously.

For thee, my sweet flower, I desire long plenteous years and felicitous seasons. According to the custom of our country I cannot bequeath thee a private fortune, but by the day thou readest this my estate will have been collected into the homestead treasury. It is a liberal addition to the Family fortune, and in attaching a gift to this letter I do not feel that I am acting dishonorably. I want thee to be independent. Loving another thou hast been good to me, and now I want to make it possible for thee to wed the Manchu whom political circumstance has deprived of his inherited fortune.

In the envelope we found seven thousand pounds of British, one hundred thousand francs of French, and thirty-two thousand dollars of American Government bonds.

2

All during this year the Anti-Japanese Society was active. On the morning of the nineteenth of January I was in the shop of Ping, on the Taku Road, when a pretty little Chinese girl, about four years old, dressed in pink silk trousers and coat lined with white rabbit, came in, holding fast to her nurse's hand. The child told Ping that her uncle had given her a dollar and she wanted to purchase a doll. She inspected Ping's dolls, and finally chose one with a chubby body which he assured her could be washed all over.

Ping's clerk was wrapping up the doll when two Anti-Japanese Scouts arrived. They were exceedingly self-assured schoolboys of perhaps fifteen or sixteen years. The elder took the parcel from the clerk, examined the doll, and said it was made in Japan. Then, despite the protests of the child and her nurse, he tucked it under his arm and joined his companion in pulling merchandise from cases and shelves.

They pronounced this and that Japanese-made, and threw other goods carelessly on the floor, trampling over them so that Ping's tidy shop was soon in a disgraceful state. Ping stood by impassive. There was a policeman on duty at the corner; the shutters of the glass-fronted shop were down, so that he could easily see what was going on — but he did nothing.

When the Scouts had gathered together spoil enough to "teach a lesson," — cotton cloth, knitting wool, spools, bath towels (which plainly bore the woven-in trade-mark of a local Chinese factory), candles, bedroom slippers, and two crates of Swedish matches, — they directed the frightened young clerk to pile the merchandise in a heap in the centre of the Taku Road. Traffic was diverted to make room for it. The elder Scout laid the doll on the pyre, while the second set the whole ablaze by putting one of the lighted candles under each crate of matches. When I left, the child who had bought the doll was screaming and struggling to get away from her nurse so that she could fly at the vandals who had destroyed her treasure.

At the corner I asked the policeman why he had permitted the bonfire. He shuffled his feet uneasily, but remained silent.

When I had repeated my question three times, he replied, "As yet I have received no command to thwart anti-Japanese activities."

These words were overheard by a coppersmith with a powerful guild behind him, who seized the occasion to lecture the policeman. A crowd came away from the bonfire to listen.

"Six of our neighbors," said the coppersmith, "have been ruined in this street in nine moons. First the government collects taxes again after they have already been paid, then it lets these Anti-Japanese Scouts complete our ruin. I have not heard that the Nationalist government has prohibited the importation of Japanese goods. Such merchandise pays import duty to get here; if it were forbidden, surely it would not be allowed to pass the customs. The merchants do not stock it just to be impudent. They would not have it on their shelves if the people did not want it. Yet these schoolboys take it upon themselves to punish the merchants by seizing everything their fancy prompts them to pronounce Japanese-made, and they trample and spoil hundreds of dollars' worth of Chinese-made goods as well. By neglecting to stop the foolishness of these students, who ought to be at their books, you police are thrusting your thumbs through your own paper lanterns. It is the merchants who pay the taxes and make possible the modern luxury of a policeman at every corner in a nice uniform. When there are no more merchants, you will be out of a job."

Farther down the street I saw a Japanese in military uniform photographing an anti-Japanese poster.

3

Early in May 1931 the press was filled with reports that the Nanking officials were demanding the surrender of all the foreign concessions in China. These concessions comprise only a few square acres, adding together the land at Shanghai, Canton, Chinkiang, Newchwang and Tientsin. Originally set aside by the rulers of China for the segregation of Westerners, they no longer serve that purpose. To-day Westerners in China are not segregated. Though they may not own property outside the concessions, they may live anywhere they can rent a residence. The concession areas naturally became oases during the perpetual civil war of the past twenty years, and as a consequence so many natives have taken refuge within them that the majority of the residents are now Chinese.

All the concessions stand on swamps. Only the most undesirable sites could be spared for the "barbarians" who pushed into China to barter and trade, despite every effort of the Son of Heaven to discourage them. The swamps were drained, filled in, and planted with trees. All the concessions have fine schoolhouses, adequate to educate all the children of the residents, good hospitals, modern sewage systems, and furnish water and electricity at much lower rates than any other municipal government in China has been able to do. Most of them have a comfortable balance in their private treasuries.

I frequently hear it said, over teacups in Chinese courtyards, that since China is now proclaimed a democratic Republic, the fate of the concessions should not be autocratically decided by ministers and officials, but by a ballot of all the residents. The clear implication of this is that, if the local Chinese were allowed a voice in the matter, the concessions would remain as they are now until such date as a stable government is established in China — which will be, according to the Elder of Exile, "several decades from now."

Until recently the municipal bonds of the concessions have regularly paid 6 per cent and been counted gilt-edged investments. They dropped alarmingly when it became a possibility that these areas might come under the same government as the rest of China.

Shortly after the opening of the Nanking Conference on Concessions, Su-ling told me that the House of Lui, noted for financial shrewdness, were selling, and advising all their relatives-by-marriage to sell, British Concession bonds — and buy French.   She said that the Lui clan interpreted the briskness with which England turned over the Hankow concession and the administration of the fishing village of Wei-hai-wei as evidence that "the British of this generation are eager to relinquish their inherited responsibilities and glad to find sentimental reasons to hand things over."

The countries in whose names these concessions are held reap no revenues from them.   They are entirely self-supporting except for the cost, which is probably considerable, of sending

TOWARD MONGOLIA

out and maintaining troops to gesture fighting away from the concession borders.   In spite of this, the concessions remain a potential source of trouble.   Chinese officials driven from office hide safely in them from their enemy officials — the Kuomintang has always maintained headquarters in the French Concession at Shanghai, the "Peking Presidents" always kept residences fully staffed in one or other of the Tientsin concessions, and in any civil strife the loser runs straight away for a concession.   The modern Chinese politician, with insight into Western character acquired through education in Europe or America, uses the concessions as a smoke-screen entitled "foreign aggression" when he desires to win sympathy from the

Western world as well as when he desires to distract the attention of the Chinese people away from something he is planning.

4

As I looked down from my Tientsin sitting-room window, at which I was writing the above extract in my journal, I saw a little group of nine Chinese people waiting, bewildered by the motor traffic, for the policeman to signal them that it was safe to cross the street. On that day, May 23, 1931, I entered: —

Ever since I came to live here, in April 1927, there has been a steady flux of hardy, independent, good-natured farm families passing through Tientsin en route to Manchuria beyond the Great Wall. There seem to be even more this spring than usual.

According to a census report which I heard a young Chinese economist deliver this week at the Nankai University, there are now thirty million farmers spread sparsely over the 364,000 square miles of Manchuria. At the time Japan began to take an interest in the development of those generous empty acres, laying railways to induce settlers to open virgin soil with the plough, there were only five million Chinese living in Manchuria. The Chinese Government was anxious lest overpopulous Japan should colonize in such numbers as to overshadow the Chinese, but events have proved this fear groundless. Twenty-seven million of the present population are Chinese.

"China proper is not crowded," said the economist. "One may travel for weeks in our country through fertile, uncultivated acres. Foreigners think we are overpopulated because they see only a few cities. In peace time it would have been impossible to colonize Manchuria, but circumstances have accomplished what the government could never have brought about by direct efforts. Civil war in the eighteen provinces has driven the peace-loving farmers out to settle Manchuria even more effectively than the Japanese government, with all its paternal coaxing, has been able to move its own citizens. In 1927, the most turbulent year of the revolution, over a million Chinese went into Manchuria. In 1928 half a million became farm proprietors there. In 1929 the emigrants numbered six hundred thousand, and in 1930 another half million joined them. In spite of the extreme difficulties encountered in the harsh climate, the Chinese farmer endures them with good spirit: he is unconcerned about hardship so long as he can plough, sow, and reap undisturbed."

Large numbers of these migrating peasants pass through Tientsin by boat, by train, and on foot, according to the fullness of their purses. They travel in family groups. One sees babies in the arms of their parents, and aged folk, too weak to walk, riding astride the backs of their descendants. They have their ploughs, their seed, their kitchen gods, often even the hearthstone from their old homestead; along with their clothes, their bedding, food, and incense to burn at wayside shrines, they often carry roots and cuttings from favorite rosebushes and shrubs.

Mai-da cannot look at them without tears in her eyes. She avoids the roads and streets where they are likely to be met, and always enters my house by the kitchen court because the trekkers pass by my front gate. She loves her birth-home with such passion that she can think of no worse fate than that of voluntary exile from the place where one's ancestors have dwelt. But it is not so many centuries since my own ancestors left England in search of independence and freedom. I myself, in girlhood, came here as an adopted daughter of Lin. So I feel differently. I often wander down the Willow Road to see the emigrant families who approach Tientsin on foot.

I have been intensely curious to know what manner of people these were who had suddenly deserted the graves of their ancestors to seek the Promised Land outside the Wall. All to whom I have talked have shown themselves to be resolute, gallant folk, ready to meet a new life with courage and fortitude. They are all stoutly Chinese. Not one of them will concede that there is a race in the world equal in any respect to their own. They speak of all others as "barbarians," except "our half-civilized cousins, the Japanese." They are firm in their conviction that Chinese confer a benefit upon any place they enter. They are not at all concerned about matters of government. "We have had many dynasties and many governments," they say. "Whatever the regulations, we farmers abide by them."

When I have asked about Manchuria, they replied: —

"We flee before the God of Civil War and the God of Flood. There is a King in Manchuria, but we can't remember his name. We do not know whether he is Russian, British as in Malaya, American as in San Francisco, Japanese, Manchu, or Ming. What does it matter? We have assurance from the member of our family sent to investigate that he lets farmers settle there and, beyond taking 20 per cent of the harvest, does not bother people."

5

Our garden extends on the south to the Newchwang Road, where it faces a red-brick house, built in Western style, which is part of the estate of the Chang family of Mukden. When appointed Mayor of Tientsin, Chang Hsueh-ming came to reside there. He is the second son of the late Chang Tso-lin, whom the populace called the "King of Manchuria." The oldest son is Chang Hsueh-liang, who inherited the eldership of the family and his father's rights to the dictatorship of the provinces north of the Great Wall.

Late in the spring, this elder brother flew from Mukden and stopped the night in his younger brother's household. Then he flew on to Nanking. Shortly after he had gone, Hsueh-ming's wife waved to me, as I sprayed the roses that ramble over our summerhouse, and called that she would come and help me if I wanted her. She came, and as we worked she told me that the Elder Brother had gone to try to patch up the conflicts within the Nationalist Party which made it impossible for the Nationalist Government to give attention to the care of the people, although it was now four years since the National flag was unfurled over all China.

She explained that Chang Hsueh-liang had asked Hsueh-ming to fly down to Nanking with him. She, the wife, had feigned neuralgia to keep her husband from going, as she thought the trip unwise. The homestead uncles and aunts in Mukden had tried to prevent the Elder Brother from leaving Mukden, because the Japanese authorities in Manchuria looked with disfavor on this friendship, and had warned Hsueh-liang against involving that region any further in the vortex of politics within the Wall.

Ten days later I was exercising a horse on the Race Course when Chang Hsueh-liang's plane landed in the centre of the course. Chang and his male secretary were lifted out unconscious, and carried to a closed car, in which they were taken to the Rockefeller hospital at Peking. Every effort was made to keep his serious illness secret, since such incidents always cause a run on the banks and general political unrest. Landing in the Tientsin Race Club was a part of this attempt to keep it secret. But, in that insidious way in which rumors get abroad in China, hot-cake vendors, minstrels, and clerks in shops were spreading word twenty-four hours before the plane arrived that Chang Hsueh-liang, Dictator in Manchuria, had been poisoned at Nanking.

Through June the only disturbance in the peace was the continued activity of the Anti-Japanese Scouts. School-teachers complained, in the vernacular press, that the students spent their days and nights in Anti-Japanese activities. Not only the shops, but the bridges, the railway stations, and the roads were infested by Anti-Japanese Scouts. Most of them were fresh-faced, impudent schoolboys, and schoolgirls as well; but in their ranks I also saw coarse ruffians from the lowest alleys in the city. They not only confiscated merchants' goods, but they stopped carriers and carters to rip open luggage and cases that had passed the Customs, and they accosted people in the street.

I myself was accosted, and had my blue-flowered scarf taken away. It was made in America, but the Scout who claimed it — he was a grown man — swore that it was made in Japan. Although it was faded and twice darned, I was annoyed to lose it. I argued and even appealed to the head priest of the temple I had been visiting, but a kindly Chinese gentleman in the crowd that had collected advised me to let it go. "One cannot blow out a fire with a rolling-pin," he remarked. Then a gentlewoman who had been praying at the shrine took my arm, saying: "Come away. It is best always to suit self to cir-cumstance."

Shun-ko came to visit me for the week of the Midsummer Festival. En route she had observed the Anti-Japanese ac-tivities at Peking and she became so alarmed by what she saw in and around Tientsin that she went to talk with Mayor Chang Hsueh-ming about it. Where there was an Anti-Japanese poster or an Anti-Japanese incident, she noted that there was certain to be a Japanese man in either civilian garb or military uniform quietly but industriously photographing and making notes. She was convinced that Japan was plotting some mischief and wanted the Mayor to stop the activities of the Anti-Japanese Scouts. He told her that the matter was in higher hands than his and he could do nothing.

In July, Chang Hsueh-liang's mission to Nanking appeared to have been futile. The feud between the Nationalist Party members, far from being ended, mounted to civil war. Canton arsenals were reported to be making cartridges, rifles, pistols, machine guns and smokeless powder in day and night shifts, for a revolution against President Chiang Kai-shek.

Chang Hsueh-liang's secretary died at the Rockefeller hospital. Daily bulletins were issued from our Mayor's office reporting the elder brother's progress. But no one was permitted to see him. People, even one Western consul, declared that he was dead and the truth kept secret, as his father's death was kept secret in June 1928.

On the fifth of July we dined at the Japanese Consulate. Chinese, French, Americans, British, Italians, and Scandinavians were present at this dinner. The Japanese said quite openly, with the Chinese guests listening, that if Chang Hsueh-liang was alive or did recover, he could never return to Manchuria — as his friendship with Chiang Kai-shek and his alliance with the Nationalist Party made his government quite unsuitable to conditions north of the Great Wall. As evidence of this they said that more than three hundred insults to Japan had occurred there since he inherited the dictatorship, and that, moreover, his brother, our Mayor, had made no effort to stop anti-Japanese activities here. When the Japanese were asked who would be acceptable to them, they just smiled and gave no answer.

On the morning of the sixth, I received an invitation from Mr. and Mrs. Henry Pu-yi, the Manchu ex-Emperor and Empress. They had received a gift of raspberries from the country and were going to have raspberry *fu-yung*, in which I delight, for the eleven-o'clock meal. Chou, our cook, hastily made a freezer of ice cream and accompanied me to serve it.

During this visit the ex-Empress told me that her husband had been unofficially approached by Japanese callers, as well as by his relatives, who work continuously for a monarchical restoration, and by anti-Chang Family Chinese, regarding acceptance of a throne in Manchuria, but that they were both anxious to keep free of all politics. They accompanied me to the gate when I left and said: "Do come again. We need our friends in these trying times."

All through the month, the thermometer hovered around ninety in the shade, and we had plenty of rain. The crops in the country came on excellently. I was guest on an all-day picnic arranged by the River Commission aboard their launch. The picnic was not just to give officials and their wives and members of prominent families a pleasant day: its object was to draw attention to the danger of flood. We were asked to recall that our province was a flood plain, and that the Hai River, curving in a restricted and narrow channel through and around Tientsin, is the only outlet to the sea. The complicated system of dykes and canals, which for centuries have been used to draw off surplus water, was reviewed; and the British, French, German, and Chinese engineers employed by the Commission emphasized the need of immediate improvements and repairs. History was quoted to remind us that Tientsin's past has been checkered with devastating floods. Photographs of the most recent catastrophes, in 1917 and 1924, were passed around.

I remembered that the flood mark in our house, which stands in the most elevated section of Tientsin, is at the second landing of the stairs, and that the gateman had told me how the family then in residence dwelt safely above. The engineers declared that the next flood would be worse, and that it might come any rainy season now. If so, we have a third story to retire to, but the average Chinese house has only one.

I concluded before noon that day that the government at Tientsin, like the governments in the Yangtze, Yellow River, and Grand Canal valleys, would do nothing except trust the gods not to send rain.

We were at Pei-tai-ho when the news of the Yangtze catastrophe, aggravated by fifteen breaks in the dykes of the Grand Canal, reached us by telegram from Hankow. We, and all our friends and neighbors, had loved relatives and friends in the Three Valleys. The days that followed were days of great anxiety. Telegrams and the press reported more and more breaks in the channel walls of the neglected waterways. People who knew the real terror of the flood, and there were many such among us, prayed that their loved ones should meet quick death as the waters rushed down upon them, and not survive, clinging to floating débris, to suffer starvation.

Mai-da had a Red Cross certificate. She volunteered for a corps organized to fight plague, which is an attribute of flood. Women who had planned new clothes for the autumn season gave the sums they had intended for their own wardrobes and all the other money they could get together. Western men planning "home leave" put it off a year and contributed the money to relief instead. The House of Exile gave ten thousand dollars as thank offering that their district had been saved from flood. The Emperor of Japan sent a personal gift of fifty thousand dollars in addition to the sympathy donation for flood relief sent by the Japanese people. Japanese health experts volunteered their service and went to work with the Chinese medical corps.

Mai-da wrote from Nanking that the water was so high there that it was necessary to camp the refugees on the wall. Su-ling was in the corps working below Hankow and wrote that it was impossible to describe the sad plight of the afflicted, or even to measure the extent of the flood, as the rushing water made it impossible to get out over the flood area. Airplanes circled over the flood lands, scouting for hillocks where refugees clung, and Colonel and Mrs. Lindbergh joined in making the survey when they arrived in China. Uncle Shao-chun was invited to go to the Capital and help get the water under control. But he felt that it was too late for him to be of any use. He asked instead that he be used to prepare against similar disaster in other districts. His request was not answered.

6

When I returned to Tientsin, Japanese and Chinese officials were still extremely polite to each other at dinner parties and social gatherings. It was still a serious breach of good taste to invite one nationality and leave out the other "because they do not go well together." But over cups of tea in Chinese courtyards it was common talk that the two countries were on the eve of war.

In the streets every day anti-Japanese incidents were numerous. About nine o'clock one morning I saw the candy vendor accosted by a well-dressed young man with a picket's badge, who proceeded to examine the old man's wares. I cannot imagine what the picket found, but he claimed that something was made in Japan, and gave a lesson in "national loyalty" by wrecking the portable cook-stove and emptying the bamboo sugar jar over the candyman's head.

At eleven that same day I saw two little Japanese schoolgirls baited by impudent questions and pushed about by a mob of Chinese children. The sash of one little girl was pulled off and trampled, and excitement was running high when Tientsin's most popular actor happened to peer out from his To and From the World Door. He snatched the Japanese maids inside and bolted his gates in the astonished faces of their persecutors. And at four that same afternoon pickets went down Shoe Street and commandeered all the cobblers' Formosa snakeskin, which was the fashionable shoe material this autumn.

In addition to the pickets there were numerous Anti-Japanese Scouts who tried to educate the people by street lectures. I listened to several. They all informed the passing populace that every treaty with Japan is unfair because none confers mutual benefits, only benefits to Japan. All the treaties have been signed under duress, they explained, and bear the signature of Chinese politicians who were bribed to sell their country. I secured and carefully read copies of all the Sino-Japanese treaties, and am tempted to believe that most of what the lecturers said is true. But after one of the orators had scolded the Street of Nine Blessings for more than half an hour for its indifference, I heard a man hitched behind a mule in the drawing harness of a cart remark, "We might be more sensitive to the danger of Japanese vassalage if we had ever known anything but vassalage at home."

Chang Hsueh-liang disproved the rumor that he was dead by granting interviews to all the Northern war lords. Soon after this he showed himself to the populace on the Polo Field at Peking, looking very frail on horseback; daily thereafter he took strenuous exercise in public view.

Through all this time the vernacular press gave scant heed to Sino-Japanese affairs. They were engrossed entirely with reports of the daily happenings in a civil war between President Chiang Kai-shek and the party veterans, Sun-fo and Wang Ching-wei, which continued with ruthless destruction of life and property, and a consequent undermining of the people's faith, as one body of troops pushed northward from Canton while another marched southward from Nanking. Chinese living in San Francisco, London, Paris, Berlin, Australia and Malaya telegraphed their "brothers in the homeland" to desist this internecine fighting because the country, already harassed by flood, was now menaced by Japan.

These telegrams were published for the comfort of the people. The strife, however, did not end. The Cantonese spent over two million, five hundred thousand dollars in Japan for the purchase of army equipment. The President's army bought supplies from the United States: twenty-five planes and five hundred cases of machine-gun ammunition reached Nanking in September.

7

On September 19, 1931, refugees from Manchuria began to pour into Tientsin's East Station. They carried their babes in their arms and their elders on their backs. Aside from this, they had little resemblance to the emigrants who, only a short time previously, were passing through Tientsin in a steady stream on the way to the Promised Land. They were sullen and slow to speak.

Banners were hung on both sides of the approach to the station, assuring the refugees that if they would continue on to Peking they would find shelter and two good meals a day. But most of the unfortunates appeared anxious to return to their birthplaces. They got off the trains, bought a little food from vendors, and set out on foot for the distant homes from which they originally came. As the frequent trains came in, the refugees seemed a large number, but, when I recalled the vast migration that had pushed northward through Tientsin in the past four years, my reason told me that those who returned were but a small proportion of the whole.

A refugee who would talk said that the Japanese had occupied Mukden, the seat of the Manchurian government, in the night, with practically no resistance, and the very quietness of the act, as well as the swift flight of the familiar Chinese officials who came inside the Wall in three trains, had alarmed the populace. But Japan did not want the Chinese settlers to leave. Japanese spokesmen attempted to calm the people by assuring them that it was best for them to remain in their shops and their farms. When this proved insufficient to check the exodus, Japan fought fear with fear, making the Chinese settlers more afraid to return than to stay. This strategy was carried out by having airplanes follow the refugee trains and drop bombs. It was effective.

Shortly after this, President Chiang Kai-shek, although still preoccupied with the southern advance, sent word to Mo Teh-lui, at Moscow, instructing him to bring Russia over to China's side in the dispute with Japan in Manchuria. News of his message leaked out and caused general indignation among the gentry, merchants, and craftsmen, who remembered Russia's former friendship and did not trust alliance with her. Among my Chinese acquaintances the people of every class, except the students, were united in favor of non-resistance against Japan: they wanted to trust the League of Nations to investigate and effect a fair settlement. The students, rallied as the Anti-Japanese Society, wanted war.

In considering the prestige and the license of these students, we of the West must temper our judgment by remembrance that through all the annals of the dynasties the scholars have held first place among the four classes into which Chinese society is divided. Until very recently the nation's governors have been appointed from the scholars, who were chosen on the basis of written examinations open to the sons of all classes.

China is now proclaimed a Republic; but this preciousness still clings to her scholars, and she has been so disturbed by revolution and reformation for the past twenty-one years that her present-day scholars have not had the discipline of continuous study of an established curriculum. Few of them have ever attended a school in which the year's term was not broken by civil war. Also the ideology has been changed continuously in this era.

On the Moon's Birthday two thousand students, delegates from different schools all over China, went to Hangchow to punish the Minister for Foreign Affairs, C. T. Wang, because he had not obeyed their dictation and declared war on Japan. They assumed that as a matter of course he would celebrate the festival with his wife at their lake-side home. The students assembled in force and broke open the To and From the World Gate of the most beautiful old Chinese homestead by the West Lake. They went through the courts, ripping up treasured flowers and shrubs, and through the Hall of Family Gathering, slashing ancient portraits to ribbons with their knives. In the library they tarried to destroy precious books and manuscripts which it had taken centuries to collect, and then surged into the adjoining rooms, sweeping aside, by their superior numbers and youthful energy, the women and servants who attempted to bar the way.

The vandals were busy smashing priceless porcelain when the aged, feeble Family Elder was brought from his bed to speak to them. As he appeared, the students greeted him with shouts: "Mr. Wang, come out and be bambooed!" The old gentleman quieted the mob by telling them that the homestead of Mr. Wang was on the other side of the lake.

"Very sorry!" the scholars apologized. "Our mistake." Then they hurried around the lake and demolished the beautiful Wang home. But they failed to find the Minister for Foreign Affairs. While they were wrecking his house and terrifying his kin, a telegram arrived from a scholar at Nanking announcing that the Minister was spending the festival at his desk.

Our neighbors, who are relatives of Mr. Wang's wife, received a message that evening giving the sequel to this outrageous attack. It stated that Mr. Wang, while working at his desk in the Ministry of Foreign Affairs, was set upon by three thousand other students, who beat him with bamboos and almost killed him by hurling inkpots, electric lights, and chairs at him. His faithful servants climbed through a window and succeeded in dragging him out after he had been ren-

dered unconscious. His life was despaired of for many
months, and he is still an invalid because of this outrage.

Thus one of China's most able men was eliminated from
Sino-Japanese affairs, and President Chiang Kai-shek was deprived of a loyal supporter, who had stood by him through four
years of arduous government work.

Mr. Wang was educated in classical Chinese at home. Later
he won degrees at Peiyang University, Tokyo University, and
Yale. He fought in the Revolution in 1911, and has since held
a succession of government posts. I have never heard any
Chinese deny the report that he has worked without salary
and never added one dollar to the homestead treasury because
of his government connection. He was a delegate to the Paris
Peace Conference, where he advised against the signing of the
Versailles Treaty, because he thought the Shantung clauses
gave too much to Japan. As Chiang Kai-shek's Minister for
Foreign Affairs since 1928, he had managed to induce every
Western nation which enjoyed special exemption to sign treaties
recognizing China's autonomy in tariff matters, and had entered into conversations by which every country had condi-
tionally agreed to consider the relinquishment of extra-terri-
torial rights.

No action was taken against the students. They continued
to flow in upon the Capital. Soon eighty thousand were reported camped upon the government offices demanding war.
The problem of housing and feeding them was serious, particularly since the resources of the city had already been heavily
drawn upon to take care of the flood refugees, and to support
the army. Iron gates had to be erected to safeguard all government offices.

At Tientsin, on November 3, the principal of the Middle
School attempted to read President Chiang Kai-shek's mandate
forbidding students to agitate against Japan and commanding
teachers to enforce discipline. Two hundred students set
upon the principal and injured him so seriously that later he

died in hospital.   Incidents such as this occurred all over the country.

The only result of President Chiang Kai-shek's mandate was that more students, carrying megaphones like American football leaders, boarded the trains, in all provinces, en route to Nanking, to demand that he do his duty by an immediate declaration of war against Japan.   They asked for and got free passage and free food in the diners.   Nothing was done to stop them, anywhere.   At Tientsin, when they had wrecked a stationmaster's house and lain down, three thousand strong, across the tracks, thereby stopping the Peking-Shanghai Express on which they wanted places, the Scotsman who is adviser to the Chinese railway authorities suggested that the firehose be used to drive them away.   But his advice was ignored and extra cars were attached to the train to give them place.

During all this period the rumor "To-night Japan will march on Tientsin" was voiced continuously.   The consuls took the rumor sufficiently seriously to make plans for such an emergency.   Several times they jointly advised both the Japanese Consul General and the Japanese Commander here that they thought such action unwise, "if contemplated."

I ordered a copy of the life of George Fox for the ex-Emperor, Mr. Henry Pu-yi, and when it came I presented it personally.   I found him and his wife much perturbed by callers who were using every possible means of persuasion and pressure to get him to agree to be crowned Emperor of Manchuria.   The ex-Emperor had sold his ivories privately and disposed of the lease of his house.   He had realized twenty-five thousand dollars and given the money to flood relief.   He and his wife had telegraphed President Chiang Kai-shek at Nanking and Chang Hsueh-liang at Peking, asserting their loyalty and asking for sanctuary.

They never received any reply.   The rumble of field-gun fire and rifle shot disturbed Tientsin during the last three weeks of November.   In this period of Sino-Japanese dispute, the ex-Emperor and ex-Empress were taken away "to a place of safety" by a Japanese escort, who put them on a Japanese gunboat which sped down river under cover of the night.

The ex-Empress's aunt came to me, weeping because the ex-Emperor had sworn a compact with his wife to commit suicide before he would consent to be King of Manchuria. In her sad mood, I got her to agree to be sponsor to Mai-da's marriage to Prince Erh-sung. He took on Chinese citizenship and they were married without ceremony, next day.

I have not heard directly from the ex-Empress since she was taken from Tientsin. Her aunt has had two letters. In both, her niece assured her that the Japanese were treating her and her husband with generosity and such ceremonious courtesy as is accorded a King and Queen by royalistic people. In February 1932 I read in a Japanese news bureau dispatch that Manchuria had declared its independence of China and set itself up as the sovereign state of Ankuo, which means "Land of Peace," and that the ruler of the new state was Henry Pu-yi, with the title of Genshu.

The fighting at Tientsin was sporadic — not much in the daytime and occasionally slack even after dark, then again incessant rumbling of guns from sunset until dawn. The Japanese authorities petitioned the Chinese to stop it; the Chinese handled the situation with extreme cautiousness. In the streets it was common talk that the trouble had been started by the Japanese hiring Chinese ruffians to set off rifles in various places so that they would have excuse to invade the city. The Mayor's house, adjoining ours, was the scene of many conferences with Western business men, consuls, and commanders in Northern China, in a sincere attempt to prevent Tientsin from becoming the tinder that would set war ablaze.

Scores of people were killed and injured. The Empress of Japan sent bandages made with her own hand for the Japanese wounded. The Chinese Red Cross Society nursed and doctored the Chinese wounded. The frightened populace left their homes and camped far out in the fields despite the bitter weather. In December, the careful conferences succeeded in diverting the gunfire away from Tientsin.

Sino-Japanese cannonading ceased in our streets. But all over China incident after incident tightened the tension with Japan. Bald-the-third has a passion for newspapers. She took in newspapers published in all the provinces. She made it her habit to read aloud to me each day while I dressed for dinner.

Each day civil war and internal politics distracted the Nanking Government, while Japan moved aggressively and the students clamored for war.

8

Wellington Koo accepted the Ministry of Foreign Affairs, vacated by the injured C. T. Wang. After his acceptance, the student deputation from Hsuchow succeeded in entering his office and forced him to answer eight questions on the Sino-Japanese crisis. The principal among these questions were: —

Did he agree that the League of Nations was a failure?
Would the new Ministry immediately abolish all existing treaties with Japan?
Why had an alliance with America against Japan not been cemented?

The new Foreign Minister's answers were reported to the other student groups as evasive and unsatisfactory. The Hsuchow group called for volunteers, and thirty-five thousand other students joined them in camping out in front of the national buildings in the drizzling rain. They refused to move from this place until President Chiang Kai-shek should hand them a statement announcing the date of his departure for Manchuria to fight Japan.

The President spoke to them when they had waited there a

week. He asked them to be patient during Sino-Japanese negotiations and suggested that they all might enlist in his regiments. They did not accept this suggestion. The weather became colder and they were given blankets from the office of the Minister of Military Affairs.

Japan moved warships up and down along the coast, distributing stores of ammunition in all the places where Japanese reside, "as a precaution against Chinese uprising." Car after car of guns and soldiers passed through Tientsin, and twenty and thirty Japanese men in civilian garb arrived daily via passenger trains from beyond the Great Wall. They were busy making record of the activities of the Anti-Japanese Societies. Although they were very polite, their presence did disturb the Chinese people. On the seventh of December, eight Japanese airplanes flew low over the roofs of villages; they dropped bombs in the empty fields, which tore the winter wheat up badly.

In early December Alfred Sze, who was representing China at the League of Nations conferences on Sino-Japanese affairs, resigned. He telegraphed Chiang Kai-shek that he had received so many letters and telegrams from his fellow countrymen and countrywomen, objecting to what he did and said, that he knew it was no longer right for him to speak as the voice of China. Wellington Koo resigned the Ministry of Foreign Affairs on the same day for the same reason. Jeered and booed by the students camped around the national office buildings each time he went out, Chiang Kai-shek struggled all week to hold a government together. But on the thirteenth, Hu Han-min, one of the most influential Kuomintang veterans, whose support Chiang had asked, sent a circular telegram out to the nation and to all the settlements of Chinese abroad, asking: "Who appointed young Chiang Kai-shek, of Fenghua near Ningpo, President-Dictator of all China?"

Immediately, Chiang Kai-shek announced his retirement in a circular telegram, in which he stated that during the years since he first took up the chairmanship of the national government, he had striven to carry out the teachings of Sun Yat-sen; but had met with such failure, as a result of repeated disloyalty and civil war, that he had come to the conclusion that he was incapable of uniting his country. He would only wait at Nanking until another came forward to relieve him of the government seal.

The following day, General Honjo, Commander of the Japanese Kungtung Garrison, announced that there was corruption in the Northeastern Salt Administration, dispatched Japanese troops to Jehol via Tungliao, and appointed a new Salt Commissioner, with a staff of Japanese assistants. This caused serious concern. The Japanese had stopped Chang Hsueh-liang's Manchurian income. Chang troops quartered on our province had, until now, been paid with these salt revenues. If money could not be found to pay them, they would certainly become unruly and sack towns and villages.

Incensed by this Japanese action, a girl student from Peking, seizing a policeman's rifle, led a riot which destroyed the Central Party Auditorium at Nanking, and partially demolished the Foreign Office. General Chen Ming-shu and Mr. Tsai Yuan-pei, delegated to calm the students, were both seriously injured.

From Shanghai came the report, "Mayor Chun, and a number of the Municipal employees, are prisoners in the hands of students who wrecked the local Kuomintang headquarters last night, destroyed the Chenju Station because the stationmaster was unable to find them a train on which to carry their prisoners to Nanking, burned the railway bridge, cut telephone and telegraph wires, and smashed property in the Municipal Buildings."

On the twenty-second, I saw Chang Hsueh-liang's plane fly south. I had been told that he would go to Nanking again to assure Chiang Kai-shek of his support and confer on the Sino-Japanese situation. But in a couple of hours he returned.

He landed in the field by his brother's house and held conferences there, which filled our crossroads with parked cars until long after dark. That evening Bald-the-third read: —

Chiang Kai-shek and his wife flew quietly away from the Capital shortly after dawn to-day. They left the government seals, keys to his office and the house they have occupied for the past four years, and a note expressing determination never to return to political life, but hereafter to enjoy the care-free life of private individuals at his birthplace homestead.

On the same day the following Japanese events were reported: Japanese troops marched on Chinchow, the last Chinese stronghold in Manchuria. Japanese warships anchored at Chinwantao. Japanese bombing planes circled over the roofs of seven cities within the Wall, without dropping bombs. Another car of Japanese ammunition was dispatched to Peking. Japanese Marines were landed at Foochow. The Japanese garrison was strengthened at Canton. Japanese soldiers enacted sham-battle manœuvres at Tsinan.

On December 24, in addition to further Japanese activity, incidents in civil wars in nine different provinces were reported in picturesque detail, and the editors of all Bald-the-third's papers asked how long the nation must wait before a brave man would come forward and grasp the government seal. Three days later circular telegrams, posters, and criers announced the formation of a National Government. According to the vernacular press: —

At the plenary session of the new government, when the Chinchow situation was brought up, the assembly was in a state of excitement. The majority were at first in favor of the dispatch of one hundred thousand men to repel the Japanese attack. Then someone recommended that Chang Hsueh-liang should be held accountable for the loss of national territory and be punished for it.

But Mr. Wu secured the floor and spoke in defense of Chang Hsueh-liang, averring that if he was punished the Canton party, who instigated the Japanese to invade Manchuria for the purpose of breaking up the Chiang Kai-shek government, should also be censured. Several members hotly contradicted that the Canton party had instigated Japan and pointed out that no matter what the circumstance might be, Chang Hsueh-liang, with an inheritance from his father of half a million well-trained troops, should defend his territory and protect his people from danger.

An order was then written commanding Chang Hsueh-liang to defend North China. It was further resolved that the National Government should summon a National Emergency Conference, within the next half month, to discuss measures for resisting foreign aggression, relieving flood sufferers, and pacifying the country. Thereupon the new government adjourned for the immediate future. The new officials mostly went to Shanghai. The students are also now leaving the Capital, satisfied that they have accomplished something in driving C. T. Wang, T. V. Soong, Chiang Kai-shek, and their associates away.

On the same day Chang Hsueh-liang sent instructions to a subordinate commander to be patient and not provoke the Japanese army to fight. Chang explained that, should a clash occur, handicapped as he was without money for ammunition, food, or winter clothing for the men, the entire Northeastern Army, left him in trust by his sainted father, would be annihilated.

9

After New Year, my daughter and I left Tientsin to visit in America. We traveled to Nanking on the Pukow Express. Chinese soldiers, wearing the colors of three different military governors, came on at different stages and examined passengers. Our car attendant said that, although the three governors were not exactly at war, still they did not want spies from each other's territory crossing over; so any folk who might be spies, on examination, were put off at each border. The soldiers ripped open suspicious luggage with their bayonets. Any weapons found were taken. Some people were not allowed to go further on the train. We were not bothered.

We stopped over in Nanking to visit friends. We found Nanking a city in waiting. The officials of the past four years had gone; the new officials had announced themselves — held one meeting — and disappeared. The roads, the markets, the parks, and the temples we passed were empty. Shops were mostly shuttered. In ordinary times, even if homestead gates are closed, children's voices, folklore songs, and occasionally shrill family squabbles drift over the walls. But in times of uncertainty a Chinese settlement is quiet. Nanking awaited the future with silent apprehension. There were no pilgrims even at the tomb of Sun Yat-sen, from which the silver wreath presented by the Emperor of Japan had been removed.

We visited a week at Shanghai. The late government officials and their families, of my friendship, were occupied reading the classics, attending to commercial business, embroidering slippers, teaching the poor to read and count, playing mahjongg and contract bridge, shopping, dancing, and riding. They said that they had done their best while in office, but had resigned because they were discouraged by not having a united country behind them. The newly announced government officials and their families, of my friendship, were occupied in the same ways. They said that they had taken on office, but were not yet certain just how they could help the nation, as they did not feel a united country behind them.

The Yangtze was filling up with warships of Western nations, and in Western homes I found fear that Japan would next strike at China through Shanghai. But in all the Chinese homes I entered, I found myself scoffed at when I mentioned this fear. There was no sign of Chinese defense preparations against such a Japanese move. "Japan," so the Chinese people at Shanghai said, "has no concern with this part of China."

En route to America, we visited in Japan. As always on arrival in Japan I was surprised anew by the charm of that country. The pearl beauty of sacred Fujiyama crowning the islands, where the people have made exquisite arrangement of

every detail of town and countryside so that there is nothing
ugly to be seen anywhere!   The loveliness of the flowers!   The
restrained use of bright splashes of color in garden, domicile,
temple, and dress!   The graceful courtesy of the people re-
enchanted me again.

But, in contrast to Shanghai, I found in Kobe, in Tokyo,
and in Yokohama the conviction that China and Japan were

JAPAN

on the eve of war.   In every home of my acquaintance, a
father, a husband, or a son had been notified to be ready to
fight.   In point of necessity Japan would have to secure the
attention of the Chinese officials by striking at China through
Shanghai, the country's strategic economic centre, in order to
stop the Anti-Japanese boycott, to assure future decent treatment for Japanese people resident in China, and force China

to the fulfillment of her treaty obligations. Women were knitting and stitching with sad courage to make their men ready.

I was on the ocean when fighting began at Shanghai. At Philadelphia, March 17, I received two letters. One from Tokyo. The other from Shanghai. Both were from dear friends whom I have loved since girlhood. We were all married in the same year. In each letter one sentence stood out: "My husband fell at Chapei." Both men were educated in the United States. Each took honors in political economy in one of our universities.

I did not return to China during this fighting, so I did not witness any of the incidents connected with it. My Chinese friends, even to-day, are not in accord in judgment of what occurred at Shanghai. Ever since the Northern troops had gone, early in the spring of 1927, Southern troops had occupied the Shanghai garrisons. When the Japanese struck at China through Shanghai, a Cantonese regiment under the command of a dreamy young poet was in residence there.

Although young, he was well known in his own country. Not because of his warlike characteristics (no one supposed that he had any!), but because of his classical learning and his verse. He surprised his own land, even his own homestead, by leading his soldiers in stubborn resistance.

Although Chapei was leveled, Japan did not pass!

In America I read of the fighting poet as a hero. In his own country, where he effectively checked enemy troops on a march to the Capital, there is considerable doubt as to the wisdom of what he did. The Chinese intelligentsia, who have their learning from the books of Lao-tzu, Mo-ti, Confucius, and Mencius, believe that no good can come of gun-play. Because of his classical learning and his poetry, they accepted him as one of themselves. Now they ignore him. Chinese of Western education, or who, like him, have not been abroad but have done some Western reading, understand his act and realize that there is truth in his explanation that he did what he did because a display of martial courage would add to China's world reputation.

He battled with Japan at Shanghai without reënforcement from other regiments. When the Japanese and the Cantonese guns were leveling Chapei, Chinese merchants, bankers, and homestead elders went to the fighting poet and asked him to desist, offering him a fortune to go away. He refused. Such consternation then reigned in Chinese minds, as the battle continued, that Chiang Kai-shek, in exile on his farm at Fenghua, was remembered as having been sane when the students clamored for war. He was asked to return to the helm of state, and after considerable persuasion returned.

Whether or not Japan could have fought her way through to Nanking is not known. Neither is it known whether Chiang Kai-shek would have brought his German-officered army out of Honan to assist the fighting poet or have agreed with the intelligentsia concerning a policy of non-resistance to be followed by international investigation. He had scarcely taken up the Government seal and had had no opportunity to announce his policy, when Japan withdrew from Shanghai.

Certainly the citizenry of Japan were not whole-heartedly behind the military action of Shanghai. I have three Japanese friends who were put into Tokyo prison for speaking in public against it, and a great many others who less publicly disapproved. I believe that the party who were in ascendancy in Japan when it was done weakened their home position by it, and that, even in the Western world, where for centuries national greatness has been measured by martial strength, Japan injured her reputation, not by failure to march to Nanking, but by going to Shanghai and fighting as long as she did.

After Shanghai, Japan concentrated on tightening her grip on Manchuria. In May, a Japanese division under General Hirose occupied Hulan. Fighting northeast of Harbin caused the river steamers to turn back, and interrupted traffic on the

East Manchurian Railway. In June the Nanking government issued a statement that China was not contemplating any compromise with Japan as regards the recognition of an independent state or Mr. Pu-yi's régime, announced official recognition of all Chinese generals fighting in self-defense against the Japanese armies in Manchuria, but stated that China would await the result of the League of Nations investigation of Manchurian affairs before taking national action against Japan.

Through all the spring and summer of 1932 there was trouble over the control of the Customs, Salt Gabelle, and the Posts. By July practically all the offices of the above-mentioned services had been taken over and the officials, of all nationalities, sent within the Wall. Just prior to the presentation of the Earl of Lytton's Commission report on Manchuria to the League of Nations, Japan officially recognized the independence of Manchuria under the title of "Manchukuo."

Within the Wall, although there is as yet no sign of universal uprising against Japan, as there was against Russia in 1927, there is more generous contribution than ever before to the Anti-Japanese Society, and a universal boycott of Japanese goods which has practically closed China as a Japanese market and is consequently giving business to England and America. Anti-Japanese Scouts are active as lecturers. The scholars are occupied with educating the populace concerning Japanese treaties, and they are not heckling Chiang Kai-shek's endeavors to end civil war and centralize authority.

V

ARRIVAL

1

DESPITE political trouble, life goes on pleasantly here. It was late in September, when the waterways of North China were open, that I last came to the homestead of the Lins on the Grand Canal. The boat was fitted with oar, towline and sail. The wind was favorable. We left the canal side and turned south without incident except that the First Boatman had difficulty in lighting his incense before the Goddess-ever-listening-to-the-prayers-of-mortals-who-pass-over-water. We had several baskets of provisions. Because, although the boat journey would probably occupy but one day, it is wisest when traveling to provide so as not to be fretted if there is delay.

Home-woven mats, with fragrant grass in their white reeds, freshly laundered cushion and back-rest covers of flowered cloth, paper fans decorated with pictures of folk in pretty summer gowns, green lacquer fly-swatters, and a large crimson umbrella over each compartment made travel comfortable.

We women sat in the aft compartment, the men in the fore. We were, as it happened, just the same company as on my first journey to the House of Exile: —

Shun-ko's husband, returning, sad and tired, from three futile months at Suining, where he had been one of a committee sent by the government to attempt a settlement with bandits holding a hundred provincial school teachers as hostages for a ransom of two million dollars.

His elder brother, who had been to the grain merchants in

Tientsin and arranged for the sale of the autumn harvest at double last year's price because of the extraordinary demand created by floods in other provinces.

Mai-da, called to her birth-home by a letter from the Lin Family Elder, informing her that the Wongs had agreed to sell the court into which Mai-lin's Walk runs and the three others adjoining it — for which she began to negotiate as a residence for her household immediately on her marriage with Prince Erh-sung.

Mai-da's mother and Shun-ko, who had come up to meet us. And the serving matrons — Shun-ko's Sweet Rain, Mai-da's Faithful Duck, and my Bald-the-third.

THE GRAND CANAL

We kept to the right on the water highway. On our left passed numerous boats piled high with grapes and grain. All had their sail hoisted, and the faces of boatmen, farmers, wives, and children beamed with delight in the weather. "May you have a fair wind all the way," "May the star of happiness shine on all your journey," "Raise the sail one foot and you get ten feet of road," we greeted in elated voices.

Small boys and girls darted through the more serious traffic on little boats, miraculously escaping accident by inches. Others swam in the sun-caressed bays.

With care not to encroach on the double-track boat path, men set shrimp traps, fashioned of cylinders of plaited straw. Projecting half a foot above water, they looked like the chimneys of tiny mermaid houses. Women wheeled hamper barrows down to the canal, and rubbed their laundry clean on smooth stones, using long bars of yellow soap — then moved along to rinse in clear water, which they dyed lapis-lazuli with indigo stalks.

At intervals we passed fishermen waiting for the fish called silver-shuttle-flowers, with net or otter, or catching carp with cormorants kept keen by loosening the birds' neck-straw to let them swallow every seventh fish. All along our waterway, the lotus was a luxuriant height with thick green leaves an arm's length in width. Folk in slipper boats were harvesting the leaves and the seed pods, with sharp short scythes, each harvester carefully keeping to the boundaries of property — because while reeds are common estate when they grow in untenanted soil, the lotus is so precious that there is "not one plant in China which does not have an owner."

Our sail had to be folded and the oar used whenever we came to the frequent high-arched stone bridges — many with legends carved on them, some humped like a camel's back, and a few perfect granite half-circles that cast a shadow at midday, so that we traveled through a good-luck ring.

Men and boys were at work gathering late crops and tending the winter kale. Women spread white-ribbed salted cabbage to dry on trays set below sun-warmed south walls. There were no cattle running free; all were hitched to carts — carrying beans down to canal boats, sweet potatoes up to villages, manure vats out to the winter wheat, or heaped with gourds which would later be made into wine jars. Donkeys saddled with panniers packed with orange persimmons were led gently to their destination along the worn paths that radiate from farm to walled village, from walled village to canal side.

Other donkeys, with tinkling bells sewn to their scarlet col-

lars, trotted along the paths carrying men or women — each
often astride a high wooden saddle with a downy-haired baby
snuggled in the curve of one arm — to visit in the homestead
of relatives.

Many folk traveled reclining in hammock litters swung between two shaggy ponies. A goodly number rode in mule
carts which had wheels studded with brass nails, axles that
protruded in half a foot of varnished length on either side of
the cart, and a larkspur cloth cabin with padded floor where
the travelers sat cross-legged and looked out past the mule's
rump. We saw none of the gaudy sedan chairs, green, scarlet,
or blue, that we used once to see.

But a yellow motor boat tore down the canal with noisy
speed. Other craft scuttled out of its path. Men, women,
and children stood up in their boats, and ran from canal-side
inn, field, and village, to stare at it. The speed boat was
driven by young Wong Tsin-min, who brought his craft up
abruptly beside the Lin boat and cried: "Greeting, neighbors!
May I give you a lift home? With luck I'll get you there for
the midday meal."

The Lins declined. Wong Tsin-min's index finger moved
one dashboard lever, and the motor horn was set in continuous
blast; his thumb moved another lever, and the motor boat went
down the canal like an aërolite.

"Such a boat is a menace to life," said Faithful Duck. "Our
Elder should have it prohibited by the Provincial Council."

"At Tientsin," said Mai-da's father, "the thirty-sixth Elder
of Wong invited me to accompany him to his dancing lesson."

"The Wong next-in-line-for-the-Eldership," said Sweet
Rain, "has bought a Moth plane in which to fly to and from his
new villa at Pei-tai-ho."

"Wong Ho-hsi is said to be married to a Frenchwoman,"
said Bald-the-third, and sniffed — a disgusting habit she has
when contemptuous.

"My youngest daughter went to Wong Lu-lei's seventh

birthday party," said Mai-da, "and Lu-lei bragged to her that there is not one grown-up Wong now in school, in business, or in government office, and that their family do nothing from sunrise to sunrise except eat, sleep, and play. Wongs, not in family groups, but just one man or one woman alone with an unrelated person of opposite sex, so my baby was informed, can be seen any night in the night clubs of Shanghai, of Tientsin, of Canton."

"It is difficult to build up but easy to tear down," said Mai-da's mother. "The Wong fortune was built by thirty-five prudent generations. The estates of the ancestors are inherited by their descendants, but there are always other generations to come who have also the right to inherit in their turn. Yet this unscrupulous generation will use up all that thirty-five generations achieved."

Then Shun-ko silenced this gossiping discussion with, "It is enough that we keep the snow swept from our own door. We are not called upon to concern ourselves with the hoarfrost on our neighbor's roof-tiles."

All along the canal high water and rumors of broken dykes in other districts had made the people ardent in their care of their asking-protection shrines. Each village had repaired the masonry of its shrine and plastered its shrine walls with brilliant picture and prayer posters. Every patron goddess was dressed in new silk. One had rose trousers and a Delphinium coat lined with rose. Another had an amber cloak embroidered with a phœnix in seed pearls. A third had jade earrings, a purple cap and slippers, and a red dress.

Shun-ko's husband told the boatman to stop at the Weary Pagoda so that we could listen to the wind-bells under its five-storied eaves. And Mai-da's father told us the pretty legend, for which we all begged him, of the pagoda's trek from beyond a mountain three thousand miles away.

"It was here that we first met dear Erh-sung," Shun-ko remembered.

"To us he was then only a tall, graceful skater in a claret gown and a marten-skin cap," said Sweet Rain.

"It was just at this place that he picked up two of our oranges and our daughter's heart," teased Mai-da's father.

But Mai-da's mother stubbornly refused to recall Prince Erh-sung in this location, although we all prodded her memory.

2

Bathed in golden warmth by the sun, with a favorable wind in our sail, we glided gently over the canal and came in quietness to Noonday Rest, landing at the south gate of the city some time after midday. In the paved area between the city wall and the glassy canal, a cheerful crowd of travelers awaiting passage, idle boatmen, sedan-chair bearers, and vendors were gathered. A fair girl, with rosy cheeks, dressed in a clean blue cotton gown, and with a long black braid neatly bound at the end with a reel of crimson thread, sang: "Wash your face for a penny?" And we washed.

It was the eve of the Moon's Birthday. Barbers had set down their portable paraphernalia and each had a customer on his stool. Because, on the fifteenth day of the eighth month, when the moon shines at her greatest brilliancy and is a perfect circle in symbol of conjugal unity, it is considered most important that husband and wife be together. So men were having themselves made attractive for their wives.

The Third Boatman secured the letter writer at the east end of the wharf to do a poem to his betrothed, begging her to marry him soon. The fortune teller had dropped a "no business" curtain around his umbrella. He was occupied for the day preparing a lengthy diagram, punctuated with prudent quotations from the sages, to guide a grey-silk-gowned man through the remainder of his life. But Faithful Duck only wanted to ask *one* question. She was in a quandary as to whether to say "yes" to the proposal of Prince Erh-sung's

servingman.   The silk-gowned gentleman courteously let her
have the fortune teller's attention for it.

The fan vendors had their tiered racks filled with pieces of
fragrant sandalwood, pillars of incense sticks, and gay paper
moon palaces inhabited by the Patron Saint of Literature.
Bald-the-third was carrying my purse, and used it, while my
attention was occupied by a toy vendor, to purchase sandalwood, incense pillars, and a palace to burn next day as an
offering for the success of the manuscript of this book, which
we were carrying to the House of Exile for criticism.

The toy vendors offered clay statuettes of the Moon Hare,
the Moon Toad, the Old Man of the Moon, the Lady of the
Moon, the Woodcutter, the Emperor who visited the Moon,
and the Cassia Tree.   Also all the accessories for a child to
enact all the moon legends on the nursery floor.   Made by the
toy vendors and their families, no two figures were exactly
alike in color, or dress, or posture, as they had lightened the
tedium of modeling by permitting their fingers to follow their
imaginations in minor details.

We bargained with the toy sellers until we had secured a
gift for each child in the Garden of the House of Exile.   Then,
remembering that such festivals are forbidden under the Republic, we bought reserves against the year when we might
approach the Moon's Birthday and be unable to find toys.

I have a hearty appreciation of food.   The steam from the
barrows of the itinerant restaurants attracted me, and, while
our purchased toys were being packed in sawdust and arranged
in the Lin family boat, I loitered near.   Spiced melon, steamed
walnuts, fried prawns, broiled fowl on spits, sour-sweet-sauced
fish, vegetable marrow hashed with pork, savory soups, stews,
pastries, and puddings were cooking.   The cooks, who had all
adapted their menus to the festival, advised their customers
from behind their stoves.

"You will enjoy my moon cakes, made of shortened white
flour and stuffed with cinnamon, dates, almonds, orange peel

and sugar. . . ." "Try my melon. It is round — a symbol of perfect love between husband and wife. I have steeped the seeds in the juices of mixed herbs and put them into the melon's flesh again, as seeds suggest sons. It is green — green is the color of youth!" "I can give you sun-ripened persimmon, red and sweet, a sign of domestic happiness and peace!" "Why not feast on the jade-white root of lotus? Its tightly knit fibres will make you constant in love!" "Drink of my chestnut soup and you not only nourish your body but you cleanse your mind of all evil."

But Shun-ko's summons reminded me that a lady does not eat from barrows. We journeyed through the city gate to the quiet *posada* that the Lins always patronize at Noonday Rest. As usual, we rode in a single-file procession of closed sedan chairs. The inn host welcomed us, and bowed us to seats at the square table of rosewood inlaid with mother-of-pearl in scenes from the life of Wen Wang, which he knows to be the Lins' favorite table.

As usual, we said that we would not give a special order but would have the day's "five dishes," which cost one dollar each person. We had dishes of salted watermelon seeds and blue-grape jelly set in the centre of the table. Warm rice wine served in thimble cups, to "aid digestion." Then crisp, fried bean-flour noodles, making a nest for hashed lean beef, white-ribbed cabbage, and green pepper; a stew of tissue-thin sliced lotus root and boned wild duck; short steamed moon cakes stuffed with shredded coconut, candied lemon peel, powdered cloves, and dried grapes; a delicious baked combination of tenderloin of pork, water chestnuts, and taro; and shrimp and radish soup made with the stock of boiled chicken.

While we ate a soldier came in. He stared at us. And we stared at him.

He had arrived by sedan chair. I saw his bearers squatting with ours in the courtyard behind him. He wore breeches and a tunic of well-woven lightweight wool, tailored to fit him. His buttons, leggings, belt, and open-top holsters, filled with two pistols, were of polished brown leather. His round visorless cap and neat slippers were of brown velvet.

His manner was quiet but self-assured. Even I found the pattern of his bronzed, intelligent face and supple hands familiar.

"Camel-back's grandson!" the Lins chorused, after staring hard at him. Mai-da's father was first across the room to welcome him with tender joy.

They brought him to our table. We had two extra dishes cooked and the inn's best wine in his honor. In China, it is uncouth to converse while at meals, as etiquette demands that one should show appreciation to host and cook by giving full attention to the food. But over fruit and green tea, Camel-back's grandson asked and was answered concerning the homestead, and began his Odyssey.

He told us how the foraging soldiers had seized him and the donkey, and ordered him to fill the basket cart with produce from neighbors' property. When he refused, the soldiers had beaten him until he lost consciousness. He woke at night beside a camp fire, where the soldiers were cooking a chicken stew.

He told of weary moons as boy slave to these soldiers in a trek to the sea. Of his sorrow when his last friend, the little donkey, dropped dead on the road, and how he had not cared when they hitched him in the shafts in the donkey's place. Of better moons, as personal valet to a captain.

Of a year when his stomach touched his backbone as the army he was with drifted from one defeat to another; and of how, in Shantung, by seizing the flagstaff of the "enemy" in a battle, as it was dropped by a wounded bearer, he attracted the attention of an officer and was given the flag-sergeant's uniform and job.

Of his naïve astonishment the first time this regiment, for which he carried the flag, was sold to the owner of an army against which they had been marching. Of similar sales until he had a knapsack full of flags and was able to retreat through any "enemy" district or join up with any victorious army in the field. Of how — his education in tactics secured in the school of experience — he was now a Republican: a general with his own regiments, at the service of his country.

He had come out of Kansu to volunteer assistance in making Japan loosen her throttle grip on the Three Eastern Provinces. But, exiled and homesick for ten years, he was permitting himself the indulgence of the Moon Festival holidays at his birthplace, as now that he was a general in comfortable circumstances it was fitting that he should pay his dutiful respects to his grandfather and have his marriage contracted. He had come to the inn because he knew that if any of the homestead were traveling the canal he would find them there for the noon meal.

Entranced with Camel-back's grandson, we forgot time and lingered at the table until the First Boatman came in anxiety to say that the sun had sunk to the height of a helmeted man and that the wind had shifted directly against the home road. The boatman began to stare at the general before he was halfway through his sentence and at the end of it he gaped with astonished recognition of the little boy grown to a man.

At the wharf the general paid off his hired boat and moved into the Family boat. Shun-ko's husband called the Minstrel of Noonday Rest from the bench under the yellow-flower pine tree where he slept, and gave him a newly minted silver dollar, round and shiny like the full moon that hung in the late-afternoon sky.

We left the wharf with two boatmen on the towrope and one at the rear oar. The minstrel walked a way with us to play an accompaniment on his three-stringed guitar. We all sang Li Tai Po's hymn beginning: —

O lovely lady Moon, now round and full and brilliant,
Now like the pale crescent on the finger nail of my beloved,
From time longer than man's memory thou hast graced
The blue night sky with thy beauty,
Entering our halls by painted door and latticed window
To enchant the sleepless with thy silver loveliness.

Yet even cheered by song the boatmen pulled feebly. They
stopped often to change from towpath to a rest at the rear oar.
Softened by too much idleness, they sweated and panted in
slow mileage. We had frequently to listen to the jeering cries
of boatmen approaching from the rear and then let them pass.
Among these were boats four times our length loaded with
baked brick so that they were sunk almost to water level with
just two sneering men on their towline who left us far behind.

We tried to get men to tow. No one would take employ-
ment on the Moon Birthday night — not even for treble wages.
All the boatmen who hurried past us said that they were but
finishing a task long ago contracted for and must get home before midnight. We knocked twice at villages. To knock
was a waste of time. Men did not want work.

The sun set, but the moon gave radiant light. The towrope broke. At the wharf of the village we waited while the
Second Boatman secured a piece of rope. Then the two bits
of rope had to be spliced.

3

It was near to midnight when we came to the Lin homestead city. The gates are sealed at sunset. The city wall, thick
enough for nine horses to trot abreast on it, rises from the canal
ten times a man's height. The boatman beat against the iron-
studded gate. Finally the attention of the gateman was secured.

But he refused to open the gates before sunrise. He acknowledged that he knew all the persons who said they were

without. Excepting the foreigner whom he had known but twelve years, he had known the others from childhood. The voices from without were like the voices of these Lins and their servants and their American friend. The extra male voice might even be the voice of Camel-back's grandson grown to manhood. But voices are dangerous to trust when heard through a wall; and he was not the type of gateman who let strangers, especially in these times, into his city after nightfall when all good people were in their homes.

After much parley one of the gateman's little nephews was dispatched to the Lin homestead. While we waited, Mai-da's mother remarked that they had not arrived late at the gate since the first time I came down. But when I said that I must be bad luck, they all hastened to remind me that I had traveled this way with them many times in the interval.

Uncle Keng-lin hailed us from within the gate. One after another, in the order of our ages, we replied to our names.

The gate creaked open. We walked in. Before greeting us, Uncle Keng-lin closed the gate again, secured its locks, and pasted a fresh strip of paper over the seal he had broken. On this paper he brushed his name.

He had brought sedan chairs. In them we followed him up to the House of Exile.

Camel-back peered through the peep-hole as we approached. He recognized his Family. He undid the locks and bars of the To and From the World Gate to let us in, bowing and smiling his joy at our safe return from the perils of travel. Massed behind him were the household — young and old.

"Happiness springs up of itself in a united family," was said again and again. Sung-li, who eleven years earlier had disapproved of inviting a Westerner into the homestead, squeezed my two hands. Martyred Shao-yi's sleepy son was put into my arms. The child cuddled against my neck. Ju-i pinched my ear as she passed to greet Shun-ko.

Mai-da's brother said, "You are getting too plump, Mai-da.

I have the Wong lease ready for your signature; when you are settled at home again we must diet you."

"We were so afraid that the cruel Japanese might prevent you all from returning to safety inside the House," Sou-mai cried, running from one to another.

"The Japanese are not in this province," Shun-ko said.

"They will seize all China if we do not put them out of Manchuria," half a dozen women chorused.

"Camel-back's grandson is a general," the children whispered with brightening eyes.

Camel-back carefully barred the high gate closing the wall against the world before he received his grandson's kowtow. When the three prostrations were completed, he brushed the dust from his descendant's uniform and said, "You wear a general's uniform; but have you kept the power to take time from the Heavens?"

"I have," the grandson said proudly, as though he too counted a general's power as nothing beside this inherited talent.

"Ah, then to-night thou shalt set the Time Stick," his grand-sire said, as one conferring an honor.

Uncle Shao-chun interrupted. "The Elder is held on his bed with a fever, but desires to welcome the-one-who-was-gone-and-is-come-home. He has lifted his head from his pillow and wrapped the robe of ceremony around him. He waits for Camel-back's grandson in the south room of the Three Eastern Courtyards."

"Midnight approaches," Yu-lin reminded us, and pushed open the opaque shell lattice before the Orchid Door. Mai-da linked her arm in mine. We hurried toward the dwelling that we always have when we come home.

But Nuan ran after us, snuggled in between, and drew us to the Court of the Ginkgo Tree for a critical survey of the Altar to the Moon, now ready for illumination, which it was her duty this year to design. When we had praised her work, we went on to change our travel attire to silk dresses suitable for participation in the Moon's Birthday celebrations.

4

I stayed at the House of Exile twenty-one sunrises this visit. It was the season of making pickles and preserves. Tientsin is so near that in my five years of residence here I have formed the annual habit of going "home" to fill my jars in the House of Exile kitchens when the family jars are filled. Each morning I pickled and preserved in the homestead kitchens with the other women.

Each afternoon the Elder called us all into the library. On the first day after my arrival Yeng-peng read Mr. Edward Weeks's letter, asking me to submit a book about my Chinese years to the Atlantic Monthly Press, voicing the English words in Chinese. Each following afternoon he translated into Chinese and read aloud a section of the manuscript which I prepared in answer to this invitation and, with the Family's permission, proposed to submit.

When Yeng-peng finished reading at the end of the Hour of the Sheep on the eighteenth day, Uncle Keng-lin spoke first. He said, "It is an achievement for a talkative woman to have written so many pages."

Chen-t'ing was next: "That which is on the paper is just the usual round of days in an ordinary family and no different, except in unimportant detail, from life in thousands of other households. The polite letter writer is seeking literature. He should be sent selections from the classics that those outside-the-world may realize the greatness of China."

The Elder said, "There is no untruth in what she has put down, but there is no great truth in it either. There is no great Lin in these generations and it is a great spirit which makes a great book. There is the life story of a Lin of the T'ang period, worthy of consideration. It exemplified a great truth, and should be well worth sending to Boston if edited out of the old records in yonder cupboard."

Kuei-tzu, who is now ninety-six years of age, and dozed in her chair beside her husband during all the reading, suddenly opened her bright black eyes and spoke. "Scholarship is useless to a woman. To translate the classics is to ruin her sight to no purpose. Hunting through dusty records is a waste of good time. All she needs to know is how to manage men, which any woman can do if she is a good cook."

And she took me off to her room and gave me her method for "honey ginger": —

Peel a fresh pineapple and cut it into thick slices. Then into wedges. Remove the lining from the peel of one dozen oranges; cut the peel in strips, and boil out the bitterness; and drain. Divide the oranges into sections, taking out all the seeds. Pick up all the ginger-root you can grasp in one hand four times; peel the ginger-root and cut each root in three pieces; bring it to a five-minutes boil in cold water; then drain. Put the pineapple, the oranges with the peel, and the ginger-root into a saucepan, and pour on honey until there is a finger-length more on than is needed to cover them. Cook to the consistency of preserve.

An hour later, Shun-ko came to tell me that her husband had secured permission from the Family Council for me to submit my manuscript.

12583

DS
721
W3

WALN, NORA
        HOUSE OF EXILE.

12583

DATE DUE	
OCT 26 1995	
OCT 04 1996	

GAYLORD   PRINTED IN U.S.A.